Men's Health

Life Improvement Guides™

Stress Blasters

Quick and Simple Steps
to Take Control and Perform
under Pressure

by Brian Chichester, Perry Garfinkel
and the Editors of **Men'sHealth** Books

Reviewed by Redford B. Williams, M.D., professor of
psychiatry and director of the Behavioral Medicine Research Center
at Duke University Medical Center, Durham, North Carolina

Rodale Press, Inc.
Emmaus, Pennsylvania

Copyright © 1997 by Rodale Press, Inc.

Illustrations copyright © 1997 by Alan Baseden
Cover photograph copyright © 1997 by Walter Smith

Other titles in the *Men's Health Life Improvement Guides* series:
  Fight Fat
  Food Smart
  Powerfully Fit
  Sex Secrets
  Symptom Solver

Library of Congress Cataloging-in-Publication Data

Chichester, Brian.
    Stress blasters : quick and simple steps to take control and
perform under pressure / by Brian Chichester, Perry Garfinkel and
the editors of Men's Health Books.
        p.   cm.—(Men's health life improvement guides)
    Includes index.
    ISBN 0–87596–358–7 paperback
    1. Stress management.   2. Men—Life skills guides.
3. Men—Health and hygiene.   4. Men—Mental health.   I. Garfinkel, Perry.
II. Men's Health Books.   III. Title.   IV. Series.
RA785.C444   1997
155.9'042—dc20   96–27694

Distributed in the book trade by St. Martin's Press

2 4 6 8 10 9 7 5 3 1   paperback

—— OUR PURPOSE ——

*"We inspire and enable people to improve
their lives and the world around them."*

Stress Blasters Editorial Staff
Senior Managing Editor: **Neil Wertheimer**
Senior Editor: **Jack Croft**
Writers: **Brian Chichester, Perry Garfinkel, K. Winston Caine, Michelle Bisson, Margo Trott**
Contributing Writers: **Joely Johnson, Kathryn Piff**
Researchers and Fact Checkers: **Valerie Edwards-Paulik, Jan Eickmeier**
Copy Editor: **David R. Umla**
Series Art Director: **Charles Beasley**
Series Designer: **John Herr**
Book Designer: **Thomas P. Aczel**
Cover Designer: **Charles Beasley**
Cover Photographer: **Walter Smith**
Photo Editor: **Susan Pollack**
Illustrators: **Thomas P. Aczel, Alan Baseden**
Studio Manager: **Stefano Carbini**
Technical Artist: **Mary Brundage**
Manufacturing Coordinator: **Melinda B. Rizzo**
Office Staff: **Roberta Mulliner, Julie Kehs, Bernadette Sauerwine, Mary Lou Stephen**

Rodale Health and Fitness Books
Vice-President and Editorial Director: **Debora T. Yost**
Design and Production Director: **Michael Ward**
Research Manager: **Ann Gossy Yermish**
Copy Manager: **Lisa D. Andruscavage**
Book Manufacturing Director: **Helen Clogston**

Photo Credits
Page 142: **Bill Smith**
Page 144: **Priscilla Harmel**
Page 146: **E. C. Publications, Inc.**
Page 148: **Courtesy of Meadowlane Enterprises**
Page 150: **Terry Perret Martin**
Page 152: **Maxis**
Back flap: **FPG International**

Contents

Introduction

It's Your Life

In my previous life, I was a business editor in one of the most competitive newspaper markets in the country. Going head-to-head every day against one of the nation's largest and most respected papers was exhilarating. Deadline pressure was intense, and adrenaline was the fuel that primed the presses. For those who have never had the pleasure of working in daily newspapers, it's a world in which cynicism and even outright hostility are viewed as valued professional attributes—not as character flaws.

After 13 years, though, I found myself wondering if there was more to life than the rush that comes with getting a big story first, the intensity of sprinting to a deadline, each and every day of the year. Adrenaline is an addictive substance, and like all intoxicants, your resistance to it increases the more that you indulge in it. The highs were no longer as invigorating as they once were, and the lows had become much lower—and more common. At age 30, I had ulcers.

I didn't fully understand it at the time, but I was exhibiting the first telltale signs of job burnout. I realized that it was time to make a choice: I could either go on living life the way I had been, wallowing in cynicism, anger and stress, or I could become happy again.

Once I understood that it truly was my choice to make, the decision was easy. My wife and I had just brought a beautiful boy into the world. The question became: What kind of father did I want my son to have? Looking into his eyes, the answer became clear. It was time to regain the jolly, calm demeanor that I was once known for. So I changed careers, moving my family across country to join the fledgling staff of *Men's Health* Books.

It was one of the most important life lessons I've learned. Each of us has the power to take control of our lives and make positive changes that lead to greater self-fulfillment and happiness. The key is to decide what's *really* important to you.

That's what *Stress Blasters* is all about. We live in a society in which money is often viewed as the measure of a man. It's not. The real measure is how well you've lived your life. That's what you'll be thinking about on your deathbed, so why wait until it's too late to do anything about it? Accepting that fundamental truth is the first step to reducing stress in your life.

We're not saying that you need to don rose-colored glasses. Unless, of course, you're still wearing a Nehru jacket and love beads. But you probably do need to challenge the way that you react to the change-ups that life throws you. Not to trivialize our lives, but our response to stressful situations boils down to two choices: Laugh at the absurdity, or get frustrated at the absurdity. Research is showing that the former will help you live not just happier but healthier. The latter, research also shows, can contribute to sickness and early death.

Stress Blasters is your guide to confronting life's challenges with gusto and humor. It is packed with detailed tips on how to take control in almost every stressful situation an adult guy could face, from coping with a jerk of a coworker to mourning a death in the family. But underlying each and every one of those tips are just a few simple themes. Control what you can, and don't worry about the rest. Choose optimism over pessimism. Keep things in perspective.

Every man's life is filled with challenges, tensions and frustrations. This is life yesterday, today and tomorrow. Don't wallow in it; master it. Here's how.

Neil Wertheimer
Senior Managing Editor, *Men's Health* Books

Part One

Take Control of Your Life

Are You Stressed Out?

Take the Test and Find Out

Stop. Don't even think about turning to the next chapter. The fact that you now hold this book in your hands is a pretty good clue that stress is a topic that concerns you. So it's understandable that you want to get to all the good stuff about how to blast stress away. But before you do, it's important that you get an honest, unbiased assessment of the role that stress plays in your life.

So in the next few minutes, put yourself to the test. There are no right or wrong answers. There's no pass or fail here. Just self-knowledge.

You see, this will probably be the first—and last—stress-free test that you'll ever take. And since no one else is likely to read the results, there's no point in lying. You'd only be lying to yourself, and there's no margin in that. And there's no point trying to figure out which answers we want to hear. We're not grading these, so you'd only be wasting your time.

Here are the ground rules. Just check the response that best describes how much you agree with the statements that follow. The more checks you have agreeing with the statements, the more distress you have in your life. The less you agree with the statements, the less distress you feel. Use the results as a measuring stick. Then take the test again after you've finished reading this book and begun to apply some of the tips you'll read here. Our hope is that you'll notice how many of those checks have moved to the low-stress zone (not to mention how many friends and loved ones have moved back into your life).

The Stress-Free Stress Test

My Work	Agree Very Much	Agree Sometimes	Agree Rarely
I think about quitting my job.	☐	☐	☐
I take work home with me in the evening.	☐	☐	☐
I feel that my boss doesn't appreciate me.	☐	☐	☐
It seems as though other employees at my level are getting promoted, while I am not.	☐	☐	☐
I want to make a career change or move to another company but am not doing anything about it.	☐	☐	☐
I feel frustrated that my job does not allow me to best display my skills and abilities.	☐	☐	☐

(continued)

	Agree Very Much	Agree Sometimes	Agree Rarely
I do not get along with my co-workers.	☐	☐	☐
I blow up easily at people whom I work with or those who work for me.	☐	☐	☐
I "stuff" my feelings when my boss reprimands me or criticizes my work.	☐	☐	☐
I feel that work procedures are unfair and discriminatory.	☐	☐	☐
I do not have much personal contact with other employees.	☐	☐	☐
I am not paid what I think I deserve.	☐	☐	☐
I don't reward myself after finishing a difficult project.	☐	☐	☐
I make demands on myself that I wouldn't ask of others.	☐	☐	☐
When I succeed, I don't think I deserve it.	☐	☐	☐
My work feels routine and boring.	☐	☐	☐

My Relationships

	Agree Very Much	Agree Sometimes	Agree Rarely
When an important relationship has ended, I move on quickly.	☐	☐	☐
The people around me don't care for me or let me know it.	☐	☐	☐
I don't feel satisfied with my sex life.	☐	☐	☐
I rarely spend time with friends who know me well and accept me for who I am.	☐	☐	☐
I am dishonest about my feelings with people close to me.	☐	☐	☐
I don't talk about things that are troubling me with close friends and family.	☐	☐	☐
People don't live up to my expectations.	☐	☐	☐
I have time for other people but little for myself.	☐	☐	☐
I get jealous of other people's success.	☐	☐	☐
The more I need people, the more I push them away.	☐	☐	☐
Meeting new people makes me nervous.	☐	☐	☐

(continued)

The Stress-Free Stress Test—Continued

My Personal Style	Agree Very Much	Agree Sometimes	Agree Rarely
I tend to finish other people's sentences.	☐	☐	☐
I tend to check my watch frequently, not to find out what time it is but to find out what time it isn't.	☐	☐	☐
From the moment I wake up, I feel as though I'm already behind schedule.	☐	☐	☐
I have the feeling that everyone is doing things too slowly.	☐	☐	☐
I start many projects but finish few.	☐	☐	☐
I have trouble focusing on one thing at a time.	☐	☐	☐
I avoid new challenges and opportunities.	☐	☐	☐
I have trouble anticipating adversity and don't plan well for breakdowns.	☐	☐	☐
I can't say "no."	☐	☐	☐
I don't ask for help when I feel I'm in over my head.	☐	☐	☐
I get little satisfaction from my accomplishments.	☐	☐	☐
I fail to see the humor in situations.	☐	☐	☐
I find it hard to make time for simple personal chores, like getting a haircut.	☐	☐	☐
I set unrealistic deadlines for myself.	☐	☐	☐
I am in many situations in which I have little or no control, and that drives me batty.	☐	☐	☐
I hold in my anger and frustration.	☐	☐	☐
I worry about the future.	☐	☐	☐
I think about mistakes that I've made in the past.	☐	☐	☐
I have trouble enjoying being in the present moment.	☐	☐	☐
When I'm hurt or upset, I go off alone and brood.	☐	☐	☐
I blow up with little warning.	☐	☐	☐

(continued)

My Body	Agree Very Much	Agree Sometimes	Agree Rarely
I skip breakfast or grab coffee and a doughnut.	☐	☐	☐
I am more than a couple of pounds over my desirable weight.	☐	☐	☐
I rarely watch my intake of fat, salt and sugar.	☐	☐	☐
I smoke cigarettes.	☐	☐	☐
I smoke pot or use other drugs at least once a week.	☐	☐	☐
I put off seeing a doctor when I have a chronic ache or pain.	☐	☐	☐
My heart is racing.			
When work pressures start building up, I get one or more of the following: headache, muscle spasms, stiff neck, indigestion, tight jaw, back pain, red eyes.	☐	☐	☐
I have trouble finding time to take a break from work and go to the gym, take a walk or do some stretching at my desk.	☐	☐	☐
I eat and run, rarely slowing down to enjoy the taste of the food or the company I'm with.	☐	☐	☐
I take a variety of medications and painkillers on a regular basis.	☐	☐	☐
I watch four or more hours of television on average every day, especially right before I go to bed.	☐	☐	☐
When I am rushed, I get sloppy and careless, knocking over and bumping into things.	☐	☐	☐
I fidget.	☐	☐	☐
I have trouble falling asleep, or I wake up in the middle of the night and can't fall asleep again.	☐	☐	☐
I am tired most of the time.	☐	☐	☐
I run through the same mental tapes over and over again.	☐	☐	☐
I feel emotionally drained.	☐	☐	☐

NOTE: Thanks for advice and assistance in the preparation of this test to Esther M. Orioli, president of Essi Systems, a San Francisco–based stress research and management consulting firm and developers of the StressMap.

The Stress Epidemic

Sweeping Changes Fuel Rise

Blame the millennium. Being on the cusp of the year 2000, you could say that we are in the midst of a major social, cultural and technological sea change. The last 50 years of the twentieth century have been a time of unprecedented growth and transformation. Into the twenty-first century, we can expect the same—but more.

Alvin Toffler described *future shock* in a book by the same title as "the shattering stress and disorientation that we induce in individuals by subjecting them to too much change in too short a time."

This begins to explain the epidemic we've come to call stress. How? Stress is about change. Coping with stress is about adjusting to change. And from most social and economic indicators, we're learning to change as fast as we're learning to program the latest techno-gizmo.

Let Us Count the Ways

One of life's big stressors is lack of control. In that case, argues Georgia Witkin, Ph.D., assistant clinical professor of psychiatry and director of the Stress Program at Mount Sinai Medical Center in New York City and author of *The Male Stress Syndrome*, stress is certainly on the rise.

"In the 1970s, we lost control of our families, divorce numbers rose and families became 'extended,' " she says. "In the 1980s, we lost control of

our 'hold-on' money as financial security became more of a fairy tale. In the 1990s, we lost our time, which means that most people leave taking care of themselves for last, or not at all."

In the last 10 to 20 years of the twentieth century, we've seen significant increases in statistics that measure our collective stress levels.

According to a U.S. News/Bozell survey, seven out of ten respondents said that they felt stress at some point during a typical weekday: 30 percent said that they experience a lot of stress, and 40 percent said that they feel some stress.

In a survey conducted in 1994 for *Prevention* magazine by Abacus Custom Research of Emmaus, Pennsylvania, 54 percent of the respondents thought that they experienced more stress than their parents did. Respondents said that they blew their stack an average of five times a month. More than half (56 percent) said that stress had led them to do something irrational or destructive that they later regretted. One-quarter had not taken a week-long vacation in a year. Almost three-quarters said that stress was hurting their enjoyment of life, and half said that it was harming their health. Twenty-one percent said that stress hurt their friendships, and 19 percent said that it damaged their marriages. Fifteen percent said that stress harmed their jobs.

Between 1973 and 1993, the number of men working 49 hours or more had increased from 23.9 percent to 29.2 percent, according to Phil Rones, chief of the Division of Labor Force Statistics of the U.S. Bureau of Labor Statistics.

Contrary to popular belief, the high-powered jobs are not necessarily the most dangerous to your mental health. The most stressful workplaces are the "electronic sweatshops" and assembly lines, where a demanding pace is coupled with virtually no individual discretion.

It used to be called getting fired. Now it's called downsizing. Call it what you want, the stress is the same. Job insecurity makes the workplace more stressful than it has ever been. In a 1992 survey by Northwestern National Life Insurance Company, four in ten American workers said that their jobs are very or extremely stressful, and 46 percent of employees said that they feel "more pressure to prove their value to employers in a recession." Long-term employees forced into early retirement, companies that opt to retain consultants and save the expense of benefits packages that full-time employees would require, mergers and acquisitions that eliminate whole departments, the younger workforce and advances in technology all make work feel like a game of musical chairs. You're never sure if your desk will be occupied by someone else when you arrive in the morning.

If it's any solace, we've been busy but productive, according to Worldwatch Institute, a Washington, D.C.–based nonprofit group. The growth in output of goods and services in just one decade, from 1984 to 1994, totaled more than $4 trillion—more than from the beginning of civilization until 1950.

We've also been reproductive. Those of us born before the middle of the twentieth century have seen more growth in population during our lifetimes than occurred during the preceding four million years.

At home the stress hits just keep on coming. Even deciding who is responsible for mundane chores such as taking out the garbage carries its own stressful emotional baggage. "In the past, there were clearer sex role differentiations," says Cheryl Russell, author of *The Master Trend: How the Baby Boom Generation Is Remaking America* and former editor-in-chief of *American Demographer* magazine. "Today men and women are doing everything. They're parenting, working and sharing more domestic and household responsibilities. Everybody feels responsible for everything all the time, and that causes greater stress."

A Matter of Perspective

Meanwhile, there has been a decline in those things that could be stress blasters.

According to a Harris poll, free time has declined at least 40 percent since 1973. Since the 1980s, paid time off has actually declined. We have about 3½ fewer days off each year for vacation, holiday, sick pay and other paid absences.

Leisure time itself has become a stressor when free time is no longer free. The growth of the so-called leisure market, a by-product of America's economic boom years, put a price on relaxation. Every hobby, recreational activity and vacation costs what once was a year's wage. Overall, per capita spending on services—like foreign travel, restaurant meals, medical attention, hair and skin care and leisure industry products such as health clubs and tennis lessons—has risen 2.6 times since 1950.

Sleep, which soothes the stressed-out beast, has become a rare commodity. And the number one reason that people give for losing sleep is stress, according to data collected in a 1995 Gallup survey for the National Sleep Foundation in Washington, D.C. The survey shows that 49 percent of Americans suffer from sleep-related problems, up 36 percent from 1991. "Stress-induced insomnia is a result of the fact that we're a 24-hour-a-day society," says David N. Neubauer, M.D., associate director of the Johns Hopkins University Sleep Disorders Center in Baltimore. "We have extremely demanding schedules, and there are so many other tempting things to do than go to bed."

But let's keep this in perspective, urges Robert Sapolsky, Ph.D., professor of biological sciences and neuroscience at Stanford University and author of *Why Zebras Don't Get Ulcers: A Guide to Stress, Stress-Related Diseases, and Coping.* "I would take a traffic jam here every day over the life of a medieval peasant," he says. "It's not that we have more stressful lives. But we're more likely to succumb to stress because there are so few other devastating diseases."

The Science of Stress

Making the Mind-Body Connection

Oh, what a feeling! An almost-euphoric natural high. A throw-me-your-best-shot, take-no-prisoners kind of feeling. A surge of energy, a hyper-awareness, like someone had suddenly turned up the volume on all your senses. As though time itself had slowed down so that you could think thoughts *between* thoughts and study the seam of the fastball coming at you as if someone had turned the projector to slow motion. And things long forgotten come back in four-color detail. Behold: Superman.

Or . . .

Man, what a drag! An I-can't-take-it-anymore, wave-the-white-flag kind of misery. When moving through space itself feels like swimming in quicksand. Every moment, every action, every thought full of so much pressure that if you were a pump you could inflate the Goodyear blimp. Meanwhile, tapes of old breakups, bad meals, wasted time, lost moments and other wrong turns in life jolt you awake at 3:00 A.M. A pair of rams is using your temples for battering practice, and butterflies the size of pterodactyls are circling your intestinal system. Your heart is beating like the drum solo from "In-A-Gadda-Da-Vida." Beware: About-to-Implode Man.

This is the double-edged sword called stress. As you've surely experienced firsthand all too many times, there are two kinds of stress. There's the stress that can move your body and mind to near superhuman feats. An exhila-rating, motivating stress. That's the good stress, known as eustress to the guys in white lab coats. And there's the stress that can reduce you to a sniveling wimp. This is the not-so-good stress, known as distress.

If you thought that all stress was bad stress, you're not alone. The key is to understand the nuts and bolts of how your body and mind respond to perceived threats so that you'll be able to take stress in stride.

Prehistoric Stress

If you've read anything about stress, you've probably heard the saber-toothed tiger analogy. That's the one in which men in modern garb are invited to recall those distant days of yore, when we hung in the 'hood in loincloths, hunting and gathering our food. Suddenly, we're face-to-face with a saber-toothed tiger or some other prehistoric predator. Our choices are two: fight the nasty beast (and either have lunch or be lunch) or run back to the cave to regale friends and family with much embellished tales of heroics.

This ability has been dubbed the fight-or-flight response. You also could call it your basic survival mechanism. "Without the fight-or-flight response, we'd probably be an extinct species," says Stanford University's Dr. Robert Sapolsky.

And if you substitute a death in the family, an overdue report or that insidious voice mail for the predatory animal, it functions exactly the same way now as it did then. Here's how.

A stressor, as the name implies, is something that causes stress. It can be as tangible as that saber-toothed tiger or an oncoming train. Or it can be as intangible as that worried voice in the deep recesses of your mind that questions what will happen to you if you miss your deadline on the big project.

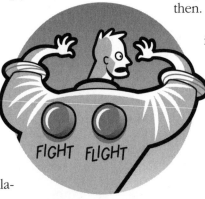

FIGHT FLIGHT

Mental stressors—worry is a big one—are one of the things that separate man from zebras, as well as modern man from his caveman cousins, who apparently worried about only immediate problems, says Dr. Sapolsky.

When something trips your stress-alert system, a danger signal rushes to your brain. From there, it travels through projections—nerves—that branch from your brain down through your spine and out to the rest of your body. The message divides. Half goes to your voluntary nervous system, which directs your skeletal system to contract and get those legs churning and those arms flailing. With some 1,030 separate skeletal muscles in your body—almost half your body weight—that's a lot of tension. The other half of the message goes from your hypothalamus, a neural center in your brain, to your autonomic nervous system. That one controls all the involuntary organ functions that happen whether you tell them to or not. (Now stay with us here, because the circuitry gets a little tricky.)

The autonomic system, for its part, subdivides into sympathetic and parasympathetic nervous systems, which serve opposite functions. The sympathetic system is the body's ultimate fire alarm. It commands the pituitary gland to release hormones into the body. Adrenaline and noradrenaline are two (these are the British terms; American scientists refer to them as epinephrine and norepinephrine). Another important class of hormones, secreted by the adrenal gland within the pituitary, are glucocorticoids, or cortisol. While epinephrine acts within seconds, glucocorticoids are activated over the course of minutes or hours.

Turn It Down

Intrusive discordant noise—street traffic, jumbo jetliners, manufacturing plants, even that subtle but constant humming of your computer—has been linked to such physical problems as high blood pressure, hypertension and learning disorders. It also has been implicated in such mental symptoms as irritability, aggressiveness, fatigue and lack of concentration. All these symptoms have been tracked back to stress.

"Virtually all the research on the physiological effects of noise has found a correlation between noise and health problems," says Evelyn Talbott, Ph.D., associate professor of epidemiology at the University of Pittsburgh Graduate School of Public Health.

Even worse for people under stress is that excessive noise can increase the risk of hypertension and other cardiovascular diseases by about 10 percent. Add to that the already-pumped-up heart activity that stress causes, and we're talking amplified concern.

More than volume, two factors—predictability and controllability—tend to influence how annoying noises are, says Jerome Singer, Ph.D., professor and chairman of the Department of Medical and Clinical Psychology at Uniformed Services University of Health Sciences in Bethesda, Maryland.

You have little control over a dripping faucet, for example, which—despite the fact that it registers a mere 55 decibels or less—can keep you up all night. It can be just as stress-invoking as the 90-decibel stream of traffic outside your office window.

Together, these chemicals flood your bloodstream. They send heart rate and blood pressure soaring. They force your throat muscles, nostril passages and your eyes to open wider. They temporarily halt digestion in your stomach and intestines. They stop the secretion of saliva and mucus. They make you sweat. They dilate the pupils of your eyes. You get goose pimples and blush.

As mentioned, the parasympathetic nervous system has the opposite job: to calm and slow the body down, promote growth and store energy. When the brain activates the sympathetic system, though, it inhibits the parasympathetic system. In other words, your brain shuts down its primary calming mechanism to force you to stay alert and ready.

The Concrete Jungle

All of this is logical in a Darwinian save-your-butt sense. You become wide-eyed to see danger better. Breathing accelerates to get more oxygen into your bloodstream. Blood rushes faster to fuel muscles tensed for action. Digestive processes are cut off so that blood can go where it's needed. Sweat cools off your body, enabling it to burn more energy.

All of this is good. There's just one problem. While the fight-or-flight response has saved more than a few lives, past and present, fighting or fleeing may not be plausible options for modern man.

"The contrast between then and now couldn't be more striking," says Reed C. Moskowitz, M.D., clinical assistant professor of psychiatry and director of the Stress Disorders Medical Services Program at New York University in New York City and author of *Your Healing Mind.* "Instead of acute physical danger, you face continual psychological and social stresses in your life. We're chronically triggering the stress response. Our bodies are prepared to fight, but we never get that release."

We may be victims of evolution, Dr. Moskowitz suggests, stuck with a response

The Man Who Invented Stress

Before Dr. Hans Selye, there was no stress. The Austrian-born endocrinologist (people who study the hormone-secreting glands of the endocrine system) who is generally credited with "discovering" stress.

"To be only a bit facetious," writes Stanford University's Dr. Robert Sapolsky in *Why Zebras Don't Get Ulcers: A Guide to Stress, Stress-Related Diseases, and Coping,* "stress physiology exists as a discipline because this man was both a very insightful scientist and somewhat inept at handling laboratory rats."

In the 1930s, it seems, Dr. Selye was a young assistant professor at McGill University in Montreal looking for a way to distinguish himself. Studying the effects on rats of a newly isolated ovarian extract, Dr. Selye injected the rodents each day but apparently "with not a great display of dexterity," Dr. Sapolsky reports. He would miss, drop them, chase them around the room or shoo them with a broom. After several months, he discovered that they had peptic ulcers, greatly enlarged adrenal glands and shrunken immune tissues. After conducting similar tests on a control group

mechanism that spins our stress wheels. And spins them again. And again. So much, in fact, that you could say that we are in perpetual preparedness, all stressed up with nowhere to go.

Endocrinologist Hans Selye, M.D., was the first to establish the link between stress and disease. In the 1930s, he gave the first definition of stress: "the nonspecific response of the body to any demand placed upon it." What he left out was the mind, which later research has shown plays an integral part in how stress affects our lives. The people who say that stress is all in people's heads may not be far from the truth, as it turns out.

The area above your shoulders gets involved in a variety of ways. One is as a

and discovering the same results, he reasoned that the one thing the two groups had in common was his klutzy handling of them. To test this theory, he put some on the roof in winter and others in the boiler room. Still others were overexercised or underwent surgical procedures. In other words, he stressed them out. The results were the same: ulcers, enlarged glands and atrophied immune tissues.

He published the results in a humble little professional paper entitled "A Syndrome Produced by Diverse Nocuous Agents," published in 1936, which rocked the medical community with his theory of what he termed the general adaption syndrome, or stress syndrome.

He went on to write *The Stress of Life* in 1956 and about 30 other books and 1,500 technical articles. For his efforts, Dr. Selye, who went on to become professor and director of the Institute of Experimental Medicine and Surgery at the University of Montreal, received 16 honorary degrees and some 50 awards, medals and honorary citizenships, including a Companion of the Order of Canada, his country's highest honor.

analyze, synthesize and basically figure out this thing called stress.

The Role of the Mind in Stress

In one of those mercifully rare songs where The Beatles actually let Ringo sing, he posed the musical question: "What goes on in your mind?" When it comes to stress, that is the key consideration.

"In our civilized environment, the stressful events are of a chronic psychological and social nature," says Dr. Moskowitz. In other words, what's going on in your mind can either make or break the stress cycle.

As Shakespeare wrote in *Hamlet*, "There is nothing either good or bad, but thinking makes it so." There's as much science as literature in those words. Dr. Moskowitz says that how we perceive and interpret what's going on is the key to whether we cope with stress or are overtaken by it.

There are, Dr. Sapolsky says, certain psychologic factors that are almost guaranteed to trip your stress-alert system. Among them: loss of control, unpredictability, lack of outlets for venting frustration, lack of sources of support and a perception that things are getting worse.

To them, you can add worry, fear, anxiety, anger, hostility, guilt, insecurity and any number of other dark thoughts that you are not required to reveal here. These kinds of thoughts trigger the same physiological reaction as any predator our prehistoric brethren encountered.

factory where the brain produces a wide assortment of chemicals that influence our responses to almost everything in our environment, including stressful situations, as new research has shown. Dr. Sapolsky notes one quick example of the hand-and-glove relationship between stress and brain chemistry. Stress depletes norepinephrine in the brain's limbic system, which regulates emotion. No one is sure why; perhaps it's because, as we saw, it's being consumed faster than usual. This drop in norepinephrine may be the reason that we feel depressed or, as we say, blue.

The other way the mind gets involved is as the thinking machine, the ivory tower where we can kick back and contemplate, ruminate,

In other words, you are what you think when it comes to stress. Perception is reality. But if we can think our way into a stress-induced funk, we can think our way out as well. That's the beautiful part of this body-mind connection stuff. There are ways—there are *always* ways. After all, we're still around. When was the last time you saw a saber-toothed tiger?

Identifying Stressors in Your Life

What Really Sets You Off?

Stress does not happen in a vacuum. There are instigators, both external and internal: things that come at you from the environment, things that bug your body and things that menace your mind. They are called stressors.

A stressor is the stimulus or event that triggers the fight-or-flight stress response. It's anything that changes the normal state, or homeostasis, of body or mind.

While there may be good stress (eustress) and bad stress (distress), there are no universals about what makes a stressor, well, stressful.

What is universal is that we will always have stressors. "Just being alive means being in a continual state of flux," explains Jon Kabat-Zinn, Ph.D., director of the Stress Reduction Clinic at the University of Massachusetts Medical Center in Worcester who is also an associate professor of medicine, lecturer and author of *Full Catastrophe Living: Using the Wisdom of Your Body and Mind to Face Stress, Pain and Illness* and *Wherever You Go, There You Are.*

Living in this state of flux should be a source of joy—not pain. The curveballs, knuckleballs and, yes, even screwballs that life throws at you are what make it exciting and interesting. You can embrace and revel in the vagaries of life, or you can wallow in worry.

It's your choice.

"It's not the potential stressor itself but how you perceive it and then how you handle it that determines whether it will lead to stress," adds Dr. Kabat-Zinn.

The Big Picture

Some stressors are big: earthquakes, the death of a spouse, the loss of a job. Some are small: getting a parking ticket (again), losing your glasses (again!), missing the train (again!!). But, once again, the size of the stressor is not so important as your perception of it and your reaction to it.

"Over a long period of time, little stressors can make you just as ill or more ill than big stressors," says C. David Jenkins, Ph.D., adjunct professor of preventive medicine and community health and professor of psychology and behavioral sciences at the University of Texas Medical Branch at Galveston.

And just to keep you on your toes, one man's stressor may well be another man's stress blaster.

"The same stressor can have a positive or a negative effect, depending on what the individual brings to it," says Glenn H. Elder, Jr., Ph.D., professor of sociology at the University of North Carolina at Chapel Hill. Playing competitive sports is an example: Some guys thrive on it; others fear it.

To further complicate the issue, every stressor does not generate the same hormonal response, notes Stanford University's Dr. Robert Sapolsky. And—hold on to your hormones—two identical stressors can cause different responses depending on how your mind perceives them.

While you can read tons of fascinating scientific stuff describing and defining stressors,

Morton Orman, M.D., author of *The 14-Day Stress Cure*, brings it down to terms that we can all relate to. Quoting a bit of wisdom that appears on many an office coffee mug, he says that "stress is created when one's mind overrides the body's basic desire to choke the living daylights out of some jerk who desperately deserves it."

So now that we've included everyone and everything as potential stressors, let's narrow the instigators down and take a closer look at a couple of internal and external stressors that men frequently encounter. And remember that there is a lot of overlap here. "Issues that begin as externals turn to internals once our minds and bodies start to grapple with them," says Dr. Orman. The trick to dealing with all of them is to keep reminding yourself that stress is in the mind—and body— of the beholder. In parts 2 and 3 of this book, we deal with specific sources of stress in the home and workplace. Here are some of the most common causes that you face almost every day.

Time

How often have you said to yourself, "There aren't enough hours in the day"? Too often, we suspect. But you know what? Twenty-four hours is the limit. The time crunch puts the stress squeeze on everyone.

You can deal with it in any number of ways. One is to do more faster. Crazy. Another is to do it all more efficiently. Pipe dream. Still another is to blow off all deadlines. Suicidal. But the best way is to completely shift your perspective on time.

It's not about being out of time or on time. It's about being "in" time, says Stephan Rechtschaffen, M.D., president of the Omega Institute in Rhinebeck, New York, which teaches healthy relaxation techniques, and author of *Time Shifting: Creating More Time to Enjoy Your Life.*

"In the present moment, there is no stress," he says. "But we have a lot of trouble with that. The 'time management' that I teach is governed by one rule: Live life in the now. We don't have to live with a chronic time shortage. We don't have to wear our watches like shackles."

Loss of Control

Biggie. Men hate to lose control. And we hate to admit that we've lost control. But the plain and simple fact is that you can't lose something you never had. And none of us have control. Most of what happens to you and around you every day is beyond your ability to manipulate. If you see yourself as a Master of the Universe, we're sorry. Now, accept it and move on.

"Men tend to interpret a greater number of situations as control situations, and they react more dramatically," says Dr. Georgia Witkin of Mount Sinai Medical Center. Her succinct advice: "Give up the struggle for control when that struggle is unrealistic." Which reminds us of the often-used "Serenity Prayer" of recovery groups: "God grant me the serenity to accept the things I cannot change, courage to change the things I can, and wisdom to know the difference."

Relationships

Parents, siblings, children, friends and— last, but hardly least—lovers. Throw in grandparents, aunts and uncles and nieces and nephews for good measure. "People are the biggest stressors," says Blair Justice, Ph.D., professor of psychology in the School of Public Health at the University of Texas Health Science Center at Houston and author of *Who Gets Sick.* "And, research shows, people are also the most commonly used method to relieve stress as well." Go figure.

"Relationship stress for men is about fear of intimacy, about attachment dilemmas that often seem insoluble," says Samuel Osherson, Ph.D., honorary research psychologist at Harvard University Health Services and author of *Wrestling with Love.* How do you solve them?

"You have to shift from angry isolation to forgiveness. You have to reframe your world and make deep internal changes."

He adds that men especially struggle with ambivalent feelings about their fathers and about being fathers. In the former, it's about earning respect. In the latter, it's about first becoming comfortable with nurturing and then later about letting go of parental authority.

Negative Emotions

The "big three" are fear, sadness and anger, according to Dr. Orman. "These are knee-jerk reflex emotions that, for the most part, we've been programmed to feel," he says. "You may not be able to cut them off at the pass, but once these emotions occur, you can take steps to eliminate them."

The first step is to identify what the emotion is. "Don't be vague or general," says Dr. Orman. "Don't use words like *stressed out* or *upset*."

Challenge your assumptions. If someone's late, don't jump to the conclusion that he's inconsiderate or disorganized. Maybe he got stuck in traffic or had an accident. "If you think about it for a second, you may realize something is not 'bad' or 'wrong' but just different, and that goes a long way toward dissipating an emotion like anger," Dr. Orman says.

Change your pattern. If you don't speak up when someone puts you down, do. Or write a letter. Or make an appointment to meet with that person to discuss it. "Force yourself to do something other than your habitual pattern," recommends Dr. Orman.

Adopt words to live by. These would be similar to affirmations, says Dr. Orman.

How Do You Spell Stress?

Your list may include your pet's accidents on the living room carpet, the loss of a set of keys and an ex-lover who keeps making untimely reappearances in your life. We all spell stress differently.

The following assessment of the stressors in our lives was developed by Thomas H. Holmes, M.D., and his research associates at the University of Washington School of Medicine in Seattle.

In this table, events with the higher numbers (values) generally elicit greater stress responses than those with lower values. Stressors can be positive or negative events.

Event	Value
Death of a spouse	100
Divorce	73
Marital separation	65
Death of a close family member	63
Jail term	63
Personal injury or illness	53
Marriage	50
Fired from work	47
Marital reconciliation	45
Retirement	45
Change in family member's health	44
Pregnancy	40
Addition to family	39
Business readjustment	39
Sex difficulties	39
Change in financial status	38
Death of a close friend	37
Change to a different line of work	36
Change in the number of marital arguments	36
Mortgage or loan for home or business	31
Foreclosure of mortgage or loan	30

Come up with principles that are as close to truth as you can get, beliefs that enable you to see things in a positive but realistic light. For

To check your own stress levels, jot down the value of each stressor that you've experienced in the past year. Multiply it by the number of times that you experienced the stressor during the year (if more than four times, multiply by four). Add up your totals.

Dr. Holmes and his colleagues have found that people with high scores may be prone to illness. About 80 percent of people with scores higher than 300 get sick soon; about 50 percent with scores in the 200 to 299 range fall ill frequently; and about 30 percent who score between 150 and 199 are easily prone to illness.

Event	Value
Change in work responsibilities	29
Son or daughter leaving home	29
Trouble with in-laws	29
Outstanding personal achievement	28
Spouse begins or stops work	26
Starting or finishing school	26
Change in living conditions	25
Revision of personal habits	24
Change in the number of troubles with a boss	23
Change in residence	20
Different working hours or conditions	20
Change to a new school	20
Change in church activities	19
Change in type or amount of recreation	19
Change in social activities	18
Loan for items like a car or major appliance	17
Change in sleeping habits	15
Change in eating habits	15
Change in number of family gatherings	15
Vacation	13
Minor violation of law	11

example, instead of adopting *The X-Files* slogan "Trust No One" as your personal creed, try this variation: Not all people are

trustworthy, but some people are. "These values give you room to give people the benefit of the doubt," points out Dr. Orman.

Worry

Dale Carnegie was onto something long before anyone else. His book *How to Stop Worrying and Start Living* predated Alfred E. Neuman's famous *Mad* magazine motto, "What, me worry?" and Bobby McFerrin's 1988 hit "Don't Worry, Be Happy." First published in 1944, it has sold well over six million copies and was even parodied in director Stanley Kubrick's 1964 Cold War film *Dr. Strangelove or: How I Learned to Stop Worrying and Love the Bomb.*

"Worrying is at the heart of all anxiety," says psychologist Daniel Goleman, Ph.D., behavior writer for the *New York Times* and author of *Emotional Intelligence.* "Underlying worry is the vigilance for potential danger that has been essential for survival over the course of evolution." That sounds like a grand anthropological justification for spinning in an endless loop of fretting. But it does explain why worrying triggers the fight-or-flight response. Dr. Goleman suggests applying relaxation methods right at the moment the worry loop takes hold (for more information, see Relaxation Techniques on page 54) and a "healthy skepticism" to worrisome thoughts.

This advice rings true with Carnegie's, who suggests following these three rules.

- Ask yourself, "What is the worst that can possibly happen?"
- Prepare to accept it if you have to.
- Then calmly proceed to improve on the worst.

Expecting the Unexpected

Reduce Stress by Being a Man with a Plan

There is something manly about being prepared. British war hero Robert S. S. Baden-Powell knew it. That's why he made "Be Prepared" the motto of the group he founded, the Boy Scouts. He wanted boys to be ready "to take on any kind of duty at any time . . . and help other people at all times." As an early history of the Scouts put it, "Here was a virile new conception—educational and social." The motto, emblazoned on the Boy Scout badge, came from the Knights of the Middle Ages Code of Chivalry, which Baden-Powell thought would "appeal to the moral sense" of all boys.

We all admire a man with a plan. But we hold a man with a Plan B in the highest esteem. The guy who appears to be cool, calm and collected while everyone around him is running about madly either does not fathom the severity of the situation or knows something that everyone else does not. He remains unscathed by stress because he has thought about what could go wrong and has a backup plan. He knows where the escape hatch is.

He is James Bond toting every techno-gadget known to man, Bill Gates with a computer system that the competition hadn't anticipated, or a Boy Scout who wrapped his matches in a plastic bag in case of rain.

"Having an alternative backup solution is always a good idea," says the Omega Institute's Dr. Stephan Rechtschaffen. "We spend so much time stressing out about things that may go wrong, things that we had not expected. We would spend that time more wisely coming up with a detailed contingency plan."

But being prepared—poised like a cat ready to pounce, thinking several steps ahead—requires all senses to be alert, present and accounted for, ready to rock and roll. And that can take a toll on your body and the mind.

Surprise! Surprises Are Stressful

Why are unexpected events and surprises stressful? "Because they throw your body out of homeostatic balance," explains Stanford University's Dr. Robert Sapolsky. Homeostasis, for those who claim that biology wasn't offered at their high schools, is the ideal level of oxygen, acidity, temperature and other physiological factors that our bodies maintain under normal circumstances. Surprise—by definition a deviation from the norm—triggers our bodies into the classic fight-or-flight stress response. We're ready to run either from it or after it, whatever "it" is. This stressful response, when confronted with unexpected situations, is true of zebras, lions and humans.

But humans, says Dr. Sapolsky, add a stressor that zebras and other animals don't deal with. "We have this great propensity to worry ourselves sick," he says. "So we have to include as a stressor the anticipation of bad things happening. When we see things coming, we can turn on just as robust a stress response based merely on anticipation."

Butterflies in the stomach before a speech, clammy palms before a job interview and accelerated heartbeat as you knock on the door of a blind date illustrate the point in the short term. Looking ahead also can trigger stress: Will you get the raise at the end of the quarter? Will the IRS audit you . . . again? How long will your parents be around? The same goes for looking far ahead: Will it be any better in your next incarnation?

Men specifically deal with yet another mental stressor, says Dr. Samuel Osherson of Harvard University Health Services. "Men translate unexpected events to mean a loss of control, and that's a significant stressor for them," he notes. "We have a choice: to let go of trying to control everything, or do all that we can to prepare."

Be Prepared

When life's vagaries cause us to lose hair—or turn what's left of it gray—we are called anxious, neurotic, paranoid, worrywarts or worse. When we plan for the unexpected and it happens, we are called forward-thinking visionaries. Since there are about 1 million young men enrolled in the Boy Scouts, and more than 92 million alumni, you'd think that more of us would have what George Bush used to call that vision thing. Here are some key tips to keep in mind as you work toward your stress-reduction merit badge.

Be street smart. In police lingo, it's called coming up, explains Detective J. J. Bittenbinder, formerly with the Chicago Police Department, now an inspector and lecturer assigned to the Cook County Sheriff's Department in Illinois. "On the streets, police are more focused," he says. "You become more aware. You pay attention to your surroundings. If something seems unusual or out of the ordinary, you should wake up, come up a notch with all your senses. When you recognize something as a potential threat, it's not as big a threat because it can't take you by surprise," adds Bittenbinder. The same holds true in life. Practice such preventive behavior and you min-

imize surprises. (Bittenbinder discusses other ways to be prepared in Fighting Crime Fears on page 92.)

Turn to family planning. Contingency plans are critical if you're a parent, as anyone who has had the pleasure of trying to get children off to school morning after morning can attest. "Take into account things that might go wrong," says Dr. Jon Kabat-Zinn of the Stress Reduction Clinic at the University of Massachusetts Medical Center. "Get up earlier, and get everything ready beforehand. Plan what time they go to bed so that you can get them up with enough time to do everything as unrushed as possible."

Practice visualization. That's the advice of 1996 NBA Coach of the Year Phil Jackson of the Chicago Bulls. "If you visualize what's going to happen, you can react to it quickly without thinking, because you've seen it in your mind," he says. "If you think of enough variables, you've covered every possibility so that nothing will be unexpected."

To increase the number of possibilities, he suggests following Japanese Zen master Suzuki Roshi's wisdom to empty your mind and think like a beginner. As Roshi said, "If your mind is empty, it is always ready for anything; it is open to everything. In the beginner's mind there are many possibilities; in the expert's mind there are few."

Take the time to make a Plan B. People have anxiety about making plans "because plans govern the future and most of us look to the future with fear," says Dr. Rechtschaffen. "What if our plans don't work out? What if something unexpected comes along to stop us? What if. . .?"

He suggests coming up with plans that aren't so specific that they "become a weight that keeps you from seeing alternatives." That way you won't end up like Alfred E. Neuman, the mascot of *Mad* magazine. "He's the kind of guy who paints himself into a corner and then applies a second coat," says *Mad* co-editor John Ficarra.

Performing under Pressure

Rise to the Occasion

It's every boy's sports fantasy, says Phil Jackson, coach of the NBA's Chicago Bulls. "Every guy envisions himself in the final seconds of the game," he says, "counting down, 5-4-3-2-1, as he launches the last-second shot with the crowd screaming and the announcer shouting, 'It's go-o-o-o-od!' Only to be wakened from the dream by his mother calling him in from the driveway basket for dinner."

We've all had some variation of that hero-at-the-buzzer dream. It epitomizes the ability to perform the most difficult task under the most extreme pressure: the report that's due the next morning, the exam that determines your grade, meeting the future in-laws for the first time, the sales pitch, the audition for the play or the tryout for the team. All the stress signs are there: the quickened pulse, the rush of adrenaline, the profuse sweating, the butterflies. And that certain high you feel when you are sometimes able to go beyond your own limits.

"Performing under pressure is about rising to the occasion in the most stressful conditions," says James E. Loehr, Ed.D., sports psychologist with LGE Sport Science in Orlando, Florida, and author of *Toughness Training for Life*.

In sports jargon, excelling in those high-stress situations is called being in the zone or feeling it. You may call it being on a roll. Those who doubt their own abilities might call it being lucky. Dr. Loehr calls it the ideal performance state.

"It's a delicate psycho-physical balance that results in being relaxed and calm, virtually feeling no pressure even when you're under incredible pressure," he says. Contributing to this feeling is a sense of having fun. That's because when you're enjoying yourself, he explains, stress hormones such as cortisol are repressed and pleasurable chemicals such as serotonin are increased.

"We have found that when athletes were happier, felt better about themselves and were in good health, they went to the next level of performance," Dr. Loehr says.

Training for Mental Toughness

Former President Harry S. Truman put it this way: "If you can't stand the heat, get out of the kitchen." But you don't have to be an American president or a professional basketball star to learn to perform well when the heat is on. Here are some tips to keep in mind the next time the clock is ticking down and all eyes are on you.

Live in the past. Chicago Bulls superstar Michael Jordan will go down in basketball history as one of the pre-eminent clutch players of all time. "Jordan's ability to stay relaxed and intensely focused in the midst of chaos is unsurpassed," comments Coach Jackson. "While everyone else is spinning madly out of control, he moves effortlessly across the floor, enveloped by a great stillness."

Jackson discloses Jordan's secret: "He often calls up images of past successes in his mind during high-pressure situations. Rather than cloud his mind with negative thoughts, he

says to himself, 'Okay, I've been here before,' then tries to relax enough to let something positive emerge."

Get in stress shape. Like athletes training for a competition, you can train yourself mentally and physically for pressure-cooker situations. Dr. Loehr is a strong believer in being a "stress seeker" as a way to learn how to deal with pressure when it comes up. He calls it toughness training.

Just as you build muscles by working them, and then allowing for adequate recovery, you can condition yourself to perform under pressure by plunging into stressful situations that you might otherwise seek to avoid. Like taking on a high-profile project at work that requires intense deadline performance. Or going into your boss's office to ask for that raise you truly believe that you've earned. One caution: If you throw yourself into a pressure-cooker situation, Dr. Loehr says, make sure that you allow for some downtime afterward—just as you would take rest days between strength-training sessions.

Banish self-doubt. The cruelest epithet in sports is "choke." If you listen to sports talk radio these days, you'll hear it from every other caller. Teams don't lose close games anymore. They choke.

Universally symbolized by squeezing one's neck with one's hand (for dramatic effect use two hands), the concept of choking doesn't just apply to sports. Dr. Loehr says that what is really at issue is self-doubt. "The fear of failure creates failure," says Dr. Loehr. Also too much inward attention can make you wilt under pressure. "Being aware is one thing; being self-conscious is another," he notes. "Get outside your head and absorbed into the activity."

Get a role model. If actors can assume the traits of a character they play, so can you. "If you don't have the skills and inner feelings that you think you need to succeed," says Dr. Loehr, "simply project the image of someone who does." Doing so will not only change how others see you but also alter your own nervous system and brain chemistry and may be the

The Price of Pressure

Roger Maris learned firsthand the terrible toll that pressure can take on a man's body, mind and spirit. In 1961, the New York Yankees slugger eclipsed the immortal Babe Ruth's long-standing single-season home run record when he clubbed 61 round-trippers.

What should have been the most glorious season of his life turned into a living hell.

"People hated me for it, especially the press," Maris once told a writer. As the season wore on, the stress grew so great that Maris's hair started to fall out in clumps.

"Stress changes the immune status," says Harry L. Roth, M.D., professor of dermatology at the University of California in San Francisco. "In the case of Roger Maris, this hair loss sounds like *alopecia totalis* or *alopecia areata*, which are autoimmune conditions in which the body produces antibodies that cause loss of function. The other possibility is extreme shedding, called telogen hair loss, which is reported after traumas like infection, major surgery, malnutrition and stress. How stress causes hair loss in this instance is not clear, but it is an observable fact."

Maris died in 1985, at age 51, of lymphatic cancer. After his career ended in 1968, Maris said of his life: "Going after the record started off as such a dream. I was living in a fairy tale for a while. Too bad it ended so badly. It would've been a helluva lot more fun if I had never hit those 61 homers."

spark you need to jump-start your own self-confidence. He suggests modeling your facial expression and how you walk, talk and hold your head after someone whose confidence you admire.

Stress and Disease

It Can Make You Sick

Remember back to the days of vinyl records? (That was sometime after the saber-toothed tigers had disappeared.) What if you had left "Rock around the Clock" on the phonograph with the arm off so that the record played over and over and over again? Eventually, you'd have worn the grooves of that 45 down so far that even Bill Haley and His Comets would have lost their shake, rattle and roll.

That's how the constant repetition of the fight-or-flight response acts on you when those stress hormones keep rockin' around your body clock day and night.

New York University's Dr. Reed C. Moskowitz uses a similar analogy. "Stress is like having one foot on the accelerator of a car, with the other foot on the brake," he says. "We wind up stripping our gears. The chronic buildup of stress takes an enormous toll on our bodies in terms of wear and tear."

Those stressors come with increasing frequency as our lives merge into the fast lane. Because we live in relatively civilized times, we have fewer ways to burn off that hormonal buildup. We can't punch our boss (unless we're trust-fund babies). We can't run over the car that cut us off (unless we're shooting a chase scene from a Sylvester Stallone action flick). We can't kill the saber-toothed tiger (because evolution beat us to the punch). Our inability to handle stress sets off a chain reaction that results in increased vulnerability to disease.

"Each period of stress, especially if it results from frustrating,

unsuccessful struggles, leaves some irreversible chemical scars that accumulate to constitute the signs of tissue aging," wrote Dr. Hans Selye in *Stress without Distress.*

The High Cost of Stress

As many as 90 percent of office visits to primary care physicians are connected to stress, some experts estimate.

Dr. Moskowitz's partial list of stress-related illnesses includes alcoholism, anorexia, arthritis, asthma, back pain, bulimia, chronic fatigue, colitis, compulsive overeating, depression, dermatitis, drug abuse, heart disease, high blood pressure, high cholesterol, infertility, irritable bowel syndrome, migraine headaches, multiple chemical sensitivities, obesity, panic disorder, phobias, severe allergies, sexual dysfunction, tension headaches and possibly ulcers.

Long before illness sets in, stress can cause these physical symptoms involving the voluntary muscular system or the automatic nervous system: belching, bloating, blushing, chest pain, cold and sweaty hands, colds, constipation, decreased sexual desire, diarrhea, dizziness, dry mouth, ear ringing, faintness, frequent or lingering chills, frowning, gas, goose pimples, heartburn, heart palpitations, hives, jaw pain, light-headedness, muscle tension and aches, neck pain, night sweats, painful cold hands and feet, rashes, sound and light sensitivity, stammering, stuttering, swallowing difficulty, teeth grinding or temporomandibular disorder, trembling hands and lips and widening pupils.

And that's just the body. Here's the toll that stress takes on the mind: anger, anxiety, apathy, concentration problems, confusion, crying, depression, difficulty learning new information, disorganization, emotionally drained feeling, fatigue, fear of closeness, forgetfulness, frustration, hopelessness, indecisiveness, insomnia, irritability, loneliness, low energy, low self-esteem, moodiness, nervousness, nightmares, obsessions, oversleeping, poor judgment, rapid thinking, recurring negative thoughts, self-doubt, tension, trapped feeling and suicidal thoughts.

Seeking Immunity

One of the effects of the stress response is that it cuts off any body function that doesn't directly relate to repelling the perceived threat, which makes sense—provided the threat is real. Why grow fingernails when you're about to have your hand bitten off? Why fight nasty cancer cells when a Mack truck is about to make you one with a cement wall?

Similarly, when your body is reacting to stress, digestion gets interrupted and reproductive urges decrease. The same is true for your immune system, which defends against infections and illness.

Here's why. Main parts of your immune system include your thymus, bone marrow, lymph nodes, lymphatic vessels, lymph (one of the three main fluids that circulate through the body), liver and spleen. All have nerve fibers that communicate with the brain. Since there is a direct link between your immune system and your mind, psychological stress can greatly affect your body's ability to fight disease.

The thymus is the big cheese of the immune system. It produces, among other regulating hormones, white blood cells known as T lymphocytes—the good guys that promote cell immunity. The lymph group helps, too. The nodes filter the lymph and contain B lymphocytes, which promote production of antibodies when you're exposed to bacteria and virus. The liver, another player, is where lymph is produced. It contains large cells that do a full frontal attack on foreign substances that invade our bodies. The spleen destroys old blood cells and also produces lymphocytes.

Hopefully you're still with us here, because here's the kicker. This whole interconnected immune system operates more efficiently under the parasympathetic nervous system, which controls body functions during rest and sleep. But stress arouses the sympathetic nervous system, which basically knocks out the parasympathetic system. As more and more hormones such as epinephrine, norepinephrine and cortisol are released, they trigger chemical changes that decrease the amount of white blood cells in the blood, thereby decreasing your level of immunity.

Naturally, the guys in the white coats have a big word for this whole process. It's called immunosuppression.

Making the Connection

Most of us have learned the hard way about the connection between stress and disease. It's the headache when we're under the gun or the cold that we catch when we're frazzled. But there is more than just anecdotal evidence that the two are linked. Studies have scientifically corroborated that stress can lead to or exacerbate the following physical problems. And thanks to the field of psychoneuro-immunology, it has been shown that mental stress can cause physical distress.

Heart disease. For a long time, there was just anecdotal evidence that stress caused heart attacks. But since the 1970s, there has been a growing body of research that shows a direct link between stress and high blood pressure, cholesterol, clogging of the arteries, hypertension, diabetes and other conditions.

For example, a long-term Harvard University study found that men who experienced symptoms of anxiety—fear of strange people, nervousness, the jitters, cold sweats (all signs that have been related to stress)—were as much as four times more likely to suffer sudden cardiac death than those without those symptoms. The study ranked anxiety right up there with smoking, excessive drinking, high sodium intake and lack of exercise as risk factors in heart disease. The Montreal Heart Institute found that heart attack survivors suffering from depression have three to four times the risk of dying within six months as nondepressed survivors. Depression is another indicator of stress. Similarly, in another study, emotional distress has been related to mortality in patients with coronary heart disease. In still another study, New Yorkers working in high-strain jobs—such as air traffic controllers and bus drivers—had higher blood pressure.

Why is the heart such a vulnerable victim of stress? Simple, says Stanford University's Dr. Robert Sapolsky. "The cardiovascular stress response basically consists of making the heart and blood vessels work harder for a while, and if you do that on a regular basis, they will wear out, just like any pump or hose you buy."

Back pain. The muscles of your back are particularly vulnerable to the constant contraction and relaxation that the stress response puts them through, says Willibald Nagler, M.D., physiatrist in chief at New York Hospital–Cornell Medical Center in New York City. That's especially true of the lower back because "so many parts of all the nerves to the lower extremities come through the lower spine," Dr. Nagler says. "The lumbar (lower) spine is a fine-tuned organization of bones that demands a lot of adjustment every time we sit or stand."

The best way to avoid back pain caused by stress is to "stay limber by doing stretching exercises every day when you're not under stress," suggests Dr. Nagler. "Well-stretched muscles can tolerate a lot more pain than stiff ones. Also, move around a lot. Don't sit in one place." For back pain and muscle spasms, he recommends ice packs, not heat. "Ice decreases the sensory nerves' ability to conduct painful stimuli."

Headaches. "We still really don't know exactly why stress causes headaches," says Seymour Diamond, M.D., director of the Diamond

Ulcers and Stress

Though ulcers are one of the oldest irregularities of the body known to mankind—Byzantine physician Paul of Aegina mentions them as far back as the seventh century—its causes are still a mystery.

Until recently, stomach ulcers—holes in the lining of the stomach walls that can cause bleeding and other unsavory repercussions—were considered the worrier's disease. The pioneering stress research of Dr. Hans Selye went a long way to making that connection. Peptic ulcers were among the trio of symptoms his stressed-out laboratory rats exhibited during his first experiments. And as you yourself may have experienced, your stomach can turn into a cauldron when you're feeling under the gun.

It turns out, however, that "stress doesn't cause ulcers," says Steven Peikin, M.D., professor of medicine at Robert Wood Johnson Medical School in Camden, New Jersey, and author of *Gastrointestinal Health*. "But stress can aggravate a pre-existing condition by enhancing the output of gastric acid."

Many doctors attribute ulcers to a tough little bacterium called *Helicobacter pylori*, or simply *H. pylori*, but even that theory is not universally accepted.

It's not even known for sure how stress aggravates a condition that already exists, but Stanford University's Dr. Robert Sapolsky suggests one of several possibilities. "Ul-

Headache Clinic in Chicago and author of *The Hormone Headache*. What is known, he says, is that stress hormones make the muscles of the neck and scalp tighten. There's a reflex swelling of blood vessels in those areas that causes the pain we commonly call headache, whether episodic or migraine. Episodic, or tension, headaches are caused by bosses yelling, children crying and other garden-variety daily tensions.

cers are not formed so much during the stressor as during the recovery," he says.

Since the stress reaction cuts down on hydrochloric acid secretion (that's the highly corrosive acid that breaks down food and aids digestion), your stomach produces less of the protective mucus and bicarbonate it needs to coat the stomach walls against that acid. If you're under stress for a while, that protective lining can become dangerously thin. Once the stress ends and your body starts secreting acid again, your defenses are down. "If you repeatedly go through this cycle of sustained periods of decreased hydrochloric acid secretion followed by periods of normal secretion, an ulcer will eventually emerge," says Dr. Sapolsky.

If stress does exacerbate ulcers, Dr. Peikin recommends acetaminophen, a good short-term pain reliever. Avoid aspirin and nonsteroidal anti-inflammatory drugs such as Advil, Motrin and Nuprin, whose active ingredient is ibuprofen.

"These drugs inhibit the production of chemicals in the stomach that protect its lining," says pharmacist John Gould, of Emmaus, Pennsylvania. Also try Tagamet HB or Pepcid AC, two popular over-the-counter heartburn-relief drugs (drugs that block the production of a chemical that releases acid in the stomach).

"We're all living hectic computer-controlled lives, which can certainly increase the number of episodic headaches that we're getting," he says. For common tension headaches, he recommends aspirin, "probably one of the greatest discoveries ever made," he says. Migraines, on the other hand, are related more to psychological problems, he notes, and often can be treated with counseling, relaxation exercises and prescription drugs. "Migraines can be an inherited disorder related to neurological manifestations in the brain," he adds. Interesting, migraines don't usually occur during times of stress, but a while after.

Colds. Several important studies have shown that psychological stress increases susceptibility to cold viruses. Besides depleting the immune system's ability to fight viruses, stress also makes us breathe more rapidly, sometimes twice the normal rate, says Dr. Georgia Witkin of Mount Sinai Medical Center. This hyperventilation dries up the mucous membranes in the respiratory system. They become more irritable and less protected against bacteria and viruses. Cortisol levels are down, and inflammations are up. Temperature regulation goes on the blink. Achoo!

"The way you handle a stress cold is the same as any cold," says Jeffrey Jahre, M.D., clinical associate professor at Temple University in Philadelphia and chief of infectious diseases at St. Luke's Hospital in Bethlehem, Pennsylvania. "Eat nourishing food, drink plenty of fluids and get rest. These are the pillars of good health. You basically should change some of the things that may have made you more susceptible in the first place."

Indigestion. When the stress button gets pushed, Dr. Witkin explains, the rhythmic smooth muscle contractions (called peristalsis) that push food through the intestinal system slow down, probably because digestion takes a backseat to basic survival needs. Also, gastric glands diminish their output, making absorption of food more difficult. The release of glucocorticoids indirectly increases the amount of stomach acid, which, in turn, leads to heartburn and worse gastrointestinal problems.

Overcoming Anger

Prevent a Hostile Takeover

Ben Franklin, a man who actually had time to go fly a kite, once said: "Anger is never without a reason, but seldom a good one."

Sure, they seem like perfectly good reasons at the time. Like the jerk who cuts you off on the highway. Or the boss who takes all the credit for your accomplishments at the staff meeting. Or getting sent into voice-mail purgatory. Or the new neighbor who apparently thinks that Metallica played at full blast will soothe men's souls. On any given day, if you're looking for an excuse to blow your top, you won't have to wait long.

"Anger is the most seductive of the negative emotions," says psychologist Dr. Daniel Goleman. "The self-righteous inner monologue fills the mind with the most convincing arguments. Anger is energizing, even exhilarating."

It's also incredibly destructive.

The Anatomy of Anger

What happens when you get angry? There are distinct physical reactions you can and should recognize.

Your knuckles whiten, your palms turn clammy, your jaws clench, your body trembles, your cheeks flush, your heart pounds and the muscles in your face lock in a scowl. These are the body's ways of preparing for the fight half of the fight-or-flight response. For example, blood flows to the hands, making it easier to grasp a weapon or strike at a foe, Dr. Goleman explains. Heart rate increases, and a rush of hormones such as adrenaline generates a pulse of energy strong enough for vigorous action.

The universal trigger for anger is a sense of being endangered, says Dr. Goleman. Not only a physical threat but also, as he says, "it can be a symbolic threat to self-esteem or dignity, being treated unjustly or rudely, being insulted or demeaned or being frustrated in pursuing an important goal."

It's a Killer

Anger may be exhilarating, as Dr. Goleman notes, but it's the most deadly exhilaration you'll ever feel because "anger kills," warns Redford B. Williams, M.D., professor of psychiatry and director of the Behavioral Medicine Research Center at Duke University Medical Center in Durham, North Carolina. He and his wife, Virginia Williams, Ph.D., are co-authors of a book by just that title.

In *Anger Kills*, the Williamses amass a convincing body of evidence that would convert even the most dyed-in-the-wool defender of anger as a healthy emotional outlet. Basically, they show that people exhibiting the psychological behaviors commonly known as Type A—always in a hurry, easily moved to anger and hostility and highly competitive and ambitious—develop heart disease more often than their more laid-back counterparts (known as Type Bs). In stressful situations, Type A's show increased blood flow to their muscles and increased blood levels of several stress hormones (adrenaline, noradrenaline and cortisol). All this means that their bodies are taxed more than others.

Dr. Williams and his colleagues did some interesting studies, showing that it's the hostility trait of Type A's that puts people at greatest risk. Hostility can magnify the impact of blood cholesterol levels. A hostile man with high cholesterol will have an increased chance of clogging his arteries. Hostile people also have weaker immune systems—never a good thing—and weakened parasympathetic nervous systems, which function as a sort of brake to calm the rush of fight-or-flight hormones. Hostile people are also unhappy, socially isolated and feel greater stress at work.

Dr. Williams identifies three specific traits of the hostile person that are most harmful: cynicism, anger and aggression.

"Hostile people are more sensitive to signals of things going wrong in their environment, and stress only amplifies their sensitivities," he says. "They have a very short fuse. They have a tendency to blame others quickly. In traffic, it's always the other guy who is 'stupid or dumb.' "

Before you check your own level of hostility in "Feeling Hostile?" on page 26, read these encouraging comments. "Hostility is a habit that can change if you apply some emotional intelligence, combining being mindful of when it is aroused, regulating it once it has begun and practicing empathy—hearing the feelings behind what is said," Dr. Goleman says.

"Trusting others goes a long way toward diffusing hostility," Dr. Williams adds. "Practicing a variety of strategies can help you change biological patterns of behavior that you may have been born with but don't have to die from."

Turning Away from Anger

Before stress triggers your next outburst and stages another emotional hijacking that threatens your health and your relationships, try some of these anger-altering approaches.

Avoid venting. "There is a widespread belief that has achieved almost mythological status that the way to get rid of anger is to express it," says Mark Epstein, M.D., a psychiatrist in Manhattan and author of *Thoughts without a Thinker*. It's not. In fact, catharsis—the vent to rage—typically pumps up the brain's arousal, leaving people feeling more

angry, not less. Dr. Epstein suggests neither venting nor suppressing anger. "People afraid of their anger act prematurely trying to get rid of it," he says. "The point is to recognize the anger coming on. Then become aware of its effect on your body. That will take you out of focusing on what's happening in your mind."

Nip anger in the bud. Question the assumptions that fuel anger in the first place, suggests Dr. Goleman. Consider the jerk who just cut you off in traffic. Maybe he had to swerve out of the way of the jerk in front of him. By challenging your assumptions, you may find that your anger is unjustified. "The earlier in the anger cycle, the better," he says.

Open your trusting heart. Because of their cynical distrust of others, hostile people feel stress when they have to let go of being in charge. To reverse that, Dr. Williams suggests relinquishing control in small inconsequential matters and building trust step-by-step until you may even let someone else pick the restaurant or drive the car without you throwing a fit. Also, to practice empathy, he recommends using an inner dialogue to "step into the other person's shoes and imagine things going on with him that may justify his behavior."

Write it off. Literally. Capture cynical or hostile thoughts as they arise and write them down, says Dr. Williams. In this way, you can reappraise and challenge their foundations in a reasonable and reasoned fashion.

Chill. Ease anger by cooling down. Walk away from whatever is irking you and keep walking, says Dr. Goleman. The exercise will do you good. It will also help distract you from the anger if you practice deep breathing and muscle relaxation, he adds.

Be assertive, not aggressive. Controlling anger "doesn't mean ignoring injustices," says Dr. Williams. "Assertion, as opposed to aggression, allows you to ask for others to change a specific behavior" without demanding it. Keep your requests short and simple, for example, "Would you please let me finish what I'm saying?" Preface it with an understanding of another person's point of view.

Feeling Hostile?

About 20 percent of the general population has levels of hostility high enough to be dangerous to their health, according to Dr. Redford B. Williams of Duke University Medical Center.

Another 20 percent has very low levels. The rest fall somewhere in between. The following self-assessment test, based on a questionnaire designed by Dr. Williams and his colleagues, measures what he calls three toxic aspects of hostility—cynicism, aggression and anger—that point to a hostile personality. Circle the letter that best corresponds with your response to the statement. As with all self-tests, this one works only if you're honest.

1. *A teenager drives by my yard with the car stereo blaring acid rock.*
   a. I begin to understand why teenagers can't hear.
   b. I can feel my blood pressure starting to rise.

2. *The person who cuts my hair trims off more than I wanted.*
   a. I tell him what a lousy job he did.
   b. I figure that it'll grow back, and I resolve to give my instructions more forcefully next time.

3. *I am in the express checkout line in the supermarket, where a sign reads: "No more than ten items, please."*
   a. I pick up a magazine to pass the time.
   b. I glance ahead to see if anyone has more than ten items.

4. *The newspaper contains a prominent news story about drug-related crime.*
   a. I wish the government had better educational/drug programs, even for pushers.
   b. I wish we could put every drug pusher away for good.

5. *There have been times when I was very angry with someone.*
   a. I was always able to stop short of hitting him.
   b. I have, on occasion, hit or shoved him.

6. *There is a really important job to be done.*
   a. I prefer to do it myself.
   b. I am apt to call on friends or co-workers to help.

7. *Someone treats me unfairly.*
   a. I usually forget about it rather quickly.
   b. I am apt to keep thinking about it for hours.

8. *Someone is being rude or annoying.*
   a. I am apt to avoid him in the future.
   b. I might have to get rough with him.

9. *I see a very overweight person walking down the street.*

    a. I wonder why this person has such little self-control.

    b. I think that he might have a metabolic defect or a psychological problem.

10. *I am talking with my wife or girlfriend.*

    a. I often find my thoughts racing ahead to what I plan to say next.

    b. I find it easy to pay close attention to what she is saying.

11. *Life is full of little annoyances.*

    a. They often seem to get under my skin.

    b. They seem to roll off my back unnoticed.

12. *I disapprove of something that a friend has done.*

    a. I usually keep such disapproval to myself.

    b. I usually let him know about it.

13. *I recall something that angered me previously.*

    a. I feel angry all over again.

    b. The memory doesn't bother me nearly as much as the actual event.

14. *I see people walking around the mall.*

    a. Many of them are either shopping or exercising.

    b. Many are wasting their time.

15. *Someone is hogging the conversation at a party.*

    a. I look for an opportunity to put him down.

    b. I soon move to another group.

Scoring

To score your cynicism level, give yourself a point for each time your answer agrees with the letter in parentheses after these numbered questions: 3 (b), 6 (a), 9 (a), 10 (a), 14 (b).

To score your anger level, give yourself a point for each time your answer agrees with the letter in parentheses after these numbered questions: 1 (b), 4 (b), 7 (b), 11 (a), 13 (a).

To score your aggression level, give yourself a point for each time your answer agrees with the letter in parentheses after these numbered questions: 2 (a), 5 (b), 8 (b), 12 (b), 15 (a).

Now add all the points to get your total hostility rating. If your total is 3 or less, your hostility is probably below the level that would put you at risk of developing health problems. Any score above 3 and your hostility level may become a health risk.

The Science of Relaxation

Reversing Eons of Evolution

Scientists, philosophers and other people gushing with gray matter have debated for years whether the biocomputer we call the human body is indeed an independent, self-programming gizmo or—as behaviorist John B. Watson once said—nothing more than a preprogrammed, fully assembled "organic machine ready to run."

The complex relationship between mind and body is still the subject of considerable scientific and medical debate. But when it comes to stress, the connection seems clear. Numerous studies have found that there appears to be a strong link between what's rolling around your cranial cavern and what's going on in the rest of your body.

"There are a lot of ways that we can create stress, but much of what happens in your body is determined first in your mind," says Phil Nuernberger, Ph.D., president of Mind Resource Technologies, an executive consulting firm in Honesdale, Pennsylvania, and author of *The Quest for Personal Power: Transforming Stress into Strength* and *Freedom from Stress.*

Do You Mind?

Understanding the link between mind and body is crucial when it comes to understanding why relaxation techniques are so effective in relieving stress.

"This mind-body notion is understood mostly in Eastern philosophies, because Easterners went inside the body in their explorations. Westerners have long looked outside," Dr. Nuernberger says. "Stress is inside the body, not outside. To understand it, you have to understand what's going on in the inside."

Even early researchers like Albert Ellis realized that mental thoughts, particularly irrational ones, can color the world we live in for the worse. In his 1961 book *A Guide to Rational Living*, Ellis concluded that negative thoughts can cause anxiety, anger and depression. Those, in turn, can lead to stress.

While there is little doubt that a link exists between your thoughts and your body's physical reaction to stress, exactly how it works and how much it comes into play at any given moment is considerably less clear.

But research has shown that relaxation appears to counter what Harvard University physiologist Walter B. Cannon first described as the body's physiological fight-or-flight response to stressful situations. Cannon, in researching this response, found that the body undergoes a series of biochemical and physiological changes in times of stress.

After Cannon, pioneer stress researcher Dr. Hans Selye built upon the fight-or-flight principle and discovered that any problem—real or imagined—causes the stress reaction.

Moreover, almost every body system is affected by stress, including cardiovascular, digestion, immunity, reproduction and growth. In many people, stress seems to favor one system over another. That's why some people get upset stomachs or diarrhea when they're stressed, while others get headaches, muscle aches and so on.

The question then became how to turn off this intense physiological response. The answer came from Herbert Benson, M.D., associate professor of medicine at Harvard Medical School in his 1975 book *The Relaxation Response.* Dr. Benson found that when we relax, a number of measurable physical changes occur within as little as three minutes after our stress—real or perceived—has passed. Relaxation changes include a drastic slowing down of heart rate, respiration rate and metabolism and an easing of muscle tension.

Perhaps more important, relaxation affects us chemically, too. When you're relaxed, for example, your insulin levels remain normal (unless, of course, you're diabetic). Stress, however, triggers changes in insulin levels, perhaps contributing to the onset of adult diabetes in chronic stress cases. There's also evidence suggesting that relaxation is chemically better for your moods. From what scientists can tell, relaxation results in more regulated levels of norepinephrine, a stress hormone that's turned on and off like a faucet during times of stress. This on/off relationship with norepinephrine under stress may contribute to depression by keeping the body out of whack.

Moreover, others have found that relaxation seems to trigger an increase in interleukin-1, an essential link in the immune system. In one study, blood samples drawn every five minutes from volunteers who listened to relaxation tapes and practiced relaxation techniques had greater levels of interleukin-1 than they did when the volunteers were asked to fill out forms or read boring textbooks.

"Since these people weren't doing anything but a relaxation exercise, it implies that the brain has an influence over blood chemistry," says William H. Keppel, M.D., the psychiatrist at Providence Medical Center in Portland, Oregon, who conducted the study. What's more, Dr. Keppel found, people who were most skilled in relaxation were more likely to see a bigger boost in their interleukin-1 levels.

Putting It All Together

Short of strapping on a series of electrodes and monitoring your breathing, pulse and blood pressure every five minutes to make sure that you're relaxing, there are a few simple strategies you can employ to ace the science of relaxation.

Practice. This one should be a no-brainer, but it's often overlooked. You have eons of evolution backing the fight-or-flight response but precious little practice at reversing it. Learning to do so is one of the best things you can do for your body and mind. Dr. Keppel found in his studies that the people most skilled at relaxing were more likely to see a physiological benefit more often and in greater quantity than those who weren't so skilled.

"Although several months of regular practice at 30 minutes a day could boost your skills, even 10 minutes might be a useful way to start," Dr. Keppel says. (For more on exactly what to do to become a master of relaxation, see Relaxation Techniques on page 54.)

Become a manager. "You don't really want to live in a stress-free environment, because stress is what challenges us," says New York City psychiatrist Gerald N. Epstein, M.D, author of *Healing into Immortality* and *Healing Visualizations.* "Stress is, in essence, stimuli. It's what life is all about.

"Instead, become skilled at learning to relax," Dr. Epstein adds. "You can get an enormous physiological response from just a little relaxation if you work at it."

Do it for your mental health. Even if relaxation isn't having a noticeable effect on your body, it's likely having a powerful effect on your mind. One study found that cancer patients on chemotherapy had a more optimistic outlook when they practiced relaxation techniques than those who did not. Both groups still suffered side effects—nausea and vomiting—but the relaxation group felt more at ease with their treatment, more in control and more on the up-and-up.

The Bright Side of the Road

The Spice of Life

After suffering a heart attack, Arnold Lemerand of Southgate, Michigan, studiously avoided lifting heavy objects. Coming home from work one night in 1980, though, he found a five-year-old boy trapped under a cast-iron pipe screaming for help. Without stopping to think, Lemerand easily lifted the pipe, saving the child's life. At the time, Lemerand recalled thinking that the pipe must have weighed at least 300 pounds. The next day he, his two sons, reporters and the police together couldn't budge the thing. It weighed 1,800 pounds.

Heroic stress hormones saved the day—and a life. There are many amazing stories like this. They can be as dramatic as Lemerand's feat or as ordinary as the one about the advertising copywriter who pulled an all-nighter and pulled a winning slogan out of his ear, saving his job if not his life.

"Stress is the spice of life," writes pioneer stress researcher Dr. Hans Selye in *Stress without Distress.* Though he wrote the book in 1974 as a guide to "using stress as a positive force for personal achievement and happiness," it is perhaps even more timely today, with stress running rampant.

"Since stress is associated with all types of activity, we could avoid most of it by never doing anything," he writes. "Who would enjoy a life of no runs, no hits, no errors? Besides, certain types of activities have a curative effect and actually help to keep the stress mechanism in good shape."

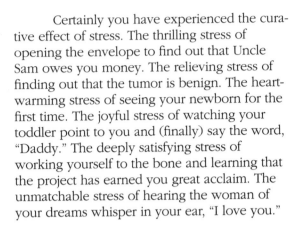

Certainly you have experienced the curative effect of stress. The thrilling stress of opening the envelope to find out that Uncle Sam owes you money. The relieving stress of finding out that the tumor is benign. The heart-warming stress of seeing your newborn for the first time. The joyful stress of watching your toddler point to you and (finally) say the word, "Daddy." The deeply satisfying stress of working yourself to the bone and learning that the project has earned you great acclaim. The unmatchable stress of hearing the woman of your dreams whisper in your ear, "I love you."

Stressed for Success

"Complete freedom from stress is death," Dr. Seyle notes.

Dr. James E. Loehr of LGE Sport Science agrees. "Without stress, the growth process comes to a screeching halt," he says. "Only with exposure to it is life sustained." Not only that but also, he contends, learning to handle larger doses of stress is the key to success in sports and in life.

Dr. Loehr has made a very good living teaching athletes like tennis star Pete Sampras, speed skater Dan Jansen, boxer Ray "Boom-Boom" Mancini and others how to attain peak performance by riding stress to the next level.

"If you want to get stronger, the best way is through exposing yourself to progressively increasing doses of stress," he says. "That's the principle behind rehabilitation therapy. Improvement is measured in terms of how much stress your muscles can withstand. The model we see in the physical realm is the same in the mental and emotional realms as well."

Stress takes a bad rap, he says. "The problem is not excessive stress," he explains. "It's the insufficient amount of healing time we allow. Recovery is when growth takes place. Recovery is healing." To ensure that time for recovery, he has developed a system called wave making, alternating between periods of stress and recovery. But, he warns, too much recovery time—that is, the absence of stress—"can be lethal because you shut down the arousal system."

Lack of recovery from real stress is not the only problem. There's also perceived stress. "Our own attitudes can cause us to be stressed even when there is no stress 'out there,'" explains Dr. Redford B. Williams of Duke University Medical Center. We also need to allow time for recovery from stress that we manufacture ourselves.

"The only true anti-aging agent is exposure to stress," Dr. Loehr says.

Stress motivates people to outdo themselves, says Dr. Blair Justice of the University of Texas Health Science Center at Houston. "You can argue that stress is necessary for a number of reasons," he says. "That imbalance between demands and resources serves to challenge us and keeps us reaching. If they were perfectly matched all the time, we might not be motivated to be creative. In the arts and in science, stress is about not being satisfied with the status quo. Dr. Selye called it eustress, good stress. We need it for stimulation and novelty. We like a certain unpredictability that stress provides. It wakes us up. It even make us laugh."

The Stress That Binds

Pulling an all-nighter to cram for a test with some classmates. Suffering through boot camp with a group of other recruits. Staying late night after night with a bunch of co-workers to finish a project. Crying in your beer with a buddy over a lost love.

And the ultimate: going into combat together and coming out at the other end, alive, to talk about it—to remember it. And talk about it. And remember it. Foxhole buddies are forged into blood brothers for life. The same holds true for those men with whom we have shared any highly stressful encounter.

Misery does love and value company. And that's another one of the unexpected bright sides of stress, says Dr. Glenn H. Elder, Jr., of the University of North Carolina at Chapel Hill. "Stress bonds men in the military," he says. "It's the great equalizer. It eliminates differences of life history. You learn interdependency; you forge a working and social unit. You understand comradeship. In fact, the strongest motive for fighting is the desire to protect your comrades, not your nation or some other abstraction. It's relation-based."

War is a harsh reality, but it can also be a metaphor for any stressful battle you've endured with another person. "Great adversity forces people onto each other," Dr. Elder says. "There's a self-understanding and mutual appreciation that comes from being able to endure great hardship and develop resilience."

Among the other physiological benefits of stress is that it serves as a natural form of Novocain. As the story of Lemerand dramatically demonstrates, "with sufficiently sustained stress, our perception of pain can become blunted," explains Stanford University's Dr. Robert Sapolsky.

Stress-induced analgesia has been observed in wounded soldiers in battle, in athletes playing under severe pain and in weekend tennis hackers who put up with sore elbows rather than sit out a set. Behind this phenomenon there is, of course, complicated neuroscience. Let it suffice to say that stress triggers the release of one type of chemical compound, called beta-endorphin, from the pituitary gland in the brain that regulates pain perception. This would account for the famed runner's endorphin high that kicks in after about a half-hour of sustained effort.

And here's a bonus benefit. Stress improves memory, and your senses grow sharper. Once again, it's that fight-or-flight survival instinct to the rescue. Enhanced thinking and sensory skills help you when you have to remember—and darn quick—where the exit door is. Or where you left that dang shotgun. Or where you left the receipt to the "misplaced" overnight package. As Dr. Sapolsky explains, short-term stress wakes up the sympathetic nervous system, increasing blood flow to the brain and thus cognition. Also, glucocorticoids strengthen connectors in the brain, aiding memory.

Dealing with Stress

So here's what it all comes down to. Stress can kill you. But life isn't worth living without it. Either way, you're going to have to deal with stress. The only question, then, is how. Either stress can run your life and ruin your health, or you can learn to laugh and roll with the punches, recognizing that the changes life has in store for you can help you attain new levels of mental and physical toughness.

Dr. Selye, after some 40-odd years of researching why people get so bent out of shape by stressful events in their lives, concluded: "Try to keep your mind on the pleasant aspects of life and on actions that can improve your situation. Try to forget everything that is irrevocably ugly or painful. This is perhaps the most efficient way of minimizing stress, by what I have called voluntary mental diversion."

Best of all, you don't have to do it alone. When it comes to stress, we're all in this together. Or, as the Irish singer Van Morrison once put it:

Let's enjoy it while we can.
Won't you help me sing my song
From the dark end of the street
To the bright side of the road.

The lyrics from "Bright Side of the Road" off Morrison's 1974 album *Into the Music* fit here because, in those four lines, he manages to sum up the collected wisdom of Dr. Seyle, Dr.

The Four Noble Truths of Stress

Siddhārtha Gautama, also known as the Buddha, didn't specifically mention stress in his Four Noble Truths, the philosophical foundation of Buddhism. But you have to think that he had an intuitive understanding of how to get to the bright side of stress. Manhattan psychiatrist Dr. Mark Epstein thinks so, too.

The Buddha concluded that life is suffering, that all suffering is caused by ignorance of the nature of reality, that suffering can be ended by overcoming said ignorance and that the suppression of suffering can be achieved by practicing morality, wisdom and concentration.

Dr. Epstein proposes his own Four Noble Truths of Stress. Taken together, they leave you believing that stress and enlightenment are but a breath away.

• Noble Truth Number One: A stress-free life is not possible. There's always stress, so don't set it up as the enemy.

• Noble Truth Number Two: The cause of stress is wanting there to be no stress, a craving for perfect existence.

• Noble Truth Number Three: There's a way out of stress. It's workable. The stress doesn't have to be destructive.

• Noble Truth Number Four: By orienting the mind properly, by learning coping skills, you can manage stress.

Sapolsky and a handful of social scientists and psychologists exploring the outer realms of human potential. What they are all saying is that a positive outlook (exercise, optimism, relaxation techniques) and some good friends (strong social support system, pets, altruistic deeds) can help you turn the corner from any dark period of stress onto the bright side of the road.

Part Two

The Stress Blaster's Arsenal

Exercise

Sending Stress on the Run

Imagine owning a car, which should be simple, considering that you probably do. Imagine that the car is built to last—this will take considerably more imagination. By last, we mean *really* last—say, 70 years or more. Now imagine that the more you drive your car, the better gas mileage it gets. Not only that but also the more you drive, the less routine maintenance it needs.

A dream come true? Not if you work at General Motors. But for consumers it *is* a dream. Yet that's the principle behind the truly amazing machine called the human body.

The human body is a breakthrough in engineering. It boasts a four-chamber, high-pressure pump called the heart that works non-stop for decades; a three-pound supercomputer called the brain that makes a Pentium chip look like a broken abacus and a 206-piece frame that not only protects all the important stuff but re-pairs itself automatically. All this wrapped in a waterproof, germ-resistant, three-layered coating that also helps regulate metabolism and body heat.

Yet for all the anatomical wonders of the human body, there's one biomechanical miracle that we often overlook, especially when it comes to stress. Your body—like vacation days for most of us—operates on a use-it-or-lose-it basis. But the more you use your body, the better it becomes.

"Exercise is truly one of those little tricks in life that can really reduce the stress of any lifestyle," says Jim Laird, Ph.D., professor of psychology at Clark University in Worcester,

Massachusetts. "No matter what you might think, exercise works. It really works."

Training Your Body

How intricately are exercise and stress re-lated? Consider the physiology of it all. When your body experiences stress, like when you're giving a big speech, what happens? Your heart races, you breathe in somewhat labored gasps, your pulse races, your face flushes and your palms sweat. Experts call this the fight-or-flight response, and it means nothing more than that your body is gearing up for action. Now consider that you're running a 5-K race, heading into the home stretch. What happens here? Your heart's racing, you're breathing faster and your blood's pounding so much that you're sweating profusely. It's essentially the same reaction.

"Your body doesn't know the difference," says Pat Etcheberry, a former Olympic javelin thrower, Pan-American Games champion, professional fitness consultant and motivational speaker for LGE Sport Science in Orlando, Florida. "The only thing that your body knows is how to adjust itself accordingly. It doesn't know the difference between mental stress and physical stress. It just reacts."

What does that mean to you? "If you train your body to handle physical stress better, it'll handle mental stress better," Etcheberry says. "On the other hand, if you lead a very quiet life and never get your pulse above zombie level, your body's not used to stress. If it ever has to react to something, well, I feel sorry for you."

If this isn't enough to prompt you to get off the couch, consider that every year, between the ages of 30 and 70, you're going to lose about 1 percent of muscle strength through natural atrophy if you don't do anything about it. Im-perceptible at first, you'll notice this loss dramatically around 60, when your 10-year-old grandkids are kicking your flabby, wrinkly butt in arm wrestling.

Moreover, government experts say that fewer than 15 percent of us ever exercise vigorously. The result? An epidemic of indolence, making America the land of the free and home of the fat.

Training Your Mind

Now you know a little about the physical benefits of exercise and how it helps safeguard you from stress. You can even measure the impact that it has. After all, you can see muscles grow and feel your endurance improve. It's harder, however, to quantify the mental benefits of exercise—harder, but not impossible.

Those who exercise regularly tend to be peppier, happier and probably have a better outlook on life. Intrigued by this long-known phenomenon, researchers have looked into it over the years. One study conducted in the mid-1990s of 188 people, ages 19 to 71, by researchers at the University of Illinois at Urbana-Champaign, found that physically active individuals are more optimistic than people who don't exercise much. This is particularly important when you consider that there's a lot of research linking optimism with increased motivation, persistence, better personal performance, goal achievement and, of course, the ability to cope with stress.

In another study, psychologists at Springfield College in Springfield, Massachusetts, studied 24 junior tennis players during their games. They found that the players who berated themselves mentally or were overly critical of their performance consistently performed worse. That is, the players who stressed themselves out mentally performed worse physically.

"Exercise gives you discipline to go inside yourself," says Gary Null, Ph.D., a nutritionist, fitness consultant, lecturer, radio talkshow host, elite athlete and motivational speaker who has more than 75 national track

and field gold medals to his credit and author of several books, including *Nutrition and the Mind*. "Touching our inner well of knowledge, pushing our potential, helps us deal with distress. Exercise is one way to do that."

Stress Training

Here are some strategies to help you achieve the maximum stress-blasting benefit from your workouts.

Get out. Where you work out has a big impact on how you burn off stress. George Eifert, Ph.D., professor of clinical psychology at West Virginia University in Morgantown, studied the effects that environment has on stress reduction during exercise. Three test groups were asked to run the same distance. The first group ran outdoors, and the other two exercised indoors on treadmills while listening to either nature sounds or nothing but their heartbeats. At the end of the experiment, the outside runners not only felt more refreshed but also had measurably lower levels of a key stress hormone. Those kept inside either experienced no changes in mood or ended up with higher stress-hormone levels than when they started.

Get your honey's helping hand. Ask your spouse or girlfriend to join in. It's time together and—just as important—it'll help you stick to it. Researchers at Indiana University in Bloomington studied 46 married couples who started an exercise routine. Sixteen of the married couples worked out together; the rest did not. After a year's time, the researchers found that the married couples who worked out together exercised more frequently and dropped out less often than individuals without spousal support.

One possible reason, Chicago State University researchers found, is that almost one in four women who took part in an exercise study had experienced sexual arousal or even orgasm while working out. Feel the burn, indeed.

Don't wait for weights. The next time you find yourself humming the Kinks old song,

"Tired of Waiting for You," while standing in line for a shot at your gym's pull-down machine, consider an escape route. "Waiting for a machine or sharing equipment can cause unnecessary stress," says Paul J. Rosch, M.D., president of the American Institute of Stress in Yonkers, New York, and clinical professor of medicine and psychiatry at New York Medical College in Valhalla. Read up on different exercises and figure out how to substitute one for another.

Heel, boy. A sneaky way to sap stress, increase exercise and escape from it all is to take your dog for a walk (or run). Just being with your pet can send stress yipping away with its tail between its legs.

Have fun. "One way to keep up with an exercise program is to find enjoyable exercise outlets," says Patch Adams, M.D., humor specialist, professional clown, lecturer and director of the Gesundheit Institute, a creativity and humor think tank in Arlington, Virginia.

"My son's school recently had a sock hop. I was the only parent dancing for two hours straight," Dr. Adams says. "I did it because the other parents know that I'm a doctor and they know I'm in my fifties, but also because I love dancing and was having fun."

Start something new. Another way to keep exercise interesting is to try something new. "I didn't take up basketball until I was 40," says Dr. Laird. "Despite my advance in years and being vertically impaired, I still have fun. For me, it's a key to stress management."

Leave competition to the pros. The surest way to turn stress-blasting exercise into another source of stress is by taking it too seriously. Remember that your goal is to ease tension—not create it by trying to be a gold medalist. "In my basketball case," Dr. Laird says, "I've pretty much realized that my basketball skills are at the point where I have to rely on

Walk on by Stress

We know, it's not macho. But walking is one of the best exercises around, especially if you're hoofing it to beat stress.

"I walk about two miles to work every morning and walk back in the afternoon," says Emmanuel Cheraskin, M.D., a food-health pioneer and author of *Diet and Disease*.

His secret, Dr. Cheraskin says, is simply recognizing the importance of walking—not just physically, but mentally as well. "I think walking is just as good as running. It's good exercise, and it's time to clear your head. I think that's why I'm in reasonably good shape at 80."

Here's how to step up your stepping-out program.

Start small. Walk for just 20 minutes to start. That's probably not more than a mile or so. After that gets easy, increase in 15-minute increments.

Pencil it in. Schedule your walking time like you

the kindness of my friends to put up with my skill level. The important thing is that I'm not out there to win."

Work on your hang time. Instead of rushing through your workout, taking a quick shower and throwing on your clothes to get back into the rat race, find a spot in the gym or outdoors where you can just hang out for 10 to 15 minutes in silence. "It's easier to achieve total relaxation when your body is in a state of postexercise fatigue," says Emmett Miller, M.D., author of *Deep Healing*. "Just sit and concentrate on your body as it brings itself back to a normal state of being." Feeling your muscles relax and your breath return to normal is a way for your mind to cool down along with your body.

Starting Over

If it's been a few years since you've exercised regularly, don't feel bad. It's never too late

would an appointment. You'll be less likely to blow it off.

Make a big to-do. Prominently mention your walking program every chance you get. Tell family, friends and co-workers. You'll feel less inclined to cheat if you know that others will ask you how your program's coming.

Change scenery. Don't get bored walking the same route every day. Take the road less traveled, including walking around a local track, hiking through the woods, exploring downtown, walking uphill or downhill, walking up and down stairs at work or just roaming the hallways (with an armful of papers, just for show, of course).

Ponder as you pound the pavement. The word *peripatetic* refers to walking or walkers, and it comes from Aristotle, the father of Western philosophy who had a habit of pacing while philosophizing. Let walking be your own time for deep thinking.

---

to start. The stress-blasting benefits of exercise will always be there waiting for you when you're ready. Here are some quick tips to help you get back in stress-free shape.

Don't start off cold. Working a cold muscle is like trying to bend a dry sponge. To work properly, muscles must be pumped up first. Loosen up for 10 to 15 minutes before starting any exercise regimen. Warm-ups increase blood flow to your muscles, raise their core temperature and prime your heart and lungs for what's to come.

Good warm-ups include jumping rope, light jogging, stair-climbing or cycling, followed by several minutes of calisthenics and light stretching.

Stretch stress away. Stretching is an often-neglected form of exercise. Take yoga, for example. It's an ancient system of stretching, posing and breathing that's supposed to bring spiritual enlightenment. Even if it doesn't do that

for you, it'll ease your stress and make you feel better. "Exercise should be a major part of your life. Stretching is a good start because you can do it anywhere and don't need special equipment or training," says nutrition expert Maye Musk, R.D., spokeswoman for the Canadian Dietetic Association and author of *Feel Fantastic.*

Stretch daily for maximal benefit. Hold each stretch for 20 to 30 seconds. Stretch only to the point of resistance, not to the point of pain. Hold stretches steady—no bouncing.

Get your heart pumping. Aerobic conditioning blasts stress because it trains your heart and lungs to handle an increased workload, which is what happens naturally when the fight-or-flight response kicks in, says Jack Groppel, a professional nutrition and fitness consultant and Etcheberry's colleague at LGE Sport Science.

"When we say that you're not tough enough, we don't mean that you're weak. We mean that you need to increase your ability to handle stress," Groppel says. "Aerobic training helps you handle stress. If you don't get aerobic exercise, there's a training effect to being a couch potato. If all you do is sit around, you're training your body to be lazy."

Exercise aerobically (cycling, hiking, running, rowing, stair-climbing) three to five days a week for 20 to 30 minutes at a clip. Stretch out and warm up first. Stop if you feel dizzy, light-headed or nauseated.

Give yourself a lift. Weight lifting is another stress blaster for several reasons. Done quickly with light weights, it helps build endurance. Done for power, it builds muscle mass, which boosts self-esteem. Plus, a good, hard workout can help you vent stress.

Remember these pointers: Start off slowly—you can always add more weight in the future; exercise your large muscle groups first; and don't neglect aerobic conditioning.

Food and Vitamins

A Tasteful Way to Ease Stress

It wasn't that long ago that anyone who mentioned food and medicine in the same sentence ran the risk of being labeled a quack. When the late Adelle Davis, an early food pioneer, wrote that diet was a direct cause for many diseases, she was dismissed as a kook. When Canadian physicians Wilfred and Evan Shute said that vitamin E could help prevent heart disease, they were called charlatans. And when Nobel laureate Linus Pauling said that vitamin C could help head off the common cold and even cancer, he was maligned by the medical community.

Today, modern medicine recognizes that pioneers like Davis, the Shutes and Pauling were on track. Thanks to stringent studies and a vast body of empirical evidence, we now know that diet, indeed, is linked to disease. People with high blood pressure are told to eat low-sodium foods. Those with diabetes are likewise put on regulated diets. People hoping to avoid heart disease are told to cut fat and boost fiber. And on and on.

When it comes to stress, most of us still aren't making the connection. Look at the harried executive who scarfs down airport hot dogs between flights. Or the busy ambulance driver who gorges on cheeseburgers and fries because it's convenient.

"Diet is usually the last front a person faces in the daily war on stress," declares Maye Musk of the Canadian Dietetic Association. "When you're stressed, you don't have time to think about

food or nutrition, so you head for junk: hamburgers, fries, doughnuts, sandwiches heavy on the mayo."

Neglecting the diet-stress connection can be hazardous to your health, just as ignoring the diet-disease link was years ago. "There's a major link between stress and diet," says Earl Mindell, Ph.D., registered pharmacist, nutrition professor at Pacific Western University in Los Angeles, worldwide lecturer on health and nutrition, author of *Earl Mindell's Anti-aging Bible* and a harried executive himself. While eating right won't make you any less busy, it will help you handle the bustle better.

Your Gut Reaction

To put stress and diet in perspective, take a look at what happens to the body under stress. When our fight-or-flight response kicks in, our pupils dilate and our nostrils flare. Our vision improves, blood pressure jumps, heart rate rockets and breathing quickens. The liver breaks down its stored glycogen into glucose and injects large amounts of glucose into the blood, which teams up with fat particles, called free fatty acids, for quick energy. (Glycogen is the stored form of glucose, the body's chief energy source. It's stockpiled in the liver and muscles.) The blood, which only moments ago was coursing to and from internal organs, suddenly channels into our muscles, which tense and tighten for the big showdown.

Flaring nostrils and dilated pupils are one thing, but the changes to the gut are another. Remember that blood that got diverted to your muscles? That's not good for the gut. Since the stomach is where food is absorbed, stress reduces your ability to absorb nutrients effectively. That's why you're not hungry when you're nervous, scared or mad. The body's not ready or willing to refuel.

Moreover, stress affects metabolism. Researchers know that stress alters the body's level of ubiquinone, a chemical substance also called coenzyme Q_{10}, which helps energize brain cells. Scientists know, too, that some vitamins, like riboflavin, seem to help the body cope better under stress. One study at Cornell University in Ithaca, New York, found that a good source of riboflavin seemed to help the body weather the stress of exercise better. If you're not eating healthfully, these vitamins won't be around to back you up.

"Behind every emotion there's a physical reaction with a different biochemical signature," says Jack Groppel of LGE Sport Science. To assume that these emotion-inspired chemicals don't react with, or aren't affected by, chemicals that we consume simply doesn't make sense, he says.

"Yet you'd never know that judging from what most people eat," says Dr. Emmanuel Cheraskin, who co-authored *Diet and Disease* 30 years ago, one of the few books at the time that made the connection. "There are a few enthusiasts who really watch what they eat, just like there are some who really watch their weight or exercise. But for most people, eating habits don't seem much of a concern."

If you're among that apathetic lot, Dr. Cheraskin says, "Look at the life expectancy of all the people in the world. The United States ranks around 17th. Despite being ahead in money, technology and in other ways, people in 16 other countries live longer than we do. Why? They eat better."

Stress-Free Eating Strategies

Eating to beat stress isn't much different than eating to beat other medical maladies. Here's how to get started.

Break for Lunch

Even though you can always find a seat at the Desk Café, eating while working isn't doing your body or stress levels any favors. Take time out to relax and eat.

To really unwind, you need a change of scenery says Maye Musk of the Canadian Dietetic Association. "I have a lovely office, so I enjoy eating at my desk. However, I find that it's more relaxing to meet good friends or colleagues in a pleasant atmosphere, giving me time to unwind."

And don't rush through lunch. Slowing down in the chow line is as much an attitude as an action. Savor your food. Look at it very closely as you deliberately raise it to your mouth. Feel the sensation of it on your tongue. Try to distinguish what's going on in your mouth by chewing slowly, absorbing its taste and texture. Then you'll know that you're eating because you love the food and not from habit. Stop eating when you feel comfortably full. It takes 20 minutes for the gut to let the brain know that you're full, so take your time, Musk says. You don't have to finish everything on your plate. If the portions are large, share with a friend or take the leftovers back to the office. After trying this a few times, you'll feel pleased with yourself for forming a new habit—making eating an art.

Think ahead. "When people come to me and say that they feel stressed and aren't eating healthy, I tell them to spend five minutes every evening mentally planning their menu for the next day," Musk says. That doesn't mean knowing exactly what you're going to eat but, rather, where you'll be when it's time to eat it. "If you know that you're going to be on the road, you can pack a healthy lunch instead of giving in to fast food," she explains. "If you know that you'll be in meetings, you can bring an apple or banana as a snack. Just thinking ahead helps you make better food choices."

Pack your own lunch. In line with Musk's suggestion above is to brown-bag it every day. This is a simple way to take control of what goes into your stomach. Packing your lunch not only saves money—always a stress reducer—but empowers you to take charge of your diet. Plus, if you can take your lunch to a park or a quiet part of the office, you'll be further rejuvenated.

Brown-bag the easy way. Can't find time to pack lunch every day? Take Musk's advice and mix up a big nutritious salad on Sunday, then bring a little of it each day. Or bring leftovers from dinner. Throw in an apple, banana and some low-fat yogurt and you have a true power lunch.

Don't skip breakfast. Not to sound like your mother, but eat your breakfast. It is the most important meal of the day. "We know that a good night's sleep almost totally depletes your liver of glycogen, so when you wake up, there's very little energy to draw from," Groppel says.

"Since your brain requires glucose to work normally, it means that there's nobody home mentally until you get something in your stomach," Groppel says. "Skipping any meal during the day has the same effect: It stresses your body."

Go for five. Meals a day, that is. Not King Henry VIII smorgasbords. Rather, small healthy meals—three meals, two snacks—something around 500 calories or so each. Breakfast could be a half-cup of high-

fiber cereal, a cup of yogurt and a banana. Lunch could be a roast turkey sandwich on rye bread with mustard, and an orange. By

C the Light, B a Champ

If your mind's eye picture of vitamins looks suspiciously like Barney Rubble (or, better yet, Betty), it might help to learn all that you can about vitamin C and B-complex vitamins, two powerful allies in the fight against stress.

Vitamin C

"This has to be one of the single most studied nutritional substances in the world in relation to stress, and it's the best indicator of your body's stress levels," declares Dr. Gary Null, a fitness consultant and author.

"In my own research, I've taken probably more supplemental vitamin C than any human being on Earth. I could pee an orchard," says Dr. Null, who is also a gonzo athlete with scores of track and field awards.

And while Dr. Null's extreme experiments aren't for the average person, they underscore the importance of vitamin C, levels of which sink during stress.

Good food sources include raw fruits and vegetables, especially strawberries, asparagus, brussels sprouts, watermelon, mangoes, honeydews, kiwifruit, oranges and orange juice, kale, cauliflower, broccoli, papaya and potatoes. If you must cook it, steam or stir-fry your food to avoid cooking away its vital nutrients.

B-Complex Vitamins

The vast family of B-complex vitamins has long been associated with stress, particularly riboflavin, which seems to help us cope with the physical demands of stress. Riboflavin is found in milk, cheese, yogurt, cereals and green vegetables, such as spinach and broccoli.

Also make a "B"-line for B₆, pyridoxine. This vitamin plays an enormous role in metabolizing nucleic acids, building body tissue and fortifying the immune system with antibodies and red blood cells.

Since large supplemental doses of B_6 can be lethal, stick with food sources. Elizabeth Somer, R.D., author of *Food and Mood*, suggests three servings or more of the following B_6-enriched foods whenever you're stressed: bananas, fish, baked potatoes, chicken and dark, green vegetables, such as collard greens, spinach, green peas and broccoli.

The last B-complex champion is B_{12}, or cobalamin. Doctors have given B_{12} shots for years to treat fatigue. Whether they were onto something or just cashing in on the placebo effect is unclear. But some studies indicate that B_{12}, which helps the nervous system work and the body form red blood cells, may reduce fatigue and improve neurological machinations.

"Just be warned that your body seems to lose B_{12} as you age. Most elderly people don't have nearly enough," says Ruth Winter, author of *A Consumer's Guide to Medicines in Foods*. "Sometimes people think that they're getting Alzheimer's when they're really just low in B_{12}. It affects your brain that much."

Sources include milk, fish, eggs and meats (stick to the lean varieties).

mentally and physically happy.

Strategize carbohydrates and protein. Complex carbohydrates and proteins supply energy for every vital bodily function, but they affect you differently. Not knowing this can add stress, because you could be eating the wrong thing at the wrong time and getting the wrong result.

Complex carbohydrates, found in whole grains, brown rice, fruits and vegetables, says Dr. Mindell, give the body lasting energy, as opposed to a rush of energy and subsequent crash that you get from simple carbohydrates, found in sugar and flour. Complex carbohydrates—say, in the form of fruit salad or a grapefruit—are a good way to start your day. When your energy flags, as it may in the afternoon, you should reach for protein. High-protein foods—fish, beans and skinless chicken breast—peak your mental energies.

Watch the G.I., Joe. In this case, the G.I. we're talking about is your glycemic index. Robert Haas, in his book *Eat Smart, Think Smart*, cautions against getting too much glucose too quickly. Glucose, that primary energy source, is a natural sugar made of carbon, hydrogen and oxygen. More important, it's the chemical that powers the brain. Get too much, say, by eating foods high in simple carbohydrates, and you'll crash and burn. Get too little, and you're still sluggish. Haas suggests starting your day with foods that have a low glycemic index, so you can benefit from a steady stream of energy through their natural "time-release" properties. These foods include grapefruit, skim milk, yogurt, apples, grapes and orange juice.

keeping a steady stream of healthy food coming in, your body doesn't have to wonder when its next meal is coming, which keeps it

Hobbies

How to Stamp Out Stress

If it's been so long that you've forgotten what a hobby feels like, consider this brief analogy: Recall the last time you saw a magician do a trick. Maybe it was David Copperfield. Or maybe it was just Al in Accounting doing parlor tricks at the company picnic. The point is that by watching the magic, everything else around you became secondary. Everything seemed to slow down and become still. Your attention span focused like a laser beam on the moment, and whether you were watching passively or trying to catch the magician's guilty hand, all your stress was momentarily banished. It disappeared—like magic.

This same focused, almost-Zenlike state of relaxation is the meat and potatoes of a hobby's stress-blasting ability. There's nothing magic about it. And it's a feeling that you can cultivate. Just read on. And watch . . . there's nothing up our sleeves.

Ride the Hobbyhorse

One of the best things about hobbies is that they're so flexible. They're something that you do on your own. Something based entirely on your personal tastes and preferences. But most important, you don't need to look far. Hobbies are everywhere.

"Any activity that you find engaging can be a hobby. There's no 'best hobby' for any one person," says Steve Allen, Jr., M.D., a humor specialist and physician in Ithaca, New York, who lectures widely on the benefits of humor and creativity.

"But, of course, it's all a matter of attitude," Dr. Allen adds. "Even an enjoyable hobby becomes stressful if you take it too seriously, are too competitive or see it as something that you have to do as opposed to something you want to do."

We probably don't need to sell you on hobbies. What you really need to know is how you can find time to indulge your old favorites or discover new ones. Wonder no more.

Take a cue from Bob Hope. The famous comedian's signature song is "Thanks for the Memories." And that's just what you'll be whistling if you decide to exercise your brain. Working your memory is an excellent hobby that you can do anywhere, anytime, with anything. But flex your memory muscle wisely. Don't try to remember your appointments or phone numbers. Experts say that they're better written down. Instead, memorize poetry, some good stories or a couple of jokes. Learn Hamlet's touching soliloquy, the words to your favorite country song or a decade's worth of playing stats from the NFL.

"I have four hours of poetry memorized. At the drop of a hat, I can rattle off poems about nature, love or the beauty of life," says Dr. Patch Adams of the Gesundheit Institute.

Put pets to use. There's no reason why Rover must be just man's best friend. Turn him—or your cat, fish, bird or reptile—into an engaging hobby by learning all that you can about him. Study his anatomy, his evolution, his history. You'll see your pet in a new light, learn something new and probably meet new friends if you join a kennel association, herpetological society or similar special-interest group.

Organize your interests. Collect something. It doesn't matter if it's coins, comics or stamps. A collection is a continuous project. Plus, it's something that you can show off. Dr. Adams boasts of a formidable 12,000-volume library of the world's classic literature—most of which he has read. Clark

University's Dr. Jim Laird collects Monty Python videos.

Don Morlan, Ph.D., professor of communications at Dayton University in Ohio, has combined his scholarly passion for communication with his equally compelling passion for the Three Stooges. He has collected two sets of their entire 190 video episodes and has written academic papers on them. Moreover—get this—he gets to go to an annual Stooge convention in Philadelphia in a scholarly capacity. Now *that's* a wise guy. Nyuk, nyuk, nyuk.

Tune out. If the Stooges had their own cable television channel, maybe it would be worth spending hours each day parked in front of the tube. Until that day comes, you probably ought to look for something else to do. "If you really want to reduce stress in your life and make more leisure time, cut out TV," suggests Pacific Western University's Dr. Earl Mindell.

Get a blast from your past. If it has been so long since you have done anything remotely resembling a hobby, ask yourself what you used to enjoy. Was it stamp collecting? Was it comic collecting? Hiking? Scouring your past—especially your childhood—is an excellent way to stumble upon a treasure trove of hobbies waiting to be resurrected.

Get physical. Make exercise a hobby, not a chore. A study by the American Medical Association found that 22 percent of 9,488 adults, 20 years old or older, did nothing physical during downtime. Moreover, researchers found that even the people who did something physical weren't doing enough for good health. The minimum exercise that you should aim for is roughly 30 minutes of accumulated moderate exercise on most days of the week. Paradoxically, the more you sweat to get in shape, the more energy you'll find that you have.

"And it doesn't matter if you're good at it," says Dr. Laird.

Compost Your Stress

Douglas Schar decided to write *Dump Your Stress in the Compost Pile!* while working for "extremely stressed millionaires" as a successful landscaper in Washington, D.C.

"I saw firsthand that a stressed-out person walking into a garden walks out serene," says Schar, former host of a nationally syndicated TV show *The Urban Gardener* and author of several gardening books.

So, with these tips and hoe in hand, head for the back 40—whether it's 40 inches or 40 acres. You'll grow more patient and some salad fixin's in the process.

Plant what you like. It's your garden. Grow plants that amuse you, plants that smell good, plants that look pretty, plants that taste good, plants that you've never seen before and plants that remind you of your grandmother or your first kiss. "If your garden contains plants that don't make your heart go pitter-patter," says Schar, "you won't find yourself there very often."

Wake up and smell the roses. Slow down and appreciate all the sensory experiences in the garden. Sights, sounds, the feel of the dirt in your hand.

Grow your own medicine chest. Dill seeds settle a nervous stomach. Sage soothes ulcerated skin. Chamomile heals headaches. Herbs have been used since ancient times as remedies for all varieties of ailments. There's no reason why you have to go out and buy them. And fresh from your garden, they will be that much more potent.

Humor

Take My Strife—Please

A young man is invited to a cocktail party so that he can meet all the right people and advance his career. Nervous and feeling more than a little bit out of place, he gathers his courage and strides into the main party hall . . . only to catch his toe on the carpet and fall face-first in front of everyone. The crowd gasps and, as he looks up sheepishly from his position on the floor, the young man notices that every eye in the place is on him.

So he hops to his feet, grins and quips, "I also do card tricks."

The moral of this story isn't that you should run out immediately and enroll in the Chevy Chase School of Pratfalls. (After all, look what it did for his career.) But it illustrates how humor—especially the self-deprecating variety—can defuse the most stressful situation and turn it to your advantage. The young man, of course, went on to be the hit of the party. And so can you.

Get Serious

Researchers know more about the stress-relieving role of humor now than ever before. They know that 100 laughs are the aerobic equivalent of ten minutes on a rowing machine. They know that laughing increases circulation, works abdominal muscles, oxygenizes the body and raises heart and breathing rates. They know that stress levels, measured in part by the presence of cortisol and epinephrine in our blood, plummet after a hearty hee-haw. And they know that a good laugh helps our immune systems rally. One

study of 50 married couples found that humor accounted for 70 percent of the difference between the happier couples and the unhappier ones. Still more studies show that yukking it up increases the body's number of T cells and interferon-gamma, two vital components to disease fighting. For some, this connection was made long before the raft of quantifiable evidence that we have today in favor of the stress-blasting power of humor.

"As a physician, I was trained to see a patient as a series of signs and symptoms, but I wanted to do more—that's when I started wearing clown clothes," says Dr. Patch Adams of the Gesundheit Institute.

"My biggest condemnation now is that I'm not serious enough. Well, I'd just as soon die than have someone take me too seriously," Dr. Adams says. "There's not a paper in all the scientific literature that says that seriousness has the same healing powers as humor. There's not a paper anywhere that says that seriousness will reduce stress and make you feel better. Humor will."

Enter Laughing

We're not saying that everyone should start dressing up as a clown. But if you're like most of us, you definitely need more laughter in your life. Although statistics vary, one group of researchers estimates that children laugh 400 times a day, compared to adults, who laugh just 15 times a day. This is one case where acting like a child is a compliment. So here are some ideas to help you record your own laugh track for the great sitcom of life.

Take your humor seriously. The secret to maximizing humor to minimize stress lies with giving yourself permission to be funny. One researcher, Michelle Newman, working on her doctorate at the State University of New York at Stony Brook, found that making a conscious effort to see things lightly did wonders to decrease stress. She had two groups of people view a gory accident video. Then she asked each group to describe the video seriously and humorously while wired to machines that measured their stress levels. When both groups looked on the bright side, their anxiety was lower than when they took a serious stance.

Shun unhealthy humor. "Let's face it, the sad truth is that the quintessence of today's supposed intellectual humor is that anything cleverly cynical, sarcastic or demeaning draws laughter," Dr. Adams says. "Why not concentrate instead on humor that's not at anyone's expense?"

Hang out with funny people. It keeps your wit—and tongue—sharp. And since moods are contagious, it will lift your spirits, even if you're in a mood to brood.

Organize your humor. Keep a humor diary of funny thoughts, phrases or experiences to draw upon when you're in the midst of crisis. With a bit of polishing, you can work these tidbits into jokes or witticisms to share with friends and family, or even in public speeches or presentations. "Professional comics are meticulous about this," says Joel Goodman, Ed.D., director of The HUMOR Project, a humor think tank in Saratoga Springs, New York, and a humor specialist who writes and lectures widely. "And for good reason: It works."

Joke to cope. Comedy great Steve Allen once said that tragedy plus time equals comedy. While it's true that we all must adjust to the stress of tragedy in our own way, don't be quick to rule out humor as a coping device.

"I tell patients to remember that humor is here to help us cope," says the great comic's son, Dr. Steve Allen, Jr., of Ithaca, New York. "There are times when people will see you laughing in the wake of tragedy, which will make you look a little weird, but if it makes you feel good, enjoy it."

It's a Guy Thing

Over these last few decades of sweeping societal change, barriers between men and women have crumbled like the Berlin Wall. But one bulwark remains: the Three Stooges.

"I have talked extensively to women about this at national Stooge conventions, and the reasons why they, in general, don't find the Stooges as funny as men are fascinating," says Dr. Don Morlan of Dayton University, a lifelong Stooge fan who's written serious academic papers on Larry, Moe and Curly. "It's not because the Stooges are violent, which is what a lot of people say. The Stooges are human cartoon characters. They get beat around, but in the next episode they're back intact just like Wile E. Coyote."

The real reason why many women aren't Stooge converts, Dr. Morlan says, is threefold: First, the Stooges relate to women poorly. Their movies are peppered with women who are unflatteringly portrayed as nagging, fat or ugly. Second, the Stooges aren't exactly Casonovas of comedy. They're short, ugly and not very intelligent men—which is what the average woman sees more than enough of in any given week.

But the most compelling reason why women don't like the Stooges is "because many of them are Stooge widows," Dr. Morlan says. "A woman's spouse or boyfriend gets together with fellow fans and what happens? They're doing impressions, joking around, making references and poking each other in the eyes. The women become Stooge widows, just like some women become golf or football widows."

Music

Striking a Soothing Chord

While everyone's heard that music soothes the savage beast, science has shown that music seems to soothe the savage executive, too.

"I've been in this field for 25 years, and I've had a lot of rocks thrown at me and a lot of doctors nip my ankles," says longtime music therapy advocate Cathie E. Guzzetta, R.N., Ph.D., director of Holistic Nursing Consultants and the nursing research consultant for Parkland Memorial Hospital and Children's Medical Center, both in Dallas. "But we're finding that it's possible for music to take you further into relaxation than ever before.

"There's certainly a component of quackery to some alternative therapies, but I've seen music therapy take on a whole new scientific stature," says Dr. Guzzetta, who plays violin and has authored numerous industry texts, including *Critical Care Nursing: Body, Mind, Spirit* and *Holistic Nursing*, and who produced the dynamic, instructional four-tape series, *The Art of Caring*.

"Music may not be your magic bullet, but you shouldn't rule it out automatically either," she says. "Relaxation shouldn't be an either/or proposition. Why not make the most of traditional and alternative therapies?"

Al Bumanis, director of communications for the National Association for Music Therapy in Silver Springs, Maryland, agrees. "People are just starting to realize the benefits of music as a bona fide therapy," he says. "In health care, for example, it's a very goal-oriented field. You use music to help you achieve specific treatment goals."

Getting in Tune

Before you crank up "Louie Louie" on the stereo, remember: The idea is to relax. Here are some tips and techniques to help you go with the flow.

Play favorites. Knowing your tastes and preferences is crucial to making the most of music. Try this exercise over the next couple weeks to raise your awareness: Find a quiet corner and sit in a comfortable position. Take your pulse. Then observe your breathing rate—is it fast, slow, forced, gentle? Now scan your body for tension—are you hunching your shoulders, knitting your brow, knotting your back muscles? Evaluate your mood—are you angry, tired, sad, happy?

Spend the next 20 minutes listening to one type of music that you like. Don't analyze yourself at this time. Rather, let your body respond without thinking about it. When you're done, reassess yourself. What happened to your breathing, pulse, mood and tension? Knowing how music influences your mood is critical so that you know whether it's time for Hendrix, Handel or Hank Williams; Bird, Beethoven or the Beatles; Mozart, Madonna or Metallica.

Get lost. In one of Dr. Guzzetta's early studies on heart attack patients, she found that three 20-minute sessions of music therapy were just as effective as similar relaxation sessions based on the popular "relaxation response," fathered by Herbert Benson, M.D., associate professor of medicine at Harvard Medical School and author of *The Relaxation Response*.

How did it work? Simple. Dr. Guzzetta or an assistant first talked patients through a mini head-to-toe relaxation session to prime them for the music. They then had patients choose either classical, pop or New Age music and listen to it for 20 minutes. The patients were told not to analyze the music but to let it suggest to them what to think and feel. If they became distracted, they were told to refocus on the music and continue.

"Essentially, we just told them to get lost in the music. In the end, this had a tremendous effect on lowering their tension and increasing their relaxation," Dr. Guzzetta says.

Listen as you please. No one type of music is best when it comes to relieving stress. A study at Pennsylvania State University in Altoona, Pennsylvania, found that 36 freshman and sophomore students who listened to everything from classical to easy listening for 15 minutes reported the most relaxation and satisfaction when they listened to music that they liked. But here's an interesting footnote: Just listening to any music seemed to relax them to some degree.

Tune in. Listening to music isn't just something that you can do at home or in your car. If your company policy permits, bring a small radio to work, or wear personal headphones, Bumanis suggests. It may look like goofing off, but several studies suggest that it has a positive effect on performance. Researchers at the University of Illinois, for example, conducted a study of 256 office workers at a retail firm, and found that the 75 who opted to listen to a stereo while on the job "exhibited significant improvements in performance, turnover intentions, organization satisfaction, mood states and other responses."

Be a music maker. About the only musical instrument that many of us play well is the radio, but that's no excuse not to try—as long as you don't try too hard. Learning an instrument, or even singing, can reduce tension much like listening to music. Why? Because they both engage the right side of your brain, the side associated with creativity and

Mood Music

Listen to country music and you'll get drunk, cheat on your wife and cry when your sainted mother or faithful dog dies. Heavy metal will cause you to either bang your head against the wall or bash in somebody else's brains. And rap, of course, will turn you into a gun-toting 'gangsta'. Those common stereotypes are vastly oversimplified, says Dr. Cathie E. Guzzetta of Holistic Nursing Consultants and Parkland Memorial Hospital and Children's Medical Center. The connection between music and human behavior is far more subtle, she says.

The key, Dr. Guzzetta says, lies in what music therapists call the iso-principle. The iso-principle is a fancy way of saying that music influences your mood and vice versa. So while listening to a heavy-metal paean to suicide probably won't make you leap from a bridge, it could make the idea sound more appealing if you're already feeling suicidal, Dr. Guzzetta says.

You can, however, use this music-mood connection to your advantage by allowing music to guide your feelings to a desired state, Dr. Guzzetta says. For example, say you're all keyed up after work and want to relax. Instead of immediately boring yourself with Bach, find something a little jazzier to match your mood. After ten minutes or so, switch to something a little more soothing. Ten minutes later, slow the music down to the rhythm that you want yourself to be at. You'll be "Bach" to normal in no time.

peacefulness. Such creative expressions can give you a sense of well-being, but only if you don't expect to be an expert right away.

"Drums are especially good for men, since you can beat away your stress at the same time," Bumanis says, "and you don't have to sit in the woods in front of a fire to do it."

Pets

Lassie Calm Home

For the stress-blasting benefits of pets, we could have turned first to medicine or psychology. But we didn't. Instead, we turned to one of the great philosophers of our time: Charlie Brown, the melon-headed kid from the "Peanuts" comic who summed it all up nicely when he said, "Happiness is a warm puppy."

It turns out that Charles M. Schulz's lovable loser was onto something. Warm puppies and all sorts of pets are attracting the collective clinical eye of science and stress researchers.

"I'm glad that this research has caught on. When we first started, colleagues thought it was a joke," says psychiatrist Aaron Katcher, M.D., a pioneer of studies linking pets to good health, emeritus professor of psychiatry at the University of Pennsylvania in Philadelphia, consultant to the Devereux Foundation for animal therapy and the proud owner of three miniature poodles.

Animal Instincts

Dr. Katcher's studies in the early 1980s, conducted with Alan Beck, Sc.D., professor of psychiatry at Purdue University in West Lafayette, Indiana, found a direct correlation between stress and pets. By wiring volunteers to electrodes and monitoring their vital signs, the two found that people relaxed more in front of their furred, feathered and finned friends.

"Of course there's more to stress management than just animals, but we found that pets play a pivotal role," says Dr. Beck. This should come as no surprise, he adds, considering

that 99 percent of pet owners talk to their pets, 48 percent talk to their pets like friends and 70 percent of adolescents intimately confide in family pets.

"The average family pet is perceived as a member of the family," says Dr. Beck, who has published his findings with Dr. Katcher in their book *Between People and Pets*.

Karen Allen, Ph.D., a contemporary pet researcher at the State University of New York at Buffalo, found even more encouraging evidence in studies that she conducted throughout the first half of the 1990s. In one study, Dr. Allen measured the heart rate and blood pressure of 240 married couples while they did three stressful tests under four different conditions.

"What we found is that people showed a lower stress response when they were alone with their dogs than in any other situation," Dr. Allen says. The reason, she surmises, is that pets provide unconditional support without the possibility of being judged or criticized. "Even if your spouse is the most supportive person in the world, you know there's the chance that he or she might be judging you when you're together. Your dog never will."

According to a poll by CNN and *U.S. News & World Report*, 63 percent of people surveyed said that owning a pet leads to a more satisfying life. Sixty-five percent said that it makes you a nicer person.

Pet Projects

Here's how to relax with Rover and other members of the mild wild kingdom.

Enjoy being the emperor. "Every man is Napoleon to his pet. You may come home from work after a day of being kicked by everyone from the chief executive officer to the janitor, but with your pets, you're the leader," Dr. Katcher says. Realize how important you are to them and enjoy your role as nurturer. It's okay to take pride in doing a fine job of caring for another living being.

Romp and roam. Scottish essayist Thomas Carlyle and English poet Alfred, Lord Tennyson once visited each other by sitting before a fire, smoking their pipes and not uttering a single word for three hours. *That's* companionship. Do the same with your pets. Play with them. Spend time with them. If your animal's a dog, go for a jog or roughhouse in the yard after work. If it's a bird, perch him on your shoulder while you read the paper or open your mail. Carlyle and Tennyson each had a masterful command of words, but they showed that strong bonds can be formed simply by being together.

Speak, boy, speak. Talk to your animals. Parrots and similar birds are nice because they talk back, but that's an added bonus. "If you think that your pet is listening to you, it helps you relax," Dr. Katcher says. "It's like with a psychiatrist—you feel better when you think he's listening, even if he's really asleep."

Explore the eccentric. Dogs may be man's best friend, but you can get as much companionship from virtually any animal, including those of an exotic ilk. Consider snakes, iguanas, amphibians, tarantulas, scorpions, ferrets or hedgehogs. "Their novelty is rewarding," Dr. Beck says. "Plus, as long as you like them and enjoy spending time with them, the species isn't important when it comes to stress reduction."

Promote family values. Nurturing a pet seems to help make you a better father. Do you want proof? Consider the University of Minnesota study of some 400 fathers that found that men with dogs—those who cared about their dogs—tended to have the best parenting traits.

Enjoy them at work. Pets are just as relaxing at work as they are at home. If your company policy allows, consider a pet for your desk. Good picks include bettas, also called Siamese fighting fish, which are beautiful tropical fish that can be kept in small bowls without air pumps or filters. Or consider an anole. Also called American chameleons, these tiny lizards are easy to take care of and will turn your office into Jurassic Park.

If You Can't Have Pets . . .

Admittedly, pets mean responsibility, despite the good that they bring to our lives. And if you're married to your job or spend all your time away from home, caring for one can be cumbersome at best and downright unfair to the animal at worst. Here are two alternatives to pet ownership that have the same stress-blasting benefits.

Feed the world. Set up a bird feeder in the backyard. It's the same stress-reducing concept. You'll be doing good for your feathered friends, you'll see nature in action and you can learn to identify your itinerant guests, turning your altruism into a pastime. (*Hint:* This also makes a great project to do with kids.) Another option, if you live in the sticks, is to put out a salt lick or food stand for wildlife. Same effect, different guests.

Adopt a plant. Consider a houseplant, like a hearty philodendron or snake plant. Or plant a rosebush or two in your yard. Caring for plants, especially if the payoff is a beautiful flower, is life-affirming. And don't laugh at the potential stress benefits.

"Did you ever watch people with plants? They talk to them, they stroke them, they dote on them. Taking care of plants is a model for all nurturing," says Purdue University's Dr. Alan Beck. Moreover, Dr. Beck adds, Purdue research has found that caring for plants and pets encourages nurturing behavior in children.

Positive Thinking

Mind over What's the Matter

There's a story of three bricklayers, each busily engaged in his profession. A man walks by and asks what they are doing.

"I'm laying one brick after another," says the first.

"I'm making a wall," says the second.

"I'm building a castle," says the third.

It doesn't take a building inspector to guess whose bricks will be laid the truest. Common sense suggests that the guy who takes the most pride in his work, the guy who sees the forest through the trees—or, in this case, the castle through the bricks—will be the best at what he does. And you can bet your bricks that he'll also be the least stressed and the most satisfied with his life.

Proof Positive

It's essential to understand that the way you view the world has a direct impact on how stress affects your life. "Your attitude is probably the single, most important factor in determining your level of stress in life," says Dr. Patch Adams of the Gesundheit Institute.

While that sounds enlightening coming from a modern medical expert, it's nothing new. Thousands of years ago, the ancient Greek philosopher Epictetus said, "Man is not disturbed by events, but by the view he takes of them."

Research shows that there may be something to this age-old perspective. Science has documented an elusive but obvious link between what we think and how we feel. The most celebrated case is that of Norman Cousins, an author and former editor who suffered a debilitating collagen disease. With his pain great and his prognosis poor, Cousins persuaded his doctors to let him leave the hospital, check into a hotel room and start an intensive program of humor therapy. He found that a few minutes of laughter not only brightened his mood but eased his pain. Cousins recovered fully and wrote the seminal best-selling *Anatomy of an Illness, As Perceived by the Patient.*

If positive thoughts influence us in good ways, consider the scary inverse: Negative thoughts influence us in bad ways. Researchers at the University of California at San Diego looked into this by examining the death certificates of 28,169 Chinese-Americans and 412,632 White Americans. They found that the Chinese died significantly earlier than the White Americans when they contracted a disease associated with Chinese astrology. The more traditional beliefs the Chinese person held, the more likely he or she was to die earlier than a White person in the control group.

This research was the second similar conclusion by the study's lead researcher, David P. Phillips, Ph.D., of the university's Department of Sociology. Dr. Phillips previously found that, among Jews and Chinese, mortality rates dipped right before important traditional holidays, such as Passover or the Harvest Moon Festival, only to spike afterward. Dr. Phillips's findings suggest that strong traditional beliefs may influence us physiologically.

Go East, Young Man

As we said, the mind-body connection isn't a new concept. Besides Epictetus, ancient Greeks like the physician-writer Galen proposed such a link more than 2,000 years ago. They believed that passions—

that is, strong feelings—were disease harbingers. Somewhere along the march to modern civilization, however, we lost this perspective.

It all started about 350 years ago, when our paradigm of medicine shifted dramatically away from the mind-body connection. The rise of scientific inquiry in the Western world, not to mention the ascent of the industrial age, reduced the human body, in the eyes of doctors, to a physiological machine.

With this new rational approach, the definition of good health became merely a body without illness or injury. If something went wrong with the body, chemistry (taking a pill) or hands-on repair (surgery) were the proper responses. Mental attitude, because it could not be measured, played little if any role in the process.

Such a mentality still permeates the medical establishment. The proof? Sleeping pills, diet pills, antidepression pills, muscle-relaxing pills. But, according to some of today's experts, this "body-as-machine" approach might have been a huge step backward.

"I've worked with patients in critical care units for a long time, and they often get left-brain treatment for their problems from Western medicine, when there's such a great need for right-brain, Eastern-style caring of their body, mind and spirit," says Dr. Cathie E. Guzzetta of Holistic Nursing Consultants and Parkland Memorial Hospital and Children's Medical Center.

"I've never been quite sure why modern Western medicine doesn't make more use of Eastern medical concepts," says Dr. Guzzetta. "Why should someone's health be an either/or proposition? Why not make the most of Eastern and Western medicines for the patient's benefit?"

Much Eastern doctrine, Dr. Guzzetta says, places a great deal of emphasis on

Feelings—Woe, Woe, Woe

There's a fascinating feedback loop built into your emotions that can dramatically alter your attitude, making you worse for wear if you're not careful enough to catch it.

Clark University's Dr. Jim Laird says that it's called mood-congruent memory, and the best analogy we can think of is that it's a one-person example of the contagiousness of emotions.

"Everybody's heard that moods are contagious, but with mood-congruent memory, we've found that our own moods can feed upon themselves," Dr. Laird says. "Say you're sad. If you recall memories when you're sad, you'll most likely recall other sad times.

"Because of this, your feelings can snowball without your knowing it," Dr. Laird says. "Since your memory is driven, in part, by feelings, you can unwittingly exaggerate them."

Obviously, this has serious implications for the guy who wants to cultivate a can-do attitude. So next time you're down in the dumps, pause and contemplate what it's doing to your outlook. It'll be one more reason to see the brighter side of life.

attitude. It acknowledges the connection between mind and body and how each complements the other.

Looking on the Bright Side

Stress research has revealed that the people who are most resistant to stress simply view it as a challenge to be met and mastered, not an obstacle to trip over.

Cultivating this attitude needn't be a Holy Grail quest, and you don't have to turn into

Candide or Pollyanna or wear rose-colored glasses. It starts with some minor changes in the way that you deal with stress. Here are some ideas to get started.

Practice prevention. Don't wait until stress reaches critical mass to do something about it. "The majority of people in the world should learn to convert stress into something positive before it becomes a problem," says Ann McGee-Cooper, Ed.D., international creativity consultant, lecturer and author of several books, including *You Don't Have to Go Home from Work Exhausted!* and *Building Brain Power.*

So start today with an attitude of stress prevention. By striving to see your top stressors—meeting the mortgage, getting ahead at work, finding inner peace—as challenges to overcome, you'll have a more stress-hardy attitude.

Keep perspective. Someone once said that the key to happiness is knowing not to sweat the small stuff and knowing that everything is small stuff. When faced with a daunting, stressful problem, ask yourself: What will this mean in 50 years? Or, on my deathbed, will this really matter?

"I don't define individual situations as stressful. It's my reaction that causes me stress," Dr. Adams says. "For me, it's simply a privilege to be alive. Everything else is small change."

Keep your passions burning. Tune in to whatever lights your fire, be it woodworking, volunteering, cycling or collecting dryer lint.

"You need passions outside of work. These are things that you do just for the fun of it. They rest your brain and remind you that life has a fun side," Dr. McGee-Cooper says. "Highly creative people, particularly geniuses, have a lot of interests. The mistake that people make is that they work too hard at their hobbies. Hobbies should be something that you just do to enjoy."

Talk to Yourself

Every minute of your life, you're awash in a waterfall of thoughts cascading through your mind. I'm hungry. Damn, she looks good. What's *his* problem? Please, don't ask me about my marketing proposal. #@%!% elevator!

Psychologists call this self-talk. And Albert Ellis, who conducted pioneering research on the subject in the 1960s, concluded it is the fastest way to talk yourself out of a good mood. According to Ellis, self-talk is the middle ground between stimulus and emotion. When a driver in front of you slams on his brakes and you narrowly miss locking bumpers, there's a point between the actual event (the near miss) and your emotion (fear, anger, relief) where self-talk intervenes, whether you realize it or not. Ellis's point was that if you learn to recognize and govern self-talk, you'll have more control over your thoughts and feelings.

Take control. It's common to feel stressed and apathetic once in a while, but staying that way isn't going to make it go away, says Dr. Paul J. Rosch of the American Institute of Stress and New York Medical College. Do something about it.

That's the preferred strategy of comedy great Steve Allen. When something provokes him—like global hunger, senselessly violent TV, America's falling academic standards—he takes control by writing a book, letter or joke about it.

"My opinion might not be any better than yours or the cab driver's, but when I'm bugged by injustice, I'll act on it," says Allen. "The obvious difference for me is that when you're a public figure, what you feel—even about spaghetti sauce—gets into the media."

While you won't get such preferential treatment, taking whatever action you can helps stress-proof your life and gives your attitude a boost.

Be tolerant. The next time you find your mood cloudier than London in November,

Being aware of self-talk and its influence is called cognitive therapy, and there are several flavors, including rational emotive therapy, Gestalt therapy, existential therapy and transactional analysis.

"Cognitive therapists will be quick to tell you that what they're doing is not positive thinking—it's *accurate* thinking," says Martha Davis, Ph.D., psychology professor in the Department of Psychiatry at Kaiser Permanente Medical Center in Santa Clara, California.

"With cognitive therapy, we ask the client to examine what they're telling themselves about events or stimuli that trigger internal or external responses," Dr. Davis says. "We identify distortions in what they're thinking and challenge distressing thoughts in order to come up with more accurate, less stressful, less extreme perspectives."

Take ten for empathy. It's easy to let the rude waitress cloud your day. Too easy. Take an empathy break next time. Rather than fly off the handle because your lunch is late, brainstorm ten empathetic possible reasons for the waitress's behavior. Maybe she just had a really rude customer who demeaned her; maybe her kids are sick; maybe she got stiffed on a tip; maybe she just got a speeding ticket. Habit-forming empathy goes a long way in altering your outlook—and in reducing stress.

Be an inverse paranoid. Dr. Adams has a great way of looking at life. He likes to think that everyone he meets is out to do him good. He finds that if he approaches people with this in mind, not only does he come off as more positive, but his encounters are generally friendlier and more productive.

Go to the library. There are many good self-help books that can help you foster a more positive attitude. For average people, these are adequate in pointing them down the right path. "Bibliotherapy is effective for the motivated and relatively intelligent person who's not too depressed," says Dr. Martha Davis of the Kaiser Permanente Medical Center. Her suggestion: *Ten Days to Self Esteem!* by David D. Burns, M.D., clinical associate professor of psychiatry at the Presbyterian Medical Center of Philadelphia. Or, we might suggest Dr. Davis's excellent *The Relaxation and Stress Reduction Workbook,* which contains keen advice on stopping negative thoughts, breaking the shackles of negativism and achieving positive goals.

Take a workshop. If books aren't cutting it, take a workshop on building a better attitude. Check with your local university, college, career-development office or mental health center. A hands-on approach or two on self-esteem, optimism or cognitive therapy will be far more effective for some people than reading a book.

ask yourself if it's because you're angry that someone or something hasn't lived up to your expectations. "If you are tolerant, your actions will almost always be more effective. Moreover, you can focus your assertion, money and time on the matters most important to you," say Redford B. Williams, M.D., professor of psychiatry and director of the Behavioral Medicine Research Center at Duke University Medical Center in Durham, North Carolina, and Virginia Williams, Ph.D., authors of *Anger Kills.*

Write yourself right. Keep a personal journal to express your innermost thoughts and feelings. Putting pen to paper clarifies what's rolling around your cranial cavern. And doing it for just 5 to 15 minutes a day can improve your outlook, mental health and well-being. There's no need to share your writings—you're not Thoreau—and from a health perspective, "you'll be better-off by making yourself the audience," says James W. Pennebaker, Ph.D., professor of psychology at Southern Methodist University in Dallas.

Relaxation Techniques

Learning to Let Go of Stress

Recall the most brilliant sunset you've ever seen. Perhaps you were strolling beachside, arm in arm with someone special. Maybe you were hiking and you reached a summit with an Ansel Adams overlook. Whatever the setting, recall how you felt the moment the sun's orange velvet fingers stroked the pale blue cheek of the evening sky for the last time that day. Picture its leisurely feather float from zenith to horizon, the point where it became molten lava and dripped, like a Salvador Dalí clock, over the edge of the world.

Watching a sunset is a brief interlude of peace that we've all experienced. They're among the few things in life that automatically propel us into bliss. They're Nature's psychotherapists.

Fortunately, you don't have to wait until sundown to re-create these peaceful feelings. You can do much the same indoors or on a rainy day with relaxation techniques, many of which have been scientifically proven to break the stranglehold of stress. The three most prominent techniques—breathing, progressive relaxation and autogenic training—can be done by anyone, virtually anywhere.

Getting Started

Before you read on and expect your stress to dissipate like the morning mist on some picturesque pond, know the ground rules.

"You have to remember that relaxation is a skill and, like any skill, it takes both time and practice to perfect," says Phil Nuernberger, Ph.D., president of Mind Resource Technologies, an executive consulting firm in Honesdale, Pennsylvania, and author of *The Quest for Personal Power: Transforming Stress into Strength* and *Freedom from Stress.*

How do you get started? Begin by approaching relaxation techniques like you would any other skill: Start slowly, maybe three times a week, for sessions that last 10 to 20 minutes each. Then, over time, build to a daily session or two of 20 to 30 minutes each.

"While 30 minutes might sound like a big chunk of time, what you'll get in return for that investment will be incredible," Dr. Nuernberger says. In some sessions you'll see results almost immediately. Other times, you won't. Regardless, remember that in time, say over two weeks or so, consistent practice will yield consistent and encouraging results.

Dr. Nuernberger suggests experimenting with each of the following techniques to find which suits you best. But pay careful attention to breathing. Breathing is at the heart of relaxation. Other than that, feel free to practice each technique and mix and match them as your moods dictate.

Breathing

Mastering proper breathing technique is the key to conquering stress.

"Breathing is fundamental to relaxation, and it can't be emphasized enough," says Dr. Martha Davis at Kaiser Permanente Medical Center. "People who are stressed don't breathe properly.

"To show this in class, I'll often ask my students to follow my finger as I wave it back and forth in front of their eyes," she adds. "Then I'll ask how many of them stopped breathing. If they're honest and paying attention, most will realize that they stopped breathing for a few seconds.

"If they stopped breathing with something as mundane as my waving my finger, then how often do all of us stop breathing during the more stressful moments in our lives?" Dr. Davis asks.

Dr. Nuernberger agrees. "Breathing is fundamental to our very existence. How come we're never taught to breathe the best we can?" Here's how.

Take the test. Lie on your back on the floor and place your left hand over your chest and your right hand over your belly button. Now, without consciously altering your breath, notice which hand moves. If your right hand rises first and falls last with each breath, great. You're breathing with your diaphragm, which is how it should be. An ideal breath should fill the bottom third of your lungs first, then the middle third and finally the top; it should reverse the order on exhalation. If, in the hand exercise, your left hand rises first or if it rises more than your right hand, you're a chest, or thoracic, breather.

Breathe by the book. Train yourself to belly breathe by lying on the floor with a book on your stomach. Concentrate on making the book rise and fall with each breath. Alternately, lie on your stomach and concentrate on pushing your stomach into the floor with each inhalation. Again, once you've breathed comfortably with your stomach, fill the middle and top thirds of your lungs.

Use the rhythm method. To establish a relaxing breathing rhythm, breathe deeply for a four count, pause briefly, then breathe out for a five count. Do this for a couple of minutes and it will have a tranquilizing effect on your body and mind. Counting keeps your breath regulated, and it gives your mind something to concentrate on.

Radio Days

In the future, you might not listen to the radio to relax and fall asleep at night. You'll just suck an antenna and ride an AM radio wave to Snoozeville.

Low-energy emission therapy (LEET) is a type of therapy that appears promising when it comes to inducing relaxation and curing insomnia. In LEET, you stick a specially designed, spoon-shaped radio antenna in your mouth at night. The antenna is attached by a short cord to an alarm clock–size transmitter. The transmitter emits low-intensity, low-frequency radio waves that seem to invite the body to relax and fall asleep.

Studies of animals have shown that LEET affects the brain's neuron firings. In people studies it seems to induce sleep. Two studies of 104 volunteers found that those who received LEET for 15 minutes had lowered blood pressures, more muscle relaxation and more subjective feelings of warmth than volunteers receiving bogus LEET in a control group. In another study of 30 people with chronic insomnia, researchers found that those receiving LEET slept 1½ hours longer than those who didn't.

While preliminary research looks promising, experts agree that more should be done.

Progressive Relaxation

In the late 1920s, a Chicago physician named Edmund Jacobson theorized that the body responds to stress anxiety by tensing muscles. To counter this, Dr. Jacobson offered progressive relaxation as an alternate path to relaxation. Jacobson published his findings in *Progressive Relaxation* in 1929, where he described a technique so simple that anyone could do it.

Progressive relaxation has since proved successful for depression, anxiety, insomnia, irritable bowels, high blood pressure and even stuttering.

"You need to have something besides breathing to get the most relaxation possible. For many men, it's progressive relaxation that works best because they have so much tension in their bodies that they're not aware of," Dr. Davis says. Here's how to be a progressive guy.

Get down. The basis of progressive relaxation is to flex all your muscles systematically so that when you loosen up, your entire body relaxes. Start by lying on your back on the floor in a comfortable position.

Hold tight, flex right. Each time you contract a muscle group, hold for 5 to 7 seconds with all your might. Then relax for 15 to 30 seconds before going on to the next muscle group. Take care with your back and neck. It's easy to overdo it with these muscles and hurt yourself. Ditto for the toes and calves, which can cramp up if they are suddenly tensed.

Relax suddenly. Remember that the tension part of your routine is a means, not an end. The goal is to relax entirely during the relaxation portion. To that end, completely let go once you stop contracting your muscles. Turn off the juices like a light switch and allow your muscles (and your mind) to slip into deep relaxation.

Follow orders. Now that you have the technique down, here's the order that you should follow for tensing and relaxing your muscles.

- Clench both fists, tighten your biceps and forearms and curl your arms inward as if you're striking the classic bodybuilding pose.
- Wrinkle your forehead, squint your eyes and scrunch your face muscles tightly, while flexing the muscles in your neck.
- Arch your back and take a deep breath, tightening your chest and stomach.

Tune In to Biofeedback

Many people think that biofeedback is a relaxation technique, like yoga or meditation, but it's not. Yet, biofeedback is almost as important because it is science's way of measuring how successful you are at relaxing. Pioneered by Alyce Green and Elmer Green, Ph.D., of the Menninger Foundation in Topeka, Kansas, in the late 1960s and refined through the years, biofeedback has become a high-tech way of making sure that your body's really listening when you tell it to slow down.

"It's a machine that allows you to do a relaxation technique and measure the results," explains Jon Kabat-Zinn, Ph.D., director of the Stress Reduction Clinic at the University of Massachusetts Medical Center in Worcester who is also an associate professor of medicine, lecturer and author of *Full Catastrophe Living: Using the Wisdom of Your Body and Mind to Face Stress, Pain and Illness* and *Wherever You Go, There You Are.*

Biofeedback "machines" come in all shapes and

- Pull your feet and toes back toward your shins, while curling your toes and tightening your thighs, calves and butt.

Make a tape. If you're finding this routine hard to do on your own, make a tape-recorded guide to talk you through the progression. The added benefits of a tape include being able to incorporate encouraging messages to help you relax further.

Autogenics

Autogenic relaxation falls somewhere between hypnosis and progressive relaxation. Autogenic research began with Oskar Vogt, a nineteenth-century brain physiologist who worked at the Berlin Institute in Germany. Vogt found that hypnosis subjects could put themselves into a trancelike state and that when

sizes. Some are relatively inexpensive and made for home use; others are expensive laboratory-style gizmos designed for professionals. They all do the same thing: measure physiological responses to stress. Typical measurements are made from muscle tension (the most common measurement), heart rate, blood pressure and the amount of perspiration that your skin's oozing, its electrical conductivity and its temperature. More advanced machines can measure your brain waves.

The good news is that you don't have to go bankrupt to get biofeedback. You can get similar results by simply scanning your body periodically for tension. Think of it as built-in biofeedback, says Dr. Phil Nuernberger of Mind Resource Technologies.

Another great way to get feedback on your relaxation efforts is to study yourself in a mirror. It's amazing how much tension you'll notice when you really stop and look for it.

they did, they felt warm, heavy and relaxed.

Building on that, Berlin psychiatrist Johannes H. Schultz found that you could achieve the same result by skipping the middle ground of hypnosis and concentrating instead on the warm and heavy feelings. He combined these techniques with yoga poses to form autogenic training, which he published in a book of the same name in 1932. Here are the basic steps.

Let go. Autogenic relaxation works like progressive relaxation, except instead of tensing your muscles into repose, you're talking yourself through the process. Here's the script. (Start on your back on the floor in a comfortable position. Note that you'll repeat each line a given number of times.)

- "My hands and arms are heavy and warm." (5 times)

- "My feet and legs are heavy and warm." (5 times)
- "My abdomen is warm and comfortable." (5 times) *Note:* Skip this if you have ulcers, diabetes or internal bleeding problems.
- "My breathing is deep, full and relaxed." (10 times)
- "My heartbeat is calm, regular and healthy." (10 times)
- "My forehead is cool." (5 times)

Take it slow. When you're talking yourself through the "warm and heavy" feelings, say each line slowly and sincerely, taking about five seconds to state your instructions. Pause for about three seconds, concentrating on the feeling, before going on.

Start with your dominant side. If you're right-handed, start with that hand. Then progress to your other hand. Ditto for your legs.

Watch for subconscious discharge. There's a phenomenon in autogenic relaxation called discharge that can be quite disturbing. What happens is, as your body and mind relaxes, thoughts and feelings from your subconscious can rise up, like an air bubble from the mud at the bottom of a well. These thoughts or feelings can be disturbing. Or you might feel strange sensations, like changes in weight, tingling, headaches, nausea or even hallucinations. Remember that these are normal occurrences but aren't the goal of your relaxation. Accept them, but don't linger on them. Let them pass. If they get to be too much, cancel your sessions and consider continuing under a certified autogenic instructor.

Check with your doctor. Dr. Davis recommends that people with physiological limitations, such as high or low blood pressure, diabetes or hypoglycemia check with their doctors before undertaking autogenic training. Likewise, people with low self-motivation or severe mental or emotional disorders should find another form of relaxation.

Sex

Relieving Stress Is a Pleasure

Life wasn't too stressful the first time you had sex. You might have thought so at the time. There were exams to study for, keg parties to plan and attend, women to woo and sports to play. But in retrospect you'd probably trade those youthful blues for today's mortgage-kids-career worry triumvirate any day.

Regardless of what your worries were back then, one thing was certain after your first close encounter of the carnal kind: After sex, you had nothing to worry about. Stress just disappeared. Your body quivered, your knees felt weak and it seemed like days before your heart stopped its heavy-metal drum solo. You swore that you'd just died and gone to Heaven. Your mind seemed so still and focused. And you had this unexplainable surge of energy that lasted for days.

It was during those early years of your sexual development that you learned a very valuable lesson about stress: "Sex is one of life's greatest releases of tension and stress," says Dr. Martha Davis at Kaiser Permanente Medical Center.

"Paradoxically, sex can also be a great stressor, if you let it," Dr. Davis adds. (For more information on that, see Taking the Stress Out of Sex on page 84.) Our focus here is on the many ways that sex can tame stress.

Get Physical

Just what is it about frisky business that makes us feel so good afterward? And why does a roll in the hay rock away stress? According to the experts, it's because sex is an intricate array of psychological and physiological re-

actions, both of which contribute to relieving tension and the exacting toll that it takes on the mind, body and spirit.

Physiologically speaking, sex is an intense physical release. For starters, it stimulates some of the most sensitive nerves in your body. Just consider the average sexual encounter. It generally starts with foreplay, which, if it's good, is a leisurely buildup of excitement that includes plenty of sexy kissing, licking, rubbing and stroking. All this on your skin, which is packed with 20 square feet of surface area and up to 18,000 nerve receptors in each square inch.

From foreplay, you'll typically proceed, in time, to the main course: intercourse and orgasm—Mother Nature's number one stress-blasting team event. Yet, despite its age-old reputation, orgasm is still a bit of a mystery to science. Researchers know that it relieves stress and tension, but to this day, they still aren't sure what orgasms are or how they work. For the most part, they know that orgasms seem to start in the limbic cortex, the brain's pleasure center. From there, a maelstrom of muscle contractions, nerve firings and so on account for the physical sensations: increased pulse and heart rates, delightful muscle contractions, exquisitely sensitive tingling and feelings of euphoria.

Sex on the Brain

Physical sensations in many ways are easier to map than our mental responses to sex. But the affect is no less dramatic—or soothing.

"At its best physiologically, we know that there's tremendous muscle relaxation after sex, but the same seems to happen mentally, too," says Dr. Steve Allen, Jr., of Ithaca, New York. "Sex undoes emotional tension.

"Of course, that's just the biochemical side. It goes even deeper than that," Dr. Allen adds. "Sex in a social situation is life-affirming. It's restorative in a relationship and spiritually reconnecting. Sex is closeness between two human beings at its finest."

Scientists have linked the chemistry of sex in the brain primarily to some key ingredients, including the natural uppers dopamine, norepinephrine and PEA, short for phenylethylamine. Another reason that you're so unwound after a bout of winding up in bed is because you're body's bathed, too, in oxytocin. Oxytocin, a hypothalamic hormone, is three to five times more abundant during orgasm than any other time. It's been linked to playing a key role in accounting for those warm and fuzzy feelings of attachment.

Recharging Your Batteries in Bed

Of course, there's only one thing that you want tense when you're between the sheets—and it's not your mind. Here's how to cash in on the mental and physical benefits of sex.

Get it often. If having sex helps relieve tension and stress, you'd think that *not* having sex would result in the opposite reaction. And you'd be right. "Men who are frustrated sexually tend to be tense and irritable; they often seem angry at the world," says urologist Dudley Seth Danoff, M.D., author of the book *Superpotency.* It says a lot for your grouchy boss.

Linger during the prologue. Foreplay has perhaps the most potential to sap stress in a sexual encounter. It's the only time during sex where the average guy is in complete control of the clock. Unfortunately, average guys seem more fixated on stopping the watch and getting down to business than setting new foreplay records. "Foreplay should be one of the highlights of a stress-relieving sexual encounter," Dr. Davis says, "not something you rush through." She suggests lots of intimate touching, like petting, back scratching, back rubs and the like.

Table for One

Sure, sex is a great way to relieve stress. The only problem is that it takes two. Or does it?

Masturbation is recommended by some experts as a way to enjoy the stress-releasing benefits of sex even if you don't have a partner. And it also can help relieve stress about sexual performance by helping you grow more confident with yourself and your body.

"I do everything I can to reduce stress about masturbation and to encourage it," says Bill Stayton, Th.D., family and marital sex therapist, professor of human sexuality at the University of Pennsylvania in Philadelphia and an ordained minister in the American Baptist Church.

"Most of the stress over masturbation comes from religious upbringing, but there's really nothing traditionally in religion that's against it," Dr. Stayton says. "Religion often comes across as antisexual, and I don't think that was the original intent. Masturbation is helpful in so many ways. If nothing else, it puts you in touch with your own sexual response."

"Intimate touching has a real revitalizing edge," she says.

Practice sensate focus. Sex experts suggest what they called sensate focus exercises to help train people to appreciate the finer points of sex, like touching and foreplay. Sensate focus exercises are big stress reducers because they're incredibly relaxing. And since most women rank touch as their number one sexual sense, it pays to be a handyman.

In essence, a sensate focus exercise is nothing more than concentrating on your sense of touch with no sexual goal in mind. It's more like an erotic massage that won't lead to intercourse. Here's an example of how it's done. Ask your partner to lie down and close her eyes. Straddle her hips and gently caress her face, breasts and stomach for 15 minutes. Trace the contours of her body. Her brows, cheekbones, lips. Run your fingers through her hair. Circle her breasts with gentle, nearly imperceptible strokes of your fingertips, working your way in toward her nipples.

Take your time and touch her for the enjoyment that it gives you, not with the ultimate goal of bringing about an orgasm. Hers or yours.

Take a stress holiday. Because it's harder to work spontaneous lovemaking into your life today, the next best thing is to plan a sex date. It'll be like sneaking off to a cheap motel when you were younger, except you won't be broke for the next two weeks. "A sex holiday can be a great way to break the grip of stress in your regular life," says Dr. Paul J. Rosch of the American Institute of Stress and New York Medical College. "Just getting away to concentrate on nothing else but being with your partner reduces tension and revitalizes your relationship."

Planning such an encounter also gives you plenty of time to pick up some luscious fruit, champagne, candles, incense and, perhaps, erotic toys to supplement your evening. It'll also give her time to pick out appropriately arousing accoutrements.

Expand your sexual horizons. One reason the horizontal hokeypokey was so relaxing in your sexual salad days was because it was new and exciting. But like a new job, sex, too, can grow into a dull, hackneyed routine . . . if you let it.

"Add some silliness to your sex," Dr. Allen suggests. "Or be adventurous and explore with different things. Even if you see sex as deeply spiritual or religious, God gave you a sense of humor and curiosity, right?"

Ways to start your sexual exploration include buying a sex book, changing positions, investigating novelties like sex toys, varying the

Better Than Sex

You hear people use the expression all the time. Surfing Oahu's North Shore is better than sex. A wild-mushroom appetizer you had last night was better than sex. A 1976 Jordan's Cabernet Sauvignon is better than sex. Gonzo journalist Hunter S. Thompson wrote a book about politics that he called—you guessed it—*Better Than Sex*. Although Thompson does concede that saying that high-stakes politics is better than sex "is a weird theory and often raises unsettling personal questions, it is a theory nonetheless, and on some days I've even believed it myself."

So we turned to some experts in the field of sex and asked them what, if anything, could possibly be better.

"Sharing a succulent lobster, fine wine and a sea breeze with good friends is better than sex," offers Robert T. Francoeur, Ph.D., professor of human sexuality at Fairleigh Dickinson University in Madison, New Jersey, and New York University in New York City, co-author of *The Scent of Eros* and editor of *The Complete Dictionary of Sexology*.

"Applause can sometimes be better than sex," says Helen Fisher, Ph.D., research associate in the Department of Anthropology at Rutgers University in New Brunswick, New Jersey, and author of *Anatomy of Love*.

In fact, if you're looking for the thrill, pleasure and deep satisfaction that sex gives you, there are plenty of options.

pacing, extending and varying your foreplay and having sex in an unusual location. The list is only limited by your imagination and willingness to try new things.

Be assertive. One way to ensure that sex is the most satisfying and relaxing thing you do is to make sure that the sexual needs for you both are being met. Granted, this may take considerable diplomacy if, say, you're into leather and she's into lace, but it is possible. Especially

"Anything that amps up the brain physiology can give a physical and emotional high just as sex gives a high," Dr. Fisher says. She explains that many activities that people enjoy stimulate rushes of dopamine and norepinephrine, chemicals that cause feelings of elation, exhilaration and euphoria.

"Other natural chemicals in the brain cause what's called an endorphin high in the pleasure centers of the brain," adds Dr. Francoeur, "the same centers that are triggered by orgasm."

We're sure that, with your creativity, you can add your own great alternatives to sex. And, like Thompson, some days you may even believe them yourself. Here's a starter list of ten things that Dr. Francoeur and Dr. Fisher suggest to get you panting.

- A good hunk of chocolate
- A deep belly laugh
- A 10-K run (or any aerobic workout)
- A full-body massage
- Any scent that recalls a fond memory
- Watching the sun set into the ocean
- A lively dialogue
- An afternoon of gardening
- Being around loving family
- A perfect fire in a perfect fireplace

candid conversations, "the good news is that most couples in time figure out gracious ways of handling their differences," Dr. Rosch says.

And remember: Assertiveness means communicating your thoughts, feelings and desires without defying or infringing upon hers.

Abstain from the training myth. In the original *Rocky* film, the grizzled trainer played by Burgess Meredith orders his boxer to abstain from sex before the big fight. "Women weaken legs," he tells a visibly disappointed Sylvester Stallone. Too bad. Maybe if Rocky and Adrian had done the "electric slide" the night before, Rocky could have beaten Apollo Creed and spared us the interminable sequels that followed.

Researchers at the College of St. Scholastica in Duluth, Minnesota, studied 11 men in their mid-twenties and found that their having sex 12 hours before a battery of fitness tests had no noticeable effect on performance. "It appears justified to dismiss the myth that sexual intercourse has a detrimental effect on physical performance," concluded lead scientist Tommy Boone, Ph.D., in his study.

Be a lifer. Studies conclude that sex doesn't end when the gray hair begins. Sex can be your most powerful lifelong stress blaster, even in the golden years, if you take the steps necessary to ensure it: Stay in shape, eat right and, most important, use it or lose it.

if you exercise sexual assertiveness. "The problem with couples in long-term relationships is that it's hard sometimes to get your sexual cycles and growth in sync," Dr. Rosch says.

He suggests talking honestly and openly with your partner about your sexual needs and desires. Just talk outside the bedroom and during neutral times—not when you're both hot and bothered and walking upstairs. Although this can be an awkward talk if you're not used to such

"I remember when I was in training," Dr. Allen says. "I saw one couple in their seventies who had a great sex life. They just came to us to 'make it better.' Their secret was that they realized that good sex sometimes includes erection, and sometimes doesn't. Sometimes includes intercourse, and sometimes doesn't," Dr. Allen adds. "They knew how wonderful sex could be over the long haul."

Sleep

Give a Nod to Stress

Ever have a truly restless night where you counted so many sheep that you felt like an auditor general for the wool industry?

We all have. And what does it do to us the next morning? It leaves us whipped, weary and grouchy. Now imagine this scenario played out to a lesser degree every night. While not seemingly as extreme as one bout of serious sleeplessness, moderate sleep deprivation over the long haul has a draining effect. And you can bet your fluffy pillow and down comforter that it insidiously adds to your total accumulation of stress.

Our Nation's Other Deficit

Excluding teenagers, do you know anyone who gets too much sleep? Neither do we. The problem is that whenever we need to cram something into our burgeoning schedules, we lop the minutes or hours off bedtime. Because of this, there's a good chunk of our nation stumbling through life like sleep-deprived zombies.

Health officials say that sleep deprivation may be the most pernicious, undiagnosed medical malady facing Americans today. Chronic deprivation strikes an estimated 40 million of us, with another 20 million to 30 million suffering intermittent problems.

"I don't think that many of us are getting enough sleep, because our lives are so full. People have so many things to do these days," says Dr. Martha Davis at Kaiser Permanente Medical Center.

Dr. Davis deals with many stressed-out clients who routinely

stay awake until 1:00 or 2:00 A.M., despite having to get up as early as 5:00 A.M. "When they get home from work, they want to exercise. Then they want to eat. Since they have kids, they want to spend time with the kids. Then they want time to themselves," she says. "They feel like there aren't enough hours in the day because there aren't. So they scrimp on sleep."

As a result, Dr. Davis adds, this lack of sleep compounds the stress in our lives. It saps our bodies of the vital recovery time we need, which means our energy can range from low to virtually nonexistent. And being low on sleep makes our tempers flare, our memories falter and our moods become dour. It's hard to be chipper, optimistic and energetic—and thus stress-free—when our bodies and minds are crying for a siesta.

Moreover, the problem doesn't seem likely to resolve itself, based on our collective attitude toward sleep. According to one survey from the Better Sleep Council, 88 percent of all adults interviewed ranked nutrition, exercise and sleep as equally important. Yet, while half exercised regularly, most failed to actually get a good night's sleep. In a previous Better Sleep Council study, more than half the people interviewed got their full 40 winks on a regular basis.

Snooze to Lose Stress

Here's how to hit the hay and send stress packing at the same time.

Sleep for strength. Weight lifters know the importance of what's called the recovery phase. The concept for growing muscle is simple: You work your beefy biceps one day, then let them rest the next. Sleep is life's recovery phase. Because we spend roughly one-third of our lives sleeping, people think that they can prolong productivity by scrimping on their time between the sheets. It just ain't so.

"When does your body get stronger? Not when you're working out; it gets stronger when you're resting," says former Olympian Pat Etcheberry of LGE Sport Science. "Recovery in life is the most important phase physically and mentally when it comes to peak performance."

Find your time. Find out how much sleep you really need by experimenting for the next few weeks. If you're currently getting five hours a night, try getting eight hours for the next week and pay close attention to how it makes you feel. The next week, try six hours. Then nine. Tinker around for about a month until you discover just what it takes for you to wake up refreshed, relaxed and energized. "Most people need six to eight hours of sleep a night—some more, some less—but it's important to recognize what works for you," says international creativity consultant Dr. Ann McGee-Cooper.

Be a regular guy. Once you find your optimal sleep period, stick to it regularly. By going to bed and waking up at roughly the same time every day—including weekends—your body's internal clock stays in sync. So will your stress levels.

Exercise. People who exercise regularly sleep more soundly, Etcheberry says. "Plus, if you're fit, you're going to be able to work longer and handle life's mental and physical stress better," he says. Just don't exercise two hours before bed or you'll run the risk of revving your system up so much that it won't be able to unwind when your head hits the pillow.

Be a good manager. Make sure that you're handling your daily schedule as efficiently as possible. Poor time-management skills can lead you to constantly feel rushed and deprive you of the sleep that you need. If you're biting off more than you can chew and it's making you choke sleepwise, put your pri-

Nixing Stress with Naps

Napping has the amazing ability to rejuvenate you and spur your creativity to higher levels. It also relaxes you and may even improve your health. One study showed that people who napped for 30 minutes each afternoon had a 30 percent lower incidence of heart disease than people who didn't nap at all. Other research shows that naps can improve your mental alertness for up to ten hours after you've shaken off that postnap grogginess.

If you do nap to pep you up on stressful days, consider these guidelines.

Don't make up for lost time. If you *must* nap because you're chronically beat, it means that you need better sleep at night—not a nap.

Keep it short. Naps over an hour might leave you with insomnia later on.

Nap in the afternoon. Research has found that naps around 2:00 or 3:00 P.M. are most effective because your body temperature drops around that time, making you more physiologically receptive to sleep.

orities where they should be: on your health. (For more on time management, see Time Management on page 66.)

Relax before reclining. Take a hot bath, meditate or ask your spouse for a massage before going to bed. If you're uptight and anxious before bed, your quality of sleep will be at rock bottom, Dr. McGee-Cooper says.

Avoid additives. Avoid alcohol and caffeine three hours before bed or they'll interfere with your sleep patterns. While a drink might make you feel drowsy, it'll compromise the soundness of your sleep once you drift off. Caffeine, on the other hand, simply revs up your system, making you toss and turn interminably.

Spirituality

The Path to Inner Peace

These days, as veteran rocker Lou Reed once sang, "It takes a busload of faith to get by."

But faith in what? Or whom? That, of course, is up to you. Each person has different core values, fundamental beliefs on which they base their actions. Faith in a god. Or justice. That man is good. That man is evil. That there is some divine master plan that our reason will never be able to comprehend. One thing for sure is that what you have for lunch tomorrow just isn't that significant in the face of it.

Many of the great battles of modern times have pitted the forces of faith against the forces of science. But fascinatingly, the hard lines that once existed between science and spirituality have started to blur. A belief in something greater than ourselves, research shows, helps shield us from stress and disease.

Tapping into that wellspring of spirituality may hold the key to a healthy body as well as a healthy soul.

Reason to Believe

The quiet strength of spirituality—the feeling that you've tapped into a greater meaning or life force—isn't limited to Buddhist monks or loincloth-clad gurus. It flows from within and can be a powerful source of healing.

"There's no question that spirituality, a strong faith in something, can relieve stress and make you feel calmer, more in control," says Dr. Paul J. Rosch of the American Institute of Stress and New York Medical College who studied under Hans Selye, M.D., the founder of stress research.

Modern science bears out Dr. Rosch's claims. According to research funded by the National Institute of Mental Health (NIMH), strong religious beliefs loosen the grip of depression and help you cope with serious illnesses better. One study of 850 men over age 65 found that 20 percent cited religion as "the most important thing that keeps me going." When 200 of the men were re-evaluated six months later, the researchers found that the religious men were the least depressed.

"Psychiatrists used to say religion was a neurotic way of coping, but religion may be an effective way of warding off depression," says Harold Koenig, M.D., of Duke University in Durham, North Carolina, the psychiatrist who led the NIMH study. "After all, financial support dwindles, friends die, but religion endures."

While the NIMH study focused specifically on religious convictions, some experts say that organized religion is merely a vehicle for spirituality and that the same inner strength and peace can come from within as well as from without.

"For me, I just call peace the miracle of life," says Dr. Patch Adams of the Gesundheit Institute. "If you want a big cheese responsible for that, it's a religion. To other people, the miracle of life is nature. To yet others, they say that they don't know if it's God or nature, but it doesn't matter—it's all the same to them."

Here's how to exorcise stress from your life by exercising spirituality.

Keep the faith. Sometimes it's hard to remain true to your spiritual convictions in today's world, concedes Dr. Gary Null, a fitness consultant and author.

"We, particularly as a Baby Boom generation, have done it all, seen it all, tasted it all, smelled it all, and we have absolutely nothing to live for, so we feel spiritually adrift," Dr. Null says. "I think that's one reason why so many people go into (fringe religious) movements these days." Know that it's okay to keep the faith, Dr. Null says.

In fact, the mental health benefits of religion and spirituality have been formally recognized by psychiatrists in the *Diagnostic and Statistical Manual of Mental Disorders*, the bible of mental illnesses.

Tap the power. Putting your fate in the hands of your faith can have powerful consequences. After all, it was a spiritual experience that spurred Bill Wilson, the founder of Alcoholics Anonymous, to devise his nondenominational 12-step plan to recovery. Simply rejoicing in your faith and relying on it may be all that you need to banish the trivialities of stress in daily life—and, as Wilson showed, to solve some of the big problems, too.

Let us pray. Prayer may be the fastest way to reach the inner peace that you need when the rest of life is ostensibly spinning out of control. Keeping a prayer constantly on your lips is a practice seen in Hinduism and Christianity. It's depicted best in the Russian work, *The Way of a Pilgrim*, which is about a pilgrim who learns to repeat the name of God 12,000 times a day without strain. He finds that, in time, this lip service gives way to a deeply spiritual feeling of warm peace.

Rejoice in the moment. Many Eastern religions make heavy use of meditation in their religious practices. Meditation, experts say, brings you a presence of mind. It focuses you on the here and now. But you don't have to spend your hours chanting mantras to get that bliss. You can find it nearly everywhere, every day in every direction, says Dr. Adams. The key is recognizing it.

"Your own personal spiritual miracle of life can be everywhere. I look out my window, I see a variety of vegetation, I see houses that

A Word of Prayer

Harvard Medical School's Dr. Herbert Benson pioneered the study of prayer, faith and stress reduction. He discovered that patients easily could enter a meditative state by simply sitting still in a comfortable position while repeating a word or phrase. But what Dr. Benson found next astounded him. A full 80 percent of his patients chose a word or prayer from their faith, when asked to practice his relaxation-response technique. And those who relied on faith had the best success in his stress-reduction program.

You, too, can strip stress from your life by turning prayer time into meditation time through the relaxation response. Start by getting comfortable and relaxed. Take a few deep breaths, then begin rhythmically repeating a familiar and comforting line from your faith. For Christians, it could be part of the Lord's Prayer, the Twenty-Third Psalm or a line from the Hail Mary. For Jews, it could be the Hebrew word for peace (*Shalom*), one (*Echod*), or the Name (*Hashem*).

Or try picturing in your mind a mental image of your spiritual source. If you're Christian, picture Jesus and Mary. If you're Jewish, Yahweh. If you're Hindu, Brahma, Vishnu or Siva. If you're agnostic—or just don't know what to picture—envision any saint or prophet whom you greatly respect or a relaxing nature scene. The point is to contemplate anything that embodies your sense of the divine.

human hands have built. I look around my room and see art books that are drying from a flood I had," he says. "This is all a part of the miracle of life. Could I get stressed over it? Sure. But why bother? Why not just accept life, relish it and live it to the fullest?"

Time Management

Organizing Your Life

Time is the ultimate commodity. You can spend it, invest it or waste it, but unlike money, you'll never get more of it. Like a breathtaking sunset, once a precious minute passes, it's gone forever.

Every day, we each get the same amount: 1,440 minutes. That's 525,600 minutes a year, 37,843,200 minutes an average lifetime. We use up time doing things like watching TV (up to 420 minutes a day) and working (117,060 minutes a year, beaten only by the Japanese, who average 129,060 minutes a year). Each time we grocery shop, we average 22 minutes gathering and another 8 minutes waiting in line to pay.

The point is that there's a lot of time out there and a lot that gets wasted. How do we keep it straight? Doctors think that there's an internal chronometer deep in our brains. In some people, this chronometer is a Rolex. In others, it's a knockoff. For still others, it's a crude sundial. Researchers know, for example, that our bodies seem to have internal peaks and lows, called circadian rhythms. They also know that our judgment of time can be subjective. A child, for example, doesn't develop an accurate grasp of time until the age of seven or eight. And adults in pain often underestimate the passing of time in clinical studies, while those not in pain overestimate.

Regardless of how your internal timepiece is calibrated, one thing is constant: "The pressure of the passing of time is what causes stress," says Roger Fisher, L.H.D., emeritus law professor at Harvard Law School, director of the Harvard Negotiation Project and author of numerous books on international law, negotiations and conflict resolution.

Time Is on Your Side

"This can't be overstated. It's amazing how often I see folks who really have their lives together tripping over low-level organizational things, like time management," says business consultant Paulette Ensign, president of the National Association of Professional Organizers in Austin, Texas, and owner of Organizing Solutions, a consulting firm in Bedford Hills, New York.

Since we haven't changed our Gregorian calendars to give us more than 24 hours a day, here's how to make the most of what you have.

Take the obituary test. Take 15 minutes right now and write an obituary for yourself. Is it too work heavy? Have you done the things that you've wanted to do? Are you the person that you want to be? Now write your ideal obituary. One where you've won a Pulitzer or Nobel Peace Prize, saved someone's life or rescued animals nearing extinction. Now compare the two. This will give you a global look at your life, where it's been and where it's headed. It'll also help you define your goals and highlight what's most important to you.

"When I did this, it was like . . . 'son of a gun!' " Ensign says. "It made me realize that life isn't about how much money I make. This nifty little exercise gives you a lot of perspective."

Set goals. Set pen to paper and write some goals. Nothing fancy, Ensign says. Start with five things that you'd like to accomplish in the next year, personally as well as professionally. Then do the same for the next 5 years. Then 10, 25 and over a lifetime. When you're done, you'll have a road map of what's most important to you. Knowing this and referring to it often can keep you from squandering your time doing things unrelated to your higher callings in life.

Do the math. You have five projects screaming to be done at once. Which should you do first to make best use of your time? Here's how to decide, according to Denise Dudley, Ph.D., executive vice-president of SkillPath, a management-training firm in Mission, Kansas.

1. Make a list of all your tasks, listing items in order of their long-term importance. No ties allowed; you have to make judgments.
2. Give each item an additional urgency value, according to the following scale:
- Needs to be done immediately = 1
- Needs to be done soon = 2
- It can wait = 3
3. Multiply the importance ranking by the urgency value. The resulting scores will tell you in what order you should do your projects.

Be in shape mentally and physically. Dr. Patch Adams of the Gesundheit Institute is a humor researcher, globe-trotting lecturer, professional clown, parent and husband. He writes 400 letters a month, regularly scans or reads 120 periodicals, works 80 to 100 hours a week and sleeps three to five hours a night. He's also in his fifties.

His secret? "I'm in shape. I'm in my fifties and fit as a fiddle," Dr. Adams says. "Plus, I don't waste time getting down on myself. When I tackle a task, I know that I'll do the best that I can. I don't waste time being unsure of myself."

Use the tools of the trade. There are numerous gizmos that can help you get organized: calendars, voice-activated memo pads, computer software, electronic day logs and more. But despite what the ad writers say, not every one is right for you. "There are folks living in a land of myth and magic who think that the product is going to do the work for them," Ensign says. "It won't. Buying these because you think that they'll be your miracle cure is how

you wind up with expensive paperweights."

Ensign's suggestion? Think before you buy. "If you have only a few appointments a week, a week-at-a-glance calendar might be all that you need. If you're scheduled by the nanosecond, you'll need more."

Ditto for high-tech gadgets. Don't splurge on elaborate scheduling software if you'll rely on a trusty pocket calendar or desk blotter more often.

Schedule everything. Invest 15 minutes to an hour planning your day, week or month, and include personal time. Although it may seem like a waste of time to sit and think about this stuff up front, it saves untold hours later. As for scheduling personal appointments, there's no reason that time at church or temple, a picnic with the kids or shooting hoops shouldn't take a priority in life. Treat these activities with the same reverence that you afford work and you'll enjoy them more often.

Be a time barber. In the average American household, the TV is on more than seven hours a day. If you were to cut that in half, that's enough time to take a college course, run a marathon or, well, you get the idea. Ditto for eliminating extraneous meetings at work. One study at McGill University in Montreal found that executives spend up to 60 percent of their time in meetings. And, if you can do it, wake up an hour earlier each morning. Ease into it: ten minutes a day for six days. Then you won't feel under the gun in the morning. The point is that life is full of ubiquitous time-wasters. Find them. Eliminate them. A few snips and clips to your schedule add up.

Find creative alternatives. Find innovative ways to loosen the chronological logjam. Can you work flextime at work—that is, come in earlier and leave earlier? Can you work from home one or two days a month? Can you pay a neighbor's kid to trim the lawn or clean the living room? This might seem extravagant, but it's worth the money if you can put that time to better use. Just skipping a dinner out once or twice a week can be all that it takes to raise the cash.

Vacations

Is Your Life Trip Wired?

VACATION CHECKLIST
1. Pick up tickets.
2. Tell Personnel about taking days off.
3. Contact friends and family.
4. Tell neighbors.
5. Pack in advance.
6. Clean out refrigerator. 7. Unplug appliances. 8. Stop newspaperdelivery. 9. Stopmaildelivery. 10. Cutlawnrealshort. 11. Closecurtains. 12. Turnoffwatertowashing-machine. 13. Settimersandlights. 14. Lockdoors. 15. Lockwindows. 16.Leavehousekey withneighbor. 17.Kenneldogsandcats.18.Contactcarpoolmembers.19.Packfirst-aidkitandsun-tanlotion.
P.S. Relax and have fun!

Getting Away from It All

If this reads like your vacation prep list, read on. Vacations, those bastions of rest and re-laxation, are a beastly paradox. They're supposed to relax us, but all they ever seem to do is work us up. And by the time we finally let down our hair, it's time to slick it back into a hair helmet for the working world.

All this, of course, assumes that you're even *taking* a vacation. Americans, the diverse, independent, Puritan-work-ethic creatures that we are, are among the sad minority of people who take the fewest va-cation days in the entire civilized world. Mexican workers, at 6 days a year, rank lowest; Ameri-cans, at 10 days a year, tie with their Japanese counterparts. For comparison's sake, British workers

take 22 days, French, 25, and Swedes, 30.

"Vacations can be the world's most pow-erful stress blaster for some people and a most powerful source of stress for others," says renowned stress expert Dr. Paul J. Rosch of the American Institute of Stress and New York Med-ical College. "Most of us don't put a high enough priority on making vacations a primary way of breaking up the stress in our lives."

One survey found that a quarter of all American employees do not use all their allotted vacation time because they are too busy. Another survey found that 47 percent of executives who do take vacations take work with them, and 22 percent even admit passing out business cards during their last vacation.

Some vacation stress is inherent: finding a doctor on the road, unexpected flat tires, plane and train delays, jet lag. But the big two—not vacationing enough and not stress-proofing your vacations when you do take them—are easily avoided. And they should be, when you consider that of the 150 million U.S. adult travelers, roughly one-quarter will take flight and spend more than $1,000 each this coming spring alone.

"It's sad that we turn what should be a soothing time into a seething time," says Dr. Steve Allen, Jr., of Ithaca, New York. "I know that when I take off, even if it's just for an after-noon of fly-fishing, I find myself constantly worried about time.

"On my free time, I really have to make a conscious effort to let go. To say 'whew' and slow down," Dr. Allen says. "It's easy on your free time to get in the same compulsive vein that you operate in at work."

Time Off from Stress

Here are some sugges-tions for making vacation time

the stress blaster that it should be.

Don't worry about "wasted" time. It's easy to think of vacation as misspent time. Don't. You earned it. And remember that it'll take a day or two for you to really start to unwind. Concentrate on that—not on what you're leaving behind.

Take a "me" vacation. It's not a Brady Bunch vacation, but traveling solo can be just what you and your spouse need to recharge your individual and collective batteries. Consider untraditional vacations as an occasional treat. In addition to traditional family outings, plan trips without the kids and trips just for yourself.

"Ever take kids to Disney? In an hour, you're going bonkers," Dr. Rosch says. "Or look at husbands who want to play golf and wives who want to sightsee. There's nothing wrong with doing your own thing once in a while if it's going to reduce stress."

Get exotic. Maybe you need to rough it to shake off the stress of the civilized world. Your options are endless. Or you might consider an adventure vacation, like a trip to Borneo, or a skills vacation, where you learn something, such as race-car driving, skydiving or even—yes—stress management. Consider an altruistic vacation, perhaps through the Sierra Club, where you'll do something like blaze a trail or build a bridge for a discounted vacation rate. Check with your local travel agency. Also visit a library or good bookstore to check out the innumerable books and references available.

Don't let vacation be a pacifier. While there's no question that vacations are an important factor in the stress-reduction equation, they can't be a substitute for dealing with chronic stress. "Refusing to face the problem and going off on a vacation merely ensures its continuation," write Stephen A. Shapiro, Ph.D., and Alan J. Tuckerman, M.D., in their book *Time Off: A Psychological Guide to Vacations.*

Make it a priority. Short of moving to England or France, there may not be much that you can do about getting your employer to grant you more vacation time. But at the very least, you can make sure that you take the vacation time to which you're entitled every year. The key is to make it the priority that it deserves to be.

"I'm a big believer in vacations. I think it's absolutely inhuman that people have to work for a company and all they get is two to three weeks a year. Worse yet, most companies don't even want them to take those weeks all at once," says international negotiating expert Roger Dawson, of La Habra Heights, California, professional lecturer, business consultant and author of *Roger Dawson's Secrets of Power Negotiating.*

"One thing that I did when I became a professional speaker is promise myself two months off a year," says Dawson, a native Briton who's accustomed to the more forgiving European vacation ethic. "Sometimes my office frantically calls me and says that I'm missing some lucrative speaking opportunities, but I don't want to burn out. I'm in this for the long haul."

Vacate with hobbies. One of the strongest stress-blasting cocktails is to mix a favorite hobby with a trip. Dayton University's Dr. Don Morlan takes an unusual pilgrimage to Philadelphia each year to study history's three wise men. Er, make that history's three wise guys: the Three Stooges.

Dr. Morlan, whose speciality is the communication of propaganda, has been able to carve a small academic niche for himself by scrutinizing Larry, Moe and Curly with a scholarly eye. Once a year he takes a brief sojourn by attending the annual Three Stooges Convention in the City of Brotherly Love. It's a great way for him to revel in a personal hobby and escape the hassles of the classroom. "But I don't do impressions or the Curly Shuffle," he laughs. "I'm too old, and my back's too stiff."

Wise guy.

Volunteering

It Really Is Better to Give

What does a volunteer look like? Mother Teresa? A benevolent, avuncular Burl Ives look-alike?

Most of us pigeonhole volunteers into a small stereotypical cast of characters. They're spinsters, nuns, grandfatherly figures or wild-eyed youths working for Greenpeace. They're not people like you, in the midst of the most productive years of their lives. But the truth is that anyone can be a volunteer. And we're going to let you in on a little secret: It will do you at least as much good as those you help, because volunteerism is one of the most potent stress-reducing activities you'll find. Consider this.

• Volunteering may actually lengthen your life. A ten-year study at the University of Michigan in Ann Arbor found that the death rate among men who volunteered their time and talents at least once a week was half that of men who didn't.

• Helping others, even complete strangers, gives an immediate feel-good physical benefit. People who volunteer the most feel the best.

• The average Peace Corps volunteer 30 years ago was a 22-year-old college graduate with an undergraduate liberal arts degree. In 1990, the average was a 32-year-old with a master's-level business degree.

We're not saying that you have to quit your job, join the Peace Corps and head overseas to an impoverished Third World country to gain the benefits of volunteering. You can do it in whatever time you have to spare right in your own community. In addition to the physical health benefits, there is an emotional boost unlike any other. "In each situation I knew—I could feel it—that when I was doing for others, I was also doing for myself," writes Allan Luks of the emotional uplift of volunteerism in his book *The Healing Power of Doing Good.* Luks should know: He's the head of New York City's Big Brothers/Big Sisters of America association and a lifelong activist in altruism.

Moreover, Luks found that the helper's high he experienced has lasting implications. In addition to reporting better health, 80 percent of the 3,296 people that Luks surveyed in the late 1980s felt better just remembering their good deeds. How's that for incentive?

Here's how to launch your own adventures in altruism.

Start slowly. The best thing about volunteering is that no one's forcing you to put in a 40-hour week. You call the shots. Start small. Spread yourself only as thin as you comfortably can. And if you need to cancel volunteering for a week because your life is busy, do so and don't anguish over it. Aim for quality—not quantity—volunteering.

Pick your passion. A nifty thing about volunteering is that it can be customized. Wanted to be a doctor but became an accountant instead? Volunteer for an ambulance corps or a hospital. Are you a closet comedian? Polish your act and take it to a nearby hospice or nursing home to cheer up the residents. Find a niche that suits your passions and talents and you'll get a lot more enjoyment from volunteering.

Still stuck? Try any one of these ideas to get started: help the local library, serve in a soup kitchen, blaze trails for wildlands conservancy, teach literacy, help build a house for the homeless, become a Big Brother, be a buddy at the Special Olympics, wash dogs and muck out kennels at the local humane society. You get the picture.

Part Three

Beating
Homegrown Stress

Managing Money

Advice You Can Bank On

In most cases, the money you possess doesn't cause much stress. The problem usually is the money you don't have.

Unfortunately, you don't have any control over that money. And therein lies the root of our financial stress.

"In our capitalistic system, it's sad but true—we measure a man's success by the amount of money he makes," observes Stephen M. Pollan, a nationally known financial consultant and co-author of *Surviving the Squeeze: The Baby Boomer's Guide to Financial Well-Being in the '90s, The Business of Living* and several other money-management books. "If you've made a lot of it, you're a better person. If you haven't, you're worthless."

Notice the wording: You're *worth less.*

"Not having money creates a fear that comes from a lack of faith or self-confidence," Pollan adds. "We've been led to believe that if you're not a provider, you're a failure."

Money Attitudes

This is not just psychobabble. It speaks directly to our nation's obsession with money. Certainly, men feel an obligation to provide for their loved ones. We also all like nice things, cash in the pocket and the ability to splurge now and then.

But where do you draw the line? Who is telling you that you must own a big house or get a new minivan every four years? Or that you must get a bigger raise than your co-workers, or that a fat wallet equates happiness or sexual prowess? Okay, Hollywood and Madison Avenue say that. But is

that who should be setting your values?

Here's a secret. Most rich people didn't get rich because they lusted after money. They got rich because they lusted after a personal dream—building the perfect computer, developing the essential medical tool, constructing glorious buildings.

You know it. Money does not equate with happiness. And yet money and stress remain intricately linked. "I have found consistently that 90 percent of the stress that American men feel today comes from either the absence or presence of money," says Pollan, who has been researching the field for 30 years. In one study he recalled, respondents were asked which emotions they associated with money: 71 percent said anxiety, 52 percent said depression, 52 percent said anger.

Because of men's association of money with power, self-esteem, independence and other deep-seated feelings, "money issues are one of the hardest to turn around for men," adds Herb Goldberg, Ph.D., professor of psychology at California State University in Los Angeles and author of *Money Madness* and a number of books on male psychology.

There are two essential truths about money that you need to realize.

First, attitude is half the battle. Get a good mental handle on the role money plays in your life, and financial stress greatly decreases.

Second, managing your money is far easier and less time-consuming than you think. Read a few books, take a few hours to pencil things out clearly, make a few phone calls, write a few letters and—presto!—your financial matters are well on their way to becoming manageable. And the stress relief will be palpable.

Of the two, attitude is tougher. Here are tips for getting a mental edge over your finances.

Get your priorities in order. Realize that "money can't buy me love," as those fi-

The No-Brainer Budget

If you find yourself wondering where your money went, the following monthly budget worksheet should help. Just fill in the blanks. Then take a long hard look at where you can cut back a little each month so that you increase the quantity of your savings without decreasing the quality of your life. Subtract your total monthly expenditure from your total monthly net income to get your discretionary income amount (also known as beer money, pocket money or play dough).

Living Expenses
Food _____
Clothing _____
Child care _____
Education _____
Cleaning _____
Cosmetics
and toiletries _____

Home Expenses
Mortgage/rent _____
Homeowners'
insurance _____
Utilities _____
Telephone _____
Home
furnishings _____
Home repairs/
improvements _____

Medical Expenses
Doctor/
hospital fees _____
Prescriptions _____

Nonprescription
drugs _____
Health
insurance _____

Transportation Expenses
Auto fuel _____
Auto
insurance _____
Auto
payments _____
Auto repairs _____
Parking _____
Tolls _____
Taxis _____
Trains
and buses _____
Airplanes _____

Entertainment Expenses
Books, records,
tapes, CDs _____

Cable TV _____
Dining out _____
Dues,
memberships _____
Movies, videos,
plays, concerts _____
Subscriptions _____
Take-out meals _____
Vacations _____

Business of Living Expenses
Disability
insurance _____
Life insurance _____
Property taxes _____
Professional
services _____
Postage _____
Stationery _____

Debt-Related Expenses
Banking fees _____

Credit card
interest _____
Student loan
payments _____
Other loan
payments _____
Regular savings
deposits _____

Luxuries
Jewelry _____
Gifts _____

Contributions
Tax-deductible
donations _____

Total Monthly Expenditures _____

Total Monthly Net Income _____

nancial wizards John Lennon and Paul McCartney wrote. "If you see money as simply a form of trade, and not a measure of your worth, you'll be the richer man for it," says Pollan.

Forget the Joneses. If you're working overtime to keep up with the Joneses—or whoever it is you're trying to earn as much as—you're like the donkey following the carrot dangling in front of it at the end of a pole. You'll never catch up. And when you do, says Dr. Goldberg, "there will always be someone else who makes more. So you'll never reach your goal, and you'll always be under stress, striving for that next elusive carrot."

Better, adds Pollan, to "set your own realistic goals based on your own needs and wants, not other people's."

Think logically. Ever catch yourself saying something like, "How am I going to make a $1,000 mortgage on $800 a week?" We psyche ourselves into being poor all the time. The real question is, "I make $3,200 a month—

what do I do with the $2,200 left after the mortgage?" Think like a businessman. How much money is coming in each month, and how much has to go out?

The Basics of Money Management

It's easy. There are six essential components to managing your money. The smart player makes a plan for each of these areas and then tries to live by it. Here are the basics.

Ongoing expenses. Utilities, clothes, food, mortgages and household repairs—for those without much money, making ends meet is where discussions of money usually begin and end. The thing is that most households spend without any thought or organization, and that means wasting a lot of hard-earned cash. The old-fashioned solution remains the best. Do a budget. Budgets make clear how much money is coming in, how much needs to go out, and what you're doing with what's left.

Taxes. Taxes, like death and Beatles revivals, are inevitable. So get a healthy attitude about them. They're the price you pay—literally—for membership in the community and nation, and while they may be offensive to you (depending on your politics), they're cheaper here than in most other countries. Obsessing to get every nickel you can from Uncle Sam probably isn't worth the time and aggravation.

That said, there are a lot of tax-saving strategies that make sense. In particular, any program that lets you set aside money untaxed—dependent-care accounts or retirement programs—can reap huge tax savings. Finally, don't obsess about federal taxes and ignore

Dealing with Credit Cards

If you carry a credit card, you're probably carrying a balance. That's what 70 percent of cardholders do. Based on 1995 figures, the average Visa or MasterCard cardholder carries a total balance of $3,900. With an interest rate of 18 percent, that means that you pay $702 a year to borrow money.

Knowingly wasting money—now that's stressful. Here's how to be a master to credit cards, not a slave.

Don't get addicted. Sure, credit cards are a powerful tool for handling unexpected cash shortfalls or major purchases. But more likely than not, your credit-card balance drifts upward from too many dinners out, can't-live-without-'em CDs or an impetuous do-or-die winter getaway to the tropics. When slapping down that plastic starts to feel like your solution to life's other problems, you may be dealing with a larger issue.

"Men have a propensity to anesthetize the pain of purchase by using credit cards," says financial consultant Stephen M. Pollan. "The problem is that some people have developed an addiction to spending that's similar to drug and alcohol dependency. It becomes an obsession and a sickness when we use it to fill up holes we think that we have in our lives." So next time you whip out that card, think clearly about why you aren't paying by cash or check.

Take advantage of teasers. Consolidate your debts onto one low-rate card. But here's the hitch: The majority

other forms. In particular, you can save hundreds of dollars a year in sales taxes by shopping smartly. For example, some states have no taxes on clothing. And buying merchandise through the mail often is tax-exempt.

Retirement planning. This is the hot topic in money circles, given pending troubles with Social Security and shakiness in many cor-

of teasers offer a low rate for three to six months, then the interest soars again. Look for the ones that give you a year before the rate goes up. "Use that year as a self-imposed deadline to pay off the bill," says Ruth Susswein, executive director of Bankcard Holders of America, a 16-year-old national nonprofit credit education group. If you haven't paid off the full bill, there's no law against jumping ship and transferring that balance to yet another low-rate card.

Know what you owe. Stop estimating debts in your head—lowballing some while conveniently forgetting others. Put it in writing. You can only solve a problem when you know exactly what it is.

Get a lifestyle. Dieting doesn't work. Not if it means swearing off your favorite foods and living a life of deprivation. The same principle applies to credit. "Some diets tell you to cut out everything," says Susswein. "The equivalent would be to cut up your credit cards. This is not necessarily workable. The healthier approach is to learn to live with credit."

Aim high. Common sense might dictate that you pay off your highest balance first. Then again, if you always listened to common sense, you might not be in a financial bind. You're looking for the credit-card bill that has the highest APR—annual percentage rate—not the monthly period rate. That high APR is the straw that's breaking your financial back. Pay it off first.

include a healthy match to whatever you invest. Get familiar with your company's employee benefit plan, including life insurance, long-term disability coverage and other miscellaneous programs and pensions.

Insurance. If you own a home or car, you have no choice but to buy insurance. Other types are optional. Before you buy any insurance, first identify what exactly the risks are. Maybe you don't need as much insurance as you think, or any at all. And, adds Ted Douglass, a certified financial planner and financial consultant at Merrill-Lynch in Allentown, Pennsylvania, "be cautious of insurance as an investment. It's not the best. There are too many hidden costs. If anything, it's an investment for your children."

Estate planning. What do you want to happen to your possessions and money after you die? It's important to ask yourself that question for several reasons, one of which is that if you don't answer it, the government will step in and do it for you, taking a big part for itself. Estate planning usually entails writing a will and then setting up your investments so that they pass easily on to the people, charities or pets of your choice.

Saving and investing. Investing is what you do when you have money left over from everything else. Never just invest. Set a specific financial goal and then set out to achieve it. A new refrigerator in 2 years. A vacation to Japan in 3 years. A vacation home in 10 years. A kid's college tuition in 15 years. Insane riches in 20 years.

There are high-risk and low-risk goals, long-term goals and short-term goals. There is a different strategy for each. Know what you want to achieve and invest accordingly, and you can sleep easily at night.

porate pension plans. The bottom line is not to expect the government or your former employer to take care of you after 65. Can you afford to live your last 20 years mostly on your current savings? If not, you have little choice but to start squirreling away cash. The good news is that more companies than ever are offering terrific retirement savings programs that

Buying a House

*How to Cope with the
American Dream*

Unless you have the blood pressure of a mummy, you are well within your bounds to feel more than a little stressed when it comes to buying a house.

"A house is the highest ticket item you will ever purchase," says Art Godi, owner of Art Godi Realtors in Stockton, California, and president of the National Association of Realtors. "Most people don't like to make decisions, and here's one in which you may be writing one check equivalent to a year's salary. Understandably, people need a lot of emotional support. More than ever, they need to talk through the stress and apprehension surrounding that decision."

A-hunting We Will Go

What makes buying a home so stressful? Here are five biggies and some ways to ease your agony for each.

1. The fear of making a bad decision. But what is a bad decision when it comes to buying a house? Likely, it's that it doesn't suit your needs. Second is that it doesn't hold up in value. Third might be that it had flaws that you didn't detect. It's easy to remedy all three of those. For functionality, figure out exactly how you want to use your future home (A home office? Lots of cooking? Lots of visitors?) and shop based on those needs. For value, remember all those axioms about location—they're true. As for flaws, there is no flaw that a good inspector can't find. A few

hundred dollars spent up front to truly check out a new or existing house is a small amount compared with the long-term satisfaction of knowing that your home is sound.

2. Fear of the deal. Escrows. Impound accounts. Inspections. Mortgages. Endless paperwork and jargon. Buying a home is a complex transaction, make no mistake. But it is not unfathomable. Take a few weeks to read a book about home buying. Talk to as many people as you can about their experiences. This stuff is not that hard to figure out. Don't permit yourself to slide through uninformed. Ignorance makes for stress; knowledge makes for confidence. In all situations.

3. The down payment. There's no denying that writing a check of, say, $30,000 to buy a strange home may be the most nerve-racking thing you'll ever do. But remember, it's not money spent; it's money invested. Treat your home well and you'll get all that money back and more when you sell. In the long term, real estate remains a solid place to park money.

4. The monthly costs. Start with the mortgage, add in insurance and then taxes, and your monthly check to the bank will be considerably more than the rent you paid on your one-bedroom flat. There's no denying it. But there are a couple of saving graces. First, your income taxes will drop considerably now that you have all that interest to deduct. Factor that in when the tax man knocks in April and you might discover that the disparity between renting and owning isn't so huge. Second, you're getting something for your money that has a lasting value. Each month you own a few hundred dollars more of a home. With rent, all that money goes out the window.

5. Feeling tied down. Deep inside, many men hold on to youthful notions that they'd be freer and happier if unencumbered by possessions, jobs, relationships and responsibilities. Owning a home—the

ultimate in stability and commitment—is the death knoll for such feelings. This is a personal issue that only you can resolve. But the joys of home ownership are immeasurable. Creating your ultimate environment. Having roots. Arriving. If you have doubts, talk to most anyone with a home to see what we mean.

The Buying Process

From the moment you decide to buy, the questions begin. Do I have enough money? What if I lose my job? What if my wife leaves me? How's the foundation? The roofing? The plumbing? The wiring? Will we be able to resell? Will it be too small when we have kids? Too big when they leave home? Will the neighborhood go to the dogs? Will our next door neighbor have a dog?

These questions are all a natural part of the classic fight-or-flight stress reaction to house buying, suggests Godi. "If you suppress these questions and pretend that they don't exist, you'll only increase the stress levels," Godi says. "Have you heard of buyer's remorse? It's there before, during and after the house-buying process. It *is* the process." All we can do, he says, is be prepared for it and think things through. Here are some thoughts that may ease that process.

Give yourself some credit. Before you even consider shopping for a house, find out whether you are eligible for that critical loan from a bank. Otherwise, you may be building a house of cards. Getting pre-approved for a bank loan has many benefits, the biggest probably being that you'll know exactly how much you can afford so that you won't waste time looking at houses far below or above your means. What will banks look for in you? A steady income, a career path, a stable lifestyle and a proven ability to pay off debts and manage credit all top the list.

Find a home in your range. The conventional formula is that your monthly mortgage payment should be between 28 and 36 percent of your gross income. Your monthly

payment is the sum of the principal, interest, taxes and insurance. Are you comfortable within this range? Remember that it's all based on current income levels. Are you certain your income will grow? Then you might be willing to spend on the high side.

Cruise the 'hood. Driving around the neighborhood will give you an idea of the quality of life that will surround you. You may be looking for proximity to schools and shopping (generally considered high-quality), and industry and highways (generally considered not-such-high-quality). It will also give you an idea of value. As you'll be able to tell, there are some areas where $100,000 will buy a lot of house. There are others where the same amount will buy a lot, period.

Get background on the builder. If you are interested in a new home, check out the reputation of the developer. If you're buying in a neighborhood developed by one person, knock on a couple of doors and ask about problems and pitfalls of the houses' structure. It's a good sign, but not necessarily a seal of approval, if the builder is a member of the National Association of Home Builders. If there are problems, the state contractors board regulates builders and it will—or should—know about a builder's reputation.

Play it cool. If you see a house you like—no, love—practice a poker face. Don't let on that you envision your great-grandchildren living there long after you're gone. It will only make negotiating a good price more difficult. Also, don't let your heart overrule your head. Yes, you have to love the place. But you also have to be savvy enough to let it go if the numbers don't work.

Don't buy a round house. Despite the preceding advisory, it's still wise not to buy a house with such unique features that it would appeal only to aliens, cautions Godi. And don't expect your custom-designed "value-added features" to make someone else giddy. The $5,000 you invest in a backyard batting cage for your Little Leaguer may not be all that attractive to retirees.

Getting Married

Make a Vow to Reduce Stress

The stress leading up to that moment when you stand at the altar and say "I do" is enormous. But it's nothing compared to the stress you may encounter once you're married.

More than 50 percent of marriages end in divorce, and trust us, the road leading to divorce is rarely serene. Marriage provides any number of surprises, some good, some bad, all involving potentially stressful changes to the way you eat, sleep, dress, relax and otherwise exist. You can accept the changes and grow with them, or you can resist them and resent your partner for forcing them to occur. Many choose the latter. "Relationships are the number one complaint of people who seek professional counseling today," says Frederic Flach, M.D., adjunct associate professor of psychiatry at Cornell University Medical College and attending psychiatrist at New York Hospital–Cornell Medical Center, both in New York City, and author of *Putting the Pieces Together Again* and *The Secret Strength of Depression*.

Marital stress can profoundly affect us emotionally and physically. Studies of recently married couples show that arguments adversely affect the immune system and can predispose newlyweds to illness. Luckily, this tends to improve after about the first year, according to the American Institute of Stress.

"The reasons that people end up together can be exciting or appalling," Dr. Flach says. Very often relationships are born out of unrealistic expectations or lust, which don't make for secure ties. When you don't take the time to examine why you are marrying someone before you tie the knot, you run a high risk of spending a lot of time with your stomach in knots, worrying if you made a big mistake.

Money, sex, free time, cleanliness and even who sleeps on what side of the bed can all be things that eat away at us. The challenge is to learn to communicate clearly what it is we are feeling and why, says Dr. Flach, so that we can overcome each issue as it arises. That's not necessarily an easy thing for guys to do. "Love is hard work and a huge investment of yourself," says Dr. Flach, "but the returns are astronomical."

Forming a More Perfect Union

Here are some ways to ease the stress in your marriage, whether you're approaching your first or fiftieth anniversary.

Get rid of the ghosts. Each of us brings certain expectations to a marriage, says Dr. Flach. You might want your relationship to be just like or completely unlike your parents'. Either way, these preconceived notions of how marriage should be can create enormous stress, compounded if your wife has her own hangups as well.

Think of your new family as unique from the family units you were in or around in the past, says Dr. Flach. Once you both recognize how you each see married life and what you both want out of your own relationship, the anxiety can often be alleviated.

Cancel all covert operations. Don't look to TV for good role models in marital communication. Old favorites like *I Love Lucy* and current top-rated shows like *Home Improvement* depict spouses constantly sneaking around behind their loved ones' backs in order to get what they want without having to discuss the matter.

That's not the way to establish trust or to ease tensions in a relationship, says Daniel Kegan, Ph.D., an organizational psychologist and attorney at Elan Associates in

Chicago. "The best way to handle a situation like that is to tell your spouse what it is you want and why you want it, listen to her side and come up with a solution that leaves no one feeling cheated," he says.

Socialize constructively. If you hang around guys who constantly bad-mouth their wives, then the mood might just rub off on you. "There are some studies showing that people who see others who are nasty tend to behave more nastily themselves, even around their families," says Dr. Kegan. "Those are not healthy influences on your marriage."

Think first, talk later. You're going to disagree with your spouse from time to time. It's how you disagree that will determine whether it becomes a source of stress in your marriage, says Dr. Kegan.

"Confrontations are less stressful if we can talk about what we are thinking and feeling clearly, without putting each other down, and if we devote an equal amount of energy to listening to what the other person is saying," says Dr. Kegan. That often requires taking a few minutes to collect your thoughts and figure out what it is you really mean to tell your wife before you actually speak with her. If you want her to hear you out patiently and attentively, then you need to be fair and do the same for her.

Get your timing down. Your wife is running late for work, but you have to get something off your chest. So on her way out the door, you tell her that you are unhappy with the way she spends too much time talking to her mother. You may feel somewhat relieved but only until she gets home that night after having all day to stew over how you blindsided her. Pick a time when you both can sit down and discuss things fully, says Dr. Kegan.

"You can always bring up the fact that

When to Get Help

Men mistakenly think that going to therapy means that there is something wrong with them, and that they are inept at fixing things themselves, says Dr. Daniel Kegan of Elan Associates. Nothing could be further from the truth. You haven't failed; you may just need to get more resources working in your favor. "Therapy is a place to go not to fix a broken marriage but to give husbands and wives the tools to repair the damage themselves," says Dr. Kegan.

If you are unable to describe how you are feeling most of the time, if you don't have another human being with whom you feel comfortable discussing what bothers you or if you have a persistent family problem that you just cannot resolve, you may want to consider finding a qualified therapist.

In particular, seek professional help if the stress of irreconcilable differences is hurting your health or contributing to addictive behaviors, such as excessive drinking, smoking or substance abuse, says Paul J. Rosch, M.D., president of the American Institute of Stress in Yonkers, New York, and clinical professor of medicine and psychiatry at New York Medical College in Valhalla.

you both need to talk, then if she can't devote enough time right then, schedule some other time in the near future when you both can relax and deal with the issue," says Dr. Kegan.

Watch the boomerang effect. "Dumping on your spouse when you get home from a hard day of work is like putting sugar in your own gas tank," says Dr. Kegan. What you're doing is transferring your work anxiety onto your spouse. You may walk away feeling as if you've just released your tensions, but now she's full of anxiety. And who's the likely recipient of her anxiety transfer? Rest assured, some way, somehow, it will end up back in your lap.

Splitting Chores

Sweep Away Stress

One of life's sweetest stress relievers is reaching the end of the day, or the end of the week, and knowing that there's absolutely nothing else you have to do. The problem is that those occasions come infrequently, thanks—or no thanks—to one of life's sourest nuisances. They're called chores, those bothersome obligations that range from the sublime (finishing that pro bono project for the Boys Club) to the ridiculous (refinishing the armoire that somebody else has decided should be salvaged from the garage); from the mundane (cleaning the bathroom) to the downright monumental (cleaning the rest of the garage). Some days, even minor chores are the stressful straw that can break a poor camel's back.

"Chores can be the bane of our existence, or they can leave us with a great feeling of accomplishment . . . if we finish them," says Robert Bramson, Ph.D., an organizational behavior consultant and author of *The Stressless Home*. "They can tear a relationship apart, or they can provide a shared sense of completion."

Not that long ago, this subject would not have appeared in a book for men about stress, mainly because men hardly ever participated in household chores. We went to work. She did everything around the house. Well, not quite everything. We mowed the lawn, took out the garbage, washed the car and chopped wood. Manly stuff. The rest— the laundry, shopping, cooking, ironing, vacuuming, dusting, making the beds and minding the kids (feeding, bathing and bedding)—was, quaintly put, "women's work."

Today, you won't exactly find us donning rubber gloves and cleaning aprons at the drop of a dust ball, but we are better at holding up our end of the domestic bargain. Granted, it's not yet a 50-50 proposition. Men's share of the total family workload (which includes child care) in 1965 was 20 percent, and it rose to 34 percent by the mid-1980s. Into the 1990s, that share continued to rise.

There's some health incentive for men to do their share of the household chores. In a study conducted by researchers at Johns Hopkins University School of Medicine in Baltimore, men and women wore activity and heart rate monitors for three days at home. It turns out that women pump up their heart rates longer than men while doing domestic tasks. Pushing a broom may not be the same as doing a 10-K or bench-pressing 200 pounds, but every little bit helps.

Time to Clean House

If you live alone, there is no ambiguity. If there are chores to be done, you've been elected—unless you've trained your Doberman to iron or your African violet can push a vacuum. But if you live with others of your species—parents, children, siblings, friends, wives or lovers—who does what can be a very vague area. And that uncertainty can cause stress.

"A lot of anger and resentment can build up when you don't know what's expected of you and vice versa," says Dr. Bramson. So before you decide to share your space with another person, Dr. Bramson recommends taking these three key steps.

Decide who does what. Get everyone in a room together and make a list of all the things that need to get done to keep the space that you share from resembling the town dump. Then discuss the expectations that each of you has about who is responsible for each chore. Use a flip chart. Draw lots to see who'll choose first.

"A high percentage of problems that people get into stem from crossed expectations," Dr. Bramson says. "I have a certain notion of what my job is and how to do it. You have a different notion. I do it my way and feel good. You see it and feel disappointed in me. That turns into resentment and bitterness."

Question authority. Mutual consent is essential to divvying up chores. The question of who tells someone else what to do goes to the very heart of the power and control issues that can stress family, friends and couples beyond repair. "If the answer to this question is left unclear, it can lead to a lot of trouble," Dr. Bramson says. "It comes down to trust, really. Optimally, no one tells anybody what to do." You discuss it. You negotiate. You compromise. You all decide together.

"You resolve conflicts in a manner that all parties can buy into. It's not a matter of keeping everyone happy," notes Dr. Bramson. "Usually, nobody is happy cleaning the cat's litter box. The key is to parcel out chores so that everyone thinks they're fair." The least stressful way is to try to make a chore list that matches what people would prefer to do.

Define tasks. You finally take out the garbage, and she's miffed. Why? Because, to her, taking out the garbage also means replacing the plastic liner. You didn't replace the liner. Agree when you all sit down to delegate responsibilities exactly what the chore entails, even if it seems a little compulsive.

The Paper Chase

Pat Dorff, an organizational consultant in Minneapolis, suggests the following techniques to keep your life—and your home—less cluttered.

Separate your papers. Basically, your papers fall into two groups: things that need immediate attention or have a deadline and things that don't. Find separate places for each. Let everyone in the house know where those places are. Make everyone in the house use them.

Make room for VIPs. Each adult and each kid in the house should have his own desk. Each desk should have a VIP (very important paper) drawer that is off-limits to everyone else in the house unless special permission is granted.

Make the short list. Although made in good faith, a long to-do list can be one of life's greatest stressors. "You set yourself up for certain failure by trying to do it all," says Dorff. "Make realistic lists. If you do everything on the list, guess what? You can make another to-do list."

Marry your own kind. That's a half-serious joke. "I have seen people who are savers and 'clip-aholics' married to nonsavers," says Dorff. "It causes a lot of undue stress. They battle over whether to keep or throw out every item." The resolution is to compromise. Or live separately but visit each other often.

"That old saying, 'Anything worth doing is worth doing well,' is as wrong a statement as there can be," Dr. Bramson says. "Everyone has a different notion of what a job well done is." It's a matter of perception. To avoid conflict, work it out beforehand. Agree that this needs to be so clean that you can eat off it; that can be done with a lick and a promise.

Excelling at Fatherhood

Avoid the Parent Traps

Bill McCoy is an editor at *Parents* magazine. He's also the author of *Father's Day: Notes from a New Dad in the Real World.* So you would think that he'd have the parenting thing down. So did he. Until his daughter, Amanda, came along.

"Up until the time she was born, my wife, Sharon, and I had a deliriously happy marriage," he says. "Once she was born, for the first nine months we didn't have any energy for each other, and it placed great stress on our marriage. Plus, I felt so much more financial pressure and responsibility. I spent a lot of time worrying whether I'd be able to pull this off now that I had an out-of-work wife and a helpless kid depending on me to support them. That's scary."

Then something unscheduled happened as the couple was slowly adjusting to a family of three. One evening, Bill came down to the living room after the ritual of putting Amanda to bed. Sharon offered him a glass of wine. They sat on the couch, exhausted as only new parents can be, sipping and chatting. "It was so pleasant," he recalls. "It was such a natural and comfortable way to unwind that we did it again. And again. The point was to be together without any specific agenda, to reaffirm the bond that led to our wanting to have children in the first place."

Changing Roles— And Diapers

"The stress on parents is enormous," says pediatrician T. Berry Brazelton, M.D., professor of pediatrics at Harvard University and author of, among many other child-rearing books, *Touchpoints: Your Child's Emotional and Behavioral Development.* "But it's stressful on men for different reasons. One of the differences is that men have more trouble dividing themselves psychologically between worker and parent. They talk about it more these days but don't really face it. Even at home they still carry their cordless phones around."

Parenting is particularly stressful for men because through the nine months of our partner's pregnancy, we take a backseat to the process. We're used to being in the middle of the fray, not standing on the sidelines, waiting. Then, after the baby is born, we play second or third fiddle again. When our turn to parent comes, we feel completely unprepared—no matter how many baby books we've read, classes we've attended or story-swapping sessions we've joined in on.

"We've been fed this cultural idea that, left to our own devices, men will put diapers on backward and feed babies tacos. And we buy it," McCoy says. "This lack of confidence in our ability to be caregivers can be the cause of unfounded stress, because, as I found out the first time I held my daughter, we men are just as instinctually good as women at parenting if we don't paralyze ourselves with anxiety about thinking that we don't know how."

We're not saying that if you stop thinking about it, the stress and strain of raising children will go away. You're still going to lose sleep in the beginning. Your wife and you will still crave some free time alone together. You'll still miss a night out with the boys. You're still going to lose your patience at many stages in your child's life. But remember, there is nothing like the joy of seeing your child's eyes light up when she recognizes you, hearing her utter "Daddy" for the first time, feeling her arms wrapped around your neck like you are the only thing in the world that matters, watching her achieve goals you only dreamed she could attain. These are life's ultimate stress blasters, the rewards of parenthood that put all your other worldly woes and worries into perspective.

Fatherhood: The New Frontier

Chances are fairly good that you are or will be more hands-on as a father than the generations before you. Because your father and his father may not have been the best role models, that makes this relatively new terrain for you. While that may cause a certain amount of stress in itself, it also offers the opportunity for you to chart new territory in the frontier of fatherhood.

"We create a lot of stress for ourselves as parents by thinking that we have to get it right every time," says Lawrence Kutner, Ph.D., clinical psychologist on the faculty of Harvard Medical School and author of several books, including *Your School-Age Child, Making Sense of Your Teenager* and *Parent and Child: Getting Through to Each Other.* "So give up trying to be the perfect parent." He recalls a favorite saying: God gives parents a thousand mistakes before they have to apply for a refill. Meanwhile, before that time comes, here are some ideas to keep next to the disposable diapers as you grow into your role as Dad.

Don't compete. It starts with the long accordion-folded baby pictures. Then it's whose kid walks first, whose talks first and whose writes first. It graduates to which school your child got into. Then it's "my daughter the doctor," "my son who owns the million-dollar house." Dr. Kutner suggests handling other competitive parents "by lying, but lie blatantly so that they understand that you're not buying in. You'll save yourself a lot of stress."

Catch your child being good. Most parents are real good at catching their kids being bad. "All too often we tell them what not to do," Dr. Kutner says. "I especially find myself falling into this pattern when I'm tired or under stress: 'Stop whining.' 'Don't talk with your mouth full.'

'Stay away from that.' " Compliment them on something done well and you'll see their faces light up and their self-confidence grow.

Keep things in perspective. At the time, toilet training may seem like a significant matter, but "in the long run it's much less important than many other parenting issues," says Dr. Kutner, who sometimes wonders about parents obsessed with getting their kids to go potty. He asks, "Who is being toilet trained, the child or the parent?"

Celebrate independence day. Despite what some parents may hope, children grow up. "It's critical to recognize that your child will change, and it's critical to let them know that you recognize that they're changing," notes Dr. Kutner. Times of biggest change are as toddlers and in puberty. Not coincidentally, these are ages when independence is the biggest issue. "They're testing their limits," says Dr. Kutner.

One way to honor their development and independence is to pair privileges with responsibilities. Young people like to contribute to the family; they like to feel valued. Let them demonstrate that they're not like they were last year by giving them additional roles. Then encourage them to take reasonable risks. Obviously, not with such no-no's as drugs and sex. Find things that will thrill and challenge them, from computers to rock climbing.

Don't be afraid of monsters. Monsters under the bed. Ghosts in the closet. "These are fears of things that are not there," comments Dr. Kutner. "They tell you that your child is struggling with abstract thinking." The best way to fight abstract fears is with abstract solutions. One of Dr. Kutner's "$2 solutions to $100 problems" with his own son's fear of a big growling dog under his bed was to ask his son what would make the dog go away. Together they concocted an anti-big-growling-dog spray. They drew a picture of the dog on an empty spray bottle, and his son sprayed under the bed whenever he was afraid. Almost miraculously, within 48 hours the canine had left the neighborhood for good.

Taking the Stress Out of Sex

Time to Rise and Shine

You wake up sweating and distracted. You run to catch the 8:17 A.M. On the train you put the finishing touches on a major presentation to the company's stockholders. Under extreme pressure, you give the killer presentation of a lifetime. Over a business lunch, the boss, obviously impressed with your skillful performance, adds a whole new department to the already-long list of your responsibilities. And the first report is due tomorrow morning.

You go home wiped out, fully fried. Your wife, thinking that the pressure is now off, is giving you those bedroom eyes and has nothing but the radio on. And all you can think is, "Oh no, not another performance."

Sex stressful? In your teens and twenties, you'd say nonsense. The only stress is worrying about how long you'll have to wait for the next time. You'd probably agree with Alfred E. Neuman, *Mad* magazine's original "What, me worry?" kid, who sums up his position on stress and sex this way: "I don't think you can stress sex enough."

But as you age, "thinking that you have to perform perfectly every time is stressful, especially for those who make their sexual prowess a competitive event and especially when you're under stress," says Samuel Osherson, Ph.D., honorary research psychologist at Harvard University Health Services and author of *Wrestling with Love*. "It becomes a vicious circle. As you struggle

through stressful times, your sexual interest may decline. As it declines, you get stressed that you're losing sexual interest, which is supposed to be a symbol of masculinity."

It's in the Hormones

"When it comes to sex, the definition of stress for a man is the first time he can't get it up," says Dr. Paul J. Rosch of the American Institute of Stress and New York Medical College. "The definition of panic is the second time he can't get it up."

Under normal circumstances, sex is one of the most effective—and definitely the most enjoyable—stress-blasting techniques (for more on that, see Sex on page 58). But sometimes, stress can sap your sex drive. When that happens, it doesn't mean that you've somehow become any less of a man. It's strictly a hormonal thing. And, according to Robert Sapolsky, Ph.D., professor of biological sciences and neuroscience at Stanford University and author of *Why Zebras Don't Get Ulcers: A Guide to Stress, Stress-Related Diseases, and Coping*, understanding the physiology goes a long way toward helping understand the psychology of why and how stress brings you down, so to speak. Here's how it works.

Stress causes a hormonal chain reaction in the male reproductive system that drives testosterone—the hormone responsible for your sex drive—into a tailspin. Decline in testosterone secretion is only half the problem, though. The other involves your nervous system, specifically, the opposing forces of your sympathetic and parasympathetic nervous systems. The former kicks into action in emergencies, releasing the kick-butt hormone adrenaline and several others. The latter oversees calming forces, promoting growth, energy storage and the like.

Problems arise—or, ahem, don't—when you're

having a terrific time with someone, getting all hot and bothered. Your sympathetic engines are humming along. Meanwhile, your parasympathetic pistons are trying to keep your penis from getting too sympathetic so that you don't ejaculate prematurely. Under stress, however, that tight control is nearly impossible because you're nervous and anxious, a virtual playground for sympathetic hormones. The sympathetic system has very little sympathy for your situation. Your body is getting mixed messages while you're just trying to concentrate on one move at a time.

So one of two things happens. Distracted, you listen to the wrong message and lose your erection. That's called impotency or, in kinder clinical terminology, erectile dysfunction. Or, responding to the excitation, you ejaculate before you'd like. That's the equally unappreciated premature ejaculation.

Get Intimate

If you're suffering through a bout with impotence, don't hesitate to seek professional help from a urologist or sex therapist. They deal with these problems all the time and can make sure that yours is taken care of before it gets too bad. Here are some other options to consider.

Be honest and tell her. Unlike men, women see right through the "not-tonight-honey-I-have-a-headache" excuse. "Better to come clean and talk about the stress that you're going through and the effect that it's having on your sex drive than try to perform at less than peak," says Dr. Osherson. You'll save a lot of awkward embarrassment, and you'll also win big points for your sincerity. Later, when the urge resurges, those points that you earned will be paid back in spades.

Keep the love light burning. Do little things to remind your mate that while your in-

---

> ## When Too Much Is Not Enough
>
> In Woody Allen's 1977 film *Annie Hall*, Diane Keaton's and Allen's characters are asked by their therapist how frequently they have sex. His answer: "Hardly ever, maybe three times a week." Hers: "Constantly, three times a week."
>
> If your sex life is not lively enough for you, try a little tenderness, advises Robert T. Francoeur, Ph.D., professor of human sexuality at Fairleigh Dickinson University in Madison, New Jersey, and New York University in New York City, co-author of *The Scent of Eros* and editor of *The Complete Dictionary of Sexology*.
>
> "Women are looking for much more than just intercourse. They want closeness and tenderness," Dr. Francoeur says. "Spend quality time with her. Take a block of time and just be together. Hold her. Caress her. Pamper her. Eventually, her physiological reflex responses will kick in. Sooner or later she'll be hot and horny and ready. It takes time and tenderness."

---

terest in sex may not be what it usually is, your love burns as strongly as ever. Leave love notes under her pillow or sweet messages on her office voice mail. Give her a favorite CD or a handpicked bunch of flowers. "This acknowledgment, called validation, is one of the most powerful healing tools for a relationship," says John M. Gottman, Ph.D., professor of psychology at the University of Washington in Seattle.

Hug her. Granted, this may not be as good as the real thing, but tactile expressions of love can go a long way toward compensating for the joy of sex. "As you age, you begin to understand more about sensuality than sexuality," Dr. Osherson says. "There's less pressure to make genital intercourse the major source of bodily contact."

Dueling Dual Careers

Make the Most of Mutual Funds

Money is good, and more money is better, yes? Then why would having a wife who works full-time be a source of stress?

Let's ponder this.

Maybe it's that some 1950s vision of how an American household should be still lingers in your brain. Maybe you miss coming in the door at 6:00 P.M. and having a home-cooked dinner on the table, like when you were young.

Maybe you worry about how your children will grow up without parents around in the daytime hours. Maybe you resent that our world has become so expensive that it takes two incomes to get by. Maybe, deep down, you are challenged by having a spouse who is competent, professional and on the rise.

Whew. The truth is that all and none of the above may apply. These are complicated times, and the issues and tensions run deep and personal regarding the two-career family.

Even if you have come to grips with the concept of a working wife, there are still stressors. Dual-career couples have a lot more options when it comes to how they want to run their homes but don't necessarily have the time or the interpersonal skills to make the most of their choices, say experts.

Don't Sleep with the Competition

Let's start with one of the more powerful stressors. There's a huge risk of competitiveness when both of you work. One of you may make more money or have more prestige associated with your title. One spouse may even envy the flexibility or perceived enjoyment of their mate's career. "Ours is a very competitive society, but you don't want to let that competitiveness come within your family where it can be destructive," says Dr. Frederic Flach of Cornell University Medical College and New York Hospital–Cornell Medical Center. If you see your marriage as a team effort, then your spouse's successes are also your successes, and that means that you picked a winner.

There are some advantages to having two different well-rounded people's perspectives on the family instead of loading all the decision making on one person. But it means that you have to coordinate things, says Dr. Daniel Kegan of Elan Associates, who specializes in small-group dynamics and work-related stress. Try to have a game plan with your wife so that you both can have similar expectations and responsibilities in the family that don't infringe on your careers. Sure, life is unpredictable, so you can't know what to do for everything. But you can be like a football team, says Dr. Kegan, and at least be working from the same playbook.

Here are some things that may cause stress in a two-career marriage and some ways to tackle them.

Get your mental house in order. If something deep inside you is uncomfortable with the fact that your wife works, and you let these feelings fester inside, they very well could kill your marriage in time. You need to resolve these thoughts, and the first step is to get them out in the open, preferably with your wife. Sometimes, voicing these old-fashioned notions is enough to make you realize that they might warrant challenging. Your wife needs your 100 percent support; anything short could cause trouble.

Have a financial plan. "Money is a big taboo subject. On the whole, people even find it easier to talk about sex," says Dr. Kegan. If you can't talk about money problems, they become even harder to solve.

"Millions of people are neurotically hung up on money, and very few are good at handling it," says Dr. Flach. Who earns the most in your household should be irrelevant, but deciding who's in charge of what financial matters and how is very important. That doesn't mean that one person handles everything and the other never gives the checkbook, bank accounts and retirement funds a second look. It just means that as a team, put your best player at quarterback and let the other person be the backup on the sidelines.

There's no one way to handle money that will fit every family. Some couples prefer to keep everything separate, while others decide to pool their paychecks into joint accounts. "It's always a good thing for each person to have some money that is just for them," says Dr. Flach. It's a way of having your own independence, of letting someone who isn't finance-savvy learn about monetary responsibilities and of letting the other person feel trusted.

Engage in family planning.
Just the idea of having kids is a very big deal for dual-career couples. Can you afford day care? If one of you stays home, will the other feel resentment? These are all questions that need to be addressed *before* you have a bun in the oven. It might not even be a bad idea to discuss them before your wedding, says Dr. Flach.

You don't need a binding contract. Situations change, as do minds, after all. But an established, nonconfrontational forum in which to bring up the topic again at a later date is helpful. "I sometimes see couples in my practice that are committed to being married, but only one person wants to have children. That poses big-time troubles later on," he says.

Remember, everything's relative.

When She Makes More Than You

If the old saying is true, and money really does make the world go around, then it's no wonder that men whose wives bring home heftier paychecks can feel very uncomfortable. To some guys, who gets paid more is not just a cash issue. It threatens their core beliefs about what makes a man a good husband. "There's this sense that the man in the family needs to make money to be successful, and that might not jive in today's two-career families," says Dr. Daniel Kegan of Elan Associates.

To forge a successful marriage means letting go of competition over who is the provider, the nurturer or the subordinate. Sure, she may make more than you, but you are still the husband, the father and the male role model, and no amount of money will change that. In fact, the trade-off of more responsibilities around the home may strengthen those ties. It takes some effort to get a good working balance, but in the end you both get to share the fun things, like spending more time playing with the kids, and both get help with the stressful things, like earning enough to pay the bills and keeping the house clean.

Children of a previous marriage, in-laws, your parents and even close friends can all be a source of stress for married people. They represent a part of each of your lives before you created a family of your own, so resentment or clinginess is understandable. Empathy is very important here, because if you understand how your wife might feel threatened by your ex-wife or needy of her father, you can be more aware of how you speak of or act around that person, says Dr. Flach. Eventually, she'll see that you are the most trustworthy person in her life. It has to be mutual, though, so your wife needs to be just as considerate of your feelings when it comes to relatives. Remember, you are a unit now, so what affects one of you affects the other, too.

Communicating Clearly

Listen—And Defuse Stress

Communicating today is easier than ever. We have e-mail, voice mail, overnight express mail and good ol' snail mail—the U.S. Postal Service. There are cordless, cellular and mobile phones. When a phone is out of reach, there are beepers and pagers urging you to get to one. There are telephone answering machines and fax machines. There's call waiting, call forwarding, call holding and caller ID. You can even talk from room to room through the magic of intercoms. And soon—very soon, we keep being promised—we'll all be like Captain Kirk (or Picard, for those of us who have cleaned our pates) and be able to see the person we're talking to on a screen.

Communicating? Piece of cake. No problem.

So why do we sometimes have so much trouble getting through to each other?

The Language of Stress

"When people try to communicate under stress, they become locked in their preferred language," says Suzette Haden Elgin, Ph.D., founder of the Ozark Center for Language Studies in Huntsville, Arkansas, and author of *Genderspeak: Men, Women and the Gentle Art of Verbal Self-Defense.* "It's verbal comfort food. They use the mode they have to think about least. They go on automatic."

Men, in particular, "are far more impaired in their communication at stressful times," she adds,

"because physiologically everything happens more acutely for them." Among the signs: Their pulse quickens, and their eyes dilate.

What should you do if you feel stress interfering with your ability to communicate clearly and effectively? Wait a minute. Or 20. That's not procrastination; it's intelligence. Dr. Elgin suggests that you let the moment pass. Go away and come back. Regain your composure. Try expressing yourself again, this time under less stress.

If you come home from a day of work that would make shoveling manure look like an enjoyable hands-on chore, so stressed out that intelligent interaction with yet another animate object has as much appeal as bathing in tar, Dr. Elgin offers this advice. "Before you walk in the door, write out and memorize the following announcement: 'Honey, I've had a really, *really* bad day, and I'm not fit to talk to.' Practice it until you don't feel vulnerable saying it. If your wife or girlfriend doesn't understand, say it again, slowly and with great conviction."

Sending a clear message is only half of communication. The other is receiving. It's a revolutionary new concept to some men, who find the receiving part kind of hard. To some men, listening means waiting—sometimes patiently, sometimes not—for the other person to stop opening and closing his or her mouth. For them, listening is a moment's break that allows them time to think of the next brilliant and witty thing to say.

"When both sides in a relationship expand the domain of their thinking and are willing to consider the other side's point of view and keep in mind the system as a whole, then extraordinary new possibilities emerge as imaginary but all-too-limiting boundaries in the mind dissolve," says Jon Kabat-Zinn, Ph.D., director of the Stress Reduction Clinic at the University of Massachusetts Medical Center in Worcester who is also an associate professor of medicine, lecturer and author of *Full Catastrophe Living: Using the Wisdom of Your Body and Mind to Face Stress, Pain and Illness* and *Wherever You Go, There You Are.*

And it turns out that listening is good for your health, according to James J. Lynch, Ph.D., director of Life Care Health Associates in Towson, Maryland. In a study, he found that listening helped hypertensive patients "lower their blood pressure dramatically, sometimes to lower levels than they had seen in years." He adds, "The problem in our world is that we don't listen. People don't even expect to be heard."

Here are some strategies to improve your listening skills so that you can keep up your half of the conversational bargain.

"Listen" to their bodies. "It's body language that tells us what people mean by the words they say," says Dr. Elgin. "At least 90 percent of all emotional information is carried not by words but by body language." She suggests listening to facial expressions, gestures, body position, attire and hairstyle and other accessories (watches and other jewelry) and the all-important tone and intonation of words. Men, she adds, are very good at watching people's faces when they talk but tend to miss a lot of the other body cues that tell you what they're trying to say.

Empathize, don't sympathize. Sympathy is crying when someone else cries at a funeral. Unfortunately, pity and compassion are forms of sympathy and drain us of energy and distract us from being there for someone. Empathy allows us to "see the world through someone's else's eyes," says Ronald G. Nathan, Ph.D., clinical psychologist and professor in the Department of Family Practice at Albany Medical College in New York and author of

---

The Voice of Stress

More often than not, says Dr. Suzette Haden Elgin of the Ozark Center for Language Studies, people under stress fall into one of the following communication patterns. See if any sound familiar.

• **Blaming.** Frequent use of "I, me, my"; use of absolutes like "always" and "never"; pounding fists; pointing fingers.

• **Placating.** Same as the above, except placators are desperate to please. They lean on people and pick lint off others' shoulders while criticizing them.

• **Computing.** A neutral position, accompanied by flat intonation, use of generalizations and abstractions, and little expressiveness in body or face.

• **Distracting.** Combines all of the above to effectively distract listener from the real issue at hand.

• **Leveling.** When words, body language and the speaker's inner feelings (sometimes called vibes) match. In plain English, the speaker means what he says.

Coping with the Stressed-Out People in Your Life, "without actually feeling what they feel. With empathy, we don't lose our identity."

Watch TV. Television, that medium which more often than not is the barrier to communication between consenting adults, is a great "teaching machine," says Dr. Elgin. Turn on any good public affairs show, not *Friends* or *Beavis and Butt-head* or orchestrated shouting matches like *Crossfire* but something along the lines of *Wall $treet Week* or anything on C-SPAN. You may be bored to tears but pay complete attention, "as if every word mattered to you personally," she says. "Each time your attention wanders, bring it back—no matter how many times it happens. Do this ten minutes, more than you'll ever be asked to listen to a live human being, and you'll be well-practiced in listening."

Breaking Up

It Really Is Hard to Do

Male myth Number 2,367: We take breakups "like a man." That is, stoically. In stride. She didn't mean that much to you anyway. Life goes on. There are plenty of other fish in the sea. They're a dime a dozen. Take 'em or leave 'em. And other hackneyed lines from Cliché Theater that mask what's really going on.

Who are you trying to kid? Splitting up stinks. Whether you dump her or she dumps you, it hurts. It's stressful. "Next to the death of a spouse or child, divorce is probably the most stressful event of a man's life," says Georgia Witkin, Ph.D., assistant clinical professor of psychiatry and director of the Stress Program at Mount Sinai Medical Center in New York City and author of *The Male Stress Syndrome.* And it's not just divorce. It could be the dissolution of a two-year live-in relationship or the end of a ten-day torrid affair.

We may be very good at stonewalling it, but the reality is that breaking up may be even more painful for men than it is for women. So says Zick Rubin, Ph.D., an adjunct professor of social psychology at Brandeis University in Watham, Massachusetts, and an attorney in Boston. After a three-year study of couples, Dr. Rubin concluded that "men hold on to hope longer, are less likely to initiate separations and suffer more than their partners in breakups."

"We call it the FILO effect—first in, last out," Dr. Witkin says. "Men are the first to get involved and the last to let go. The myth is that women are more romantic, but I've found that men fall in love hard."

And they fall out of love even harder.

The sad fact is that separation and divorce are increasingly part of our lifestyle. Fifty percent of the couples who wed in 1970 will wind up divorced. For married couples starting out in 1990, the likelihood of divorce was projected to be close to a staggering 67 percent.

Letting Go

You may not be able to avoid checking into a room at the Heartbreak Hotel at some point in your life, but there are steps that you can take to make sure that it doesn't become your permanent address. Here are a few recommended by experts.

Be shortsighted. Rather than being bummed about seeing a breakup as a failed long-term relationship, view it as a successful short-term relationship, suggests Jed Diamond, a licensed clinical social worker who lectures widely, teaches in the alcohol and drug studies program at the University of California at Berkeley and is the author of several books on relationships, including *Looking for Love in All the Wrong Places.*

"What's stressful about breaking up is the belief that we're not supposed to break up," says Diamond. "But new research in evolutionary psychology suggests that we may be built and programmed to break up. Maybe we're not supposed to be with one person the rest of our lives, just as you probably won't keep the same job you started in your twenties. It may be that the likelihood of being with one person for our whole lives is not very likely."

Confide in a guy. Breakups are more stressful for men than women, Diamond says, because "men tend to put all their intimacy eggs in one basket"—that basket being the woman in their lives.

"For most men," he explains, "a woman is the sole provider of his emotional well-being. Unlike women, who have stronger friendship networks than men and can get together and commiserate with those friends, men don't have friends to call on for support. Men would rather say that they're fine and suffer inside than admit to another man that their relationship has 'failed.' "

Bruce Fisher, Ed.D., founder and director of the Family Relations Learning Center in Boulder, Colorado, marriage and family therapist and author of *Rebuilding When Your Relationship Ends*, found that men have the greatest trouble with letting go. "I used to believe that men leave and move on easily," Dr. Fisher says. "Now I believe that they're more attached. The reason why it's harder is because when their relationships end, they've lost not only a love partner but also their only confidante and their only friend."

Don't play the blame game.
Men who respond to being dumped by blaming the dumper are spinning their wheels needlessly, says Mark Epstein, M.D., a psychiatrist in Manhattan and author of *Thoughts without a Thinker*. "I tell people who ask, 'How could she do this to me?' to rephrase the question without the 'me.' What feeds the stress-invoking self-defeating loop is feeling that you're having it done to you. It's better to realize that the other person has to do what she has to do."

Deal with the real problem.
Sometimes the pain and stress we feel about the loss of a relationship has more to do with losses from our past, notes Diamond. "We're dealing with the re-creation of childhood losses. It could be the loss of something larger than a particular woman. It could be related to your parents or some personal goals. If you can acknowledge that, then you can identify where the healing really needs to be done, where the loss really took place."

Rebuilding Blocks

We go through predictable stages after the dust has settled on a relationship, according to Dr. Bruce Fisher of the Family Relations Learning Center. He's the first to admit that the 19 rebuilding blocks he describes are not easy to climb. But he feels strongly that knowing the stages helps ease the stress. Here they are.

- Denial. "I can't believe this is happening to me."
- Fear. "What happens now?"
- Adaptation. "It always worked when I was a kid."
- Loneliness. "I've never felt so alone."
- Friendship. "Got a few minutes to talk?"
- Guilt/Rejection. "I should have been more understanding."
- Grief. "I feel like my guts are being ripped out."
- Anger. "I hate her. She played me like a fool."
- Letting Go. "Man, I've gotta get on with my life."
- Self-Worth. "I'm not really so bad after all."
- Transition. "I'm waking up and taking out the trash."
- Openness. "I've been hiding behind a mask."
- Love. "Could somebody really care for me?"
- Trust. "My wound is beginning to heal."
- Relatedness. "Healthy relationships help me rebuild."
- Sexuality. "I'm interested, but I'm scared."
- Singleness. "You mean it's okay?"
- Purpose. "I have goals for the future."
- Freedom. "From chrysalis to butterfly."

Learn. When you are ready to try again, remember that experience is the best teacher. Look upon your past experiences to help you do better next time, recommends Redford B. Williams, M.D., professor of psychiatry and director of the Behavioral Medicine Research Center at Duke University Medical Center in Durham, North Carolina.

Fighting Crime Fears

Safeguard Yourself from Stress

Standing at the bank cash machine, you glance nervously over your shoulder as it spits out crisp, new $20 bills and worry about the shadowy figure you see shuffling his feet just a few yards away. At home, before you turn in for the night, you make sure that all the door locks and windows are secure. When you park your car, you pull out the car stereo and lock it in the trunk. Wherever you go and whatever you do, fear of crime is your constant companion.

"If you watch TV and read the newspaper, you know that it's appropriate to feel stress thinking that there's a possibility that it will happen to you," says Constance Dancu, Ph.D., director of the Center for Cognitive and Behavior Therapy in Wilmington, Delaware, and assistant professor of the Crime Victim's Program at Allegheny University of the Health Sciences in Philadelphia. "We know that there's crime out there. I know that it can happen to any of us because of my work, but I'm not sure that many people go through the day thinking that it will happen. . . ." Dr. Dancu pauses for effect. "Until it happens."

If you think increased crime is a figment of your imagination or some promotional gimmick conceived by the producers of TV police dramas such as *NYPD Blue*, think again. According to the FBI's "Uniform Crime Reports," the violent crime index—which measures the combined level of murder, forcible rape, robbery and aggravated assault— increased by 40.3 percent between 1985 and 1994. Property crime—

which includes burglary, larceny-theft and motor-vehicle theft—rose 9.2 percent in the same period. The number of murders jumped by 22.8 percent.

"But crime isn't the number one issue in America," says Detective J. J. Bittenbinder, who had been with the Chicago Police Department for 23 years before becoming an inspector and lecturer with the Cook County Sheriff's Department in Illinois. "Fear of crime is the number one issue."

Taking Precautions

"When the bad guys—I call them goofs—hit the streets, they have a plan," says Bittenbinder. "You should, too." Knowing what to do in an emergency situation could save you precious seconds that could make the difference between life and death.

People who have been victims—whether that means your car stereo was stolen, you're a Vietnam War veteran or even a survivor of a natural disaster—"can see the world as a very dangerous place," Dr. Dancu says. "An extremely upsetting event can make people feel vulnerable. They can have their antennae up all the time, sitting at home with mace in their hand."

In the extreme, it can lead to agoraphobia and other chronic phobic reactions, including post-traumatic stress disorder. Dr. Dancu says that one strategy for overcoming the stress is to re-educate the victim. "If maladaptive behavior can be learned, so, too, can new positive coping behaviors with the right kind of intervention," says Dr. Dancu. She recommends professional counseling for people who exhibit extreme reaction to the stress of crime fears.

Meanwhile, Bittenbinder says that a healthy level of suspicion can keep you from becoming another statistic in the "Uniform Crime Reports." "Like my father said," he notes, "trust everybody, but always cut the cards."

Here are a number of cards to keep up your sleeve when you need to call a goof's bluff.

Look confident, even if you're not. "If you don't want to be prey, look like a predator," says Bittenbinder. "The goofs go for the weak-looking ones. If they see you walking with your head down, they'll think you're a wussy." Walk erect, with your head high and a strong gait. Make eye contact with shifty looking characters. Let them know that you see them and that you're not afraid.

Don't telegraph your keys. By now, everybody and his kid sister knows that you leave the key to the house under the potted plant next to the front door. Don't. Not even those cutesy key hiders like the fake thermometer or the imitation dog poo work. "The goofs aren't too smart, but they're not that stupid either," Bittenbinder says. "If you leave the keys outside, someone will find them."

Do it with mirrors. Here's an especially good tip for salesmen loading samples or shoppers with a bunch of bags to put in the trunk. Buy a convex mirror and place it inside the trunk so that you can see behind you. "A $2 investment can make you feel 500 percent safer," Bittenbinder calculates.

Spice up your life. Of the many anticrime devices you can carry, Bittenbinder recommends a canister of pepper spray. Guns can be turned against you too easily. Tear gas won't work on narcotics users or someone who's drunk. Whistles are only good as long as you blow them.

The Heat Is On

During the dog days of July and August, the rate of violent crimes—defined as murder, rape, robbery and aggravated assault—perennially reaches its highest level, according to the FBI's "Uniform Crime Reports."

It's no wonder. Heat sends stress to the boiling point. When endocrinologist Hans Selye, M.D., conducted his pioneering stress studies on laboratory rats in the 1930s, he discovered that exposing them to the heat of the boiler room made them ill. Why is that?

Stanford University's Dr. Robert Sapolsky speculates that it has to do with our internal thermometer, which likes to stay right at about 98.6°F. When it gets too high, he explains, it can trip our fight-or-flight alarm. It could also have something to do with the fact that the brain's hypothalamus, which controls the regulation of heat throughout the body, is the center that signals the release of our stress hormones.

For those who find that heat makes them hot under the collar, the best advice is to chill. Drink plenty of cool liquids, stay out of the sun, retreat to air-conditioned environments and wear face-shading hats and loose clothing, suggests Jeffrey Jahre, M.D., clinical associate professor at Temple University in Philadelphia and chief of infectious diseases at St. Luke's Hospital in Bethlehem, Pennsylvania. Consciously recognizing that heat is one of the factors that increases stress may help you take a deep breath instead of chewing out the waitress that you think is deliberately ignoring you.

Pepper spray will stop most people in their tracks, Bittenbinder says. "It's painful, but it contains no deadly chemicals. It will debilitate someone long enough for you to get away."

Aging with Grace

The Best Is Yet to Come

Always as we tromp forward, the glimmer of light in the distance ahead is bright. Then we pass a sign that says "Halfway Point," and we glimpse—for the first time—darkness at the end of the tunnel.

We spin madly and examine the hourglass. Yes, half the sand *has* sifted to the bottom. We stare in disbelief. How could this have happened? We've only just begun.

"These are the days that must happen to you," wrote poet Walt Whitman.

Classic literature tells us that midlife turmoil is universal and has ever been with us. It is a time of angst and questioning and reprioritizing, but it is not necessarily a *crisis*, notes Ross Goldstein, Ph.D., a psychologist in private practice in San Francisco. This is a time to clean out the attic, so to speak; to toss the garbage and obsolete clutter and to explore, define and chart a course for the best years that truly can lie ahead. It's a necessary reassessment, a midcourse adjustment, and is not something to shortcut or attempt to detour around, says Dr. Goldstein.

Is That All There Is?

We tend to go through reappraisals of our values and goals and directions about once every decade we are alive, says Frederic Hudson, Ph.D., a psychologist in Santa Barbara, California, and author of the widely used college text *The Adult Years*, as well as other books. The biggest single shift hits men

somewhere between ages 38 and 43, he says. This is "a shift from early adult thinking. . . . Early adults are driven not by their own voices but by the committee in their heads made up of professors and friends, peers, peer pressure, advertising and mostly of parents and siblings, and all these values and beliefs about things that must be accomplished by the time they are 40. . . . The young male has this deadline of when to arrive at happiness, success and financial wealth."

So picture a country full of vigorous young men, climbing and achieving, whatever the cost, each trying to reach the top rung of a ladder by age 40. Even if they make it, says Dr. Hudson, "they find that the ladder is up against the wrong wall.

"Even if you're the president of a large corporation," he says, "you're going to ask, 'Why am I here? It's a nice place to be, and I'm doing fine, but is this all there is?' "

Because when a male moves into what Swiss psychologist Carl Jung called "the afternoon of life," he "comes to terms with what his core values are," says Dr. Hudson. "It's in your early forties that the psychological birth of the adult takes place. That's when you really become a person. You individuate. Until then, you are marching to the beats of lots of different drummers."

Suddenly, a man finds himself wanting to love more—to be more emotionally expressive, to be a better father, to have more friends, to be a better spouse, to have a more meaningful life and to explore beauty and life's mysteries and the tugging spiritual sense that maybe he really *is* connected somehow to a bigger scheme of things, says Dr. Hudson. And he feels remorse for having failed to do or recognize these things earlier, notes Dr. Goldstein.

The remorse may translate into disillusionment

with himself as well as his current environment and relationships, Dr. Goldstein says.

A Map for the Journey

Some men whiz right through midlife, with barely a snag, and wonder what's going on with all their friends, Dr. Hudson observes. Most, though, spend some time sorting and redefining.

For the smoothest journey, consider the following advice.

Accept yourself. "Don't degenerate into character assassination and self-loathing," warns Dr. Goldstein. Cultivate an accepting attitude toward yourself that is both forgiving and encouraging. Three-fourths of the work involved in navigating through the midlife quandary is learning to accept who you are, not who you might be sometime or who you should have been, says Dr. Goldstein.

"The middle-age guy in his forties and fifties says, 'I've finally figured out that life is something to be lived one day at a time, that it is the journey and not the result that matters,' " Dr. Hudson says. "That's the beginning of elderhood."

Choose battles wisely. Know which goals you want to take on and how realistic they are, advises Dr. Goldstein. It may be necessary to extend deadlines or redefine or even discard some goals. Or set newer, higher goals. Also, savor the pleasures and give yourself credit for the small victories each day. Don't just think in terms of the big picture.

Get on the learning curve. Keep your skills sharp and stay ahead of the trends and changes—or at least apace with them. "Survival in today's work world absolutely demands life-long learning," says Dr. Goldstein.

Diversify your relationships. "You need a lot of friendships, a lot of different kinds

---

How Many Gold Chains Should You Wear?

The stereotype of the middle-age male: He buys a hairpiece—for his chest, since he now wears his shirts open enough to expose ten pounds of gold chains dangling from his neck. He drives a red Corvette, top down, and is glued to a 20-year-old babe who smiles and pouts a lot and dresses like she belongs on MTV.

The reality: "That's only a microscopic portion of men," says psychologist Dr. Ross Goldstein.

"The fact that the myth has had such a long life suggests that unconsciously there is something going on. That men have that desire. But the number of men that actually act on it is minuscule. Most men, by the time they reach that age, have enough impulse control that they don't do stupid things that mess up their lives. Their changes are much more subtle. And, maybe in some ways, more profound."

---

of people in your life. It keeps you in touch with a lot of segments of the world around you, and that's a key to staying youthful," Dr. Goldstein says. Don't overly depend on a few people, like your wife or children, for emotional fulfillment.

Avoid being judgmental. You may have been there, done that, but you really shouldn't jump to conclusions, particularly about other people and other generations, Dr. Goldstein says. "Be experimental," he says. "Be challenging, be accepting and engage in some trial and error. Try some different ways of dressing and thinking."

Take care of yourself. Now that you know that you're really going to live this long, "take care of your body as though you are going to live a long time," says Dr. Goldstein. "Get started on a fitness program. Eat wisely."

Coping with Illness

Keys to Resiliency

Everything has changed. A fickle illness or disability now controls the agenda—today, tomorrow and for an uncertain forever. No longer can you do and be on your own terms.

Chronic illness. Men are poorly equipped to handle it in themselves or in others, says Paul J. Donoghue, Ph.D., a psychologist in Stamford, Connecticut, and co-author of *Sick and Tired of Feeling Sick and Tired.*

That's because male identity and esteem are especially centered around their ability to perform, to fix things and to do and make things right, says JoAnn LeMaistre, Ph.D., clinical psychologist, instructor at Stanford University School of Medicine and author of *After the Diagnosis: From Crisis to Personal Renewal for Patients with Chronic Illness.*

Adds Marsha Goodman Landau, Ph.D., psychologist, instructor at the University of New Mexico in Albuquerque and co-author (with Robert A. Klein, Ph.D.) of *Healing the Body Betrayed*, men have a need to feel strong and independent.

Chronic illness sharply limits or ends all that, and chronic illness can't be "fixed." It sends everyone reeling in shock—and especially men, Dr. LeMaistre says.

Complicating things, says Dr. Donoghue, men aren't known for carefully and clearly expressing and discussing deeper longings, needs and feelings.

Yet, the three doctors

agree, direct expression of emotional and physical needs is an essential coping skill for anyone living with chronic illness.

Your Illness

Expect to feel fear and panic at first, says Dr. LeMaistre. She knows. She lives with multiple sclerosis. Expect to wrestle with a loss of identity and feelings of anger and depression as you come to terms with your disability, she says. Realize that some friends will drop away—not everyone can handle disability. Your job is to find new friends comfortable with someone who will never "get well soon."

"A lot of our friendships are based on having playmates that we buddy with and play sports with but that we don't really talk with," Dr. Donoghue says. "And when we can't play the sports anymore, we don't have the friendships."

Know, says Dr. LeMaistre, that you can live a full and fulfilling life, so long as you keep challenging yourself to find ways to work with and around your limitations and as long as you keep expressing compassion and empathy to others. Know also that you will have setbacks.

All three doctors are founts of insightful advice for coping. Here are a few of their best recommendations.

Keep score. Daily charting your ups and downs in a notebook or on a graph and noting the symptoms, their intensity and what you are doing and thinking at the time helps put the disabling aspect of the illness into perspective. It rarely is constant, says Dr. Landau. Charting uncovers factors that influence it positively and negatively.

Eavesdrop on your inner voice. "We talk to ourselves all day long. Either we're talking to ourselves in a way that gives us peace, or we're talking to ourselves in a way that puts us under more stress," says Dr. Donoghue. "So we need to identify the way that we're talking to ourselves and the way that we're thinking and then substitute rational, sensible, truthful and even positive thinking in place of the irrational thinking."

Write your feelings down. Talk about them if only to a notepad or diary. This helps you clarify and understand what you're going through so that you can better communicate your needs to others.

Improve the environment. If you're bedridden, make your bedroom beautiful and pleasant. Have your favorite music, colors, artwork, photos, videos, books and so on around you, Dr. Landau advises. Insist on spending some time outdoors in the sunshine. You aren't a prisoner. Find stimulating phone friends to discuss ideas with when you're housebound.

Seek support. Dr. Donoghue recommends joining a support group, someplace where you're encouraged to explore and vent deep feelings with others who understand them firsthand.

Someone Else's Illness

Men caring for someone close to them with a chronic illness are in serious danger of burnout, says Dr. LeMaistre. It is important that they care for themselves physically, spiritually and emotionally, she says. And that they have a confidante away from the caregiving relationship to whom they can talk about their feelings and frustrations and responsibilities.

Also understand that a serious chronic illness of any family member is a psyche torquer for the whole family. Try to guard against feeling angry at the ill person for the changes that the illness forces on the family. One way to avoid that, suggests Dr. LeMaistre, is to continue normal family-bonding activities,

---

How to Really Help

Everybody sends flowers when someone is ill. But when someone is chronically ill, they need more than flowers. They need real human contact. Here are some fun, almost-effortless ways to offer it, as suggested by psychologists Dr. Marsha Goodman Landau and Dr. Robert A. Klein, co-authors of *Healing the Body Betrayed*.

- Go for a walk with them.
- Run an errand for them.
- Offer a back rub.
- Carry or move something for them (the trash, some furniture).
- Clip and send a magazine or newspaper story on a subject that intrigues them.
- Help them put on a jacket.
- Share a tape, CD or great video.

---

even if the ill person cannot participate.

When a friend's family is hit with a chronic illness, rather than regularly call for reports on the ill person, express sympathy for the well members and offer to help them with their everyday duties. They are going through tough, stressful times, Dr. LeMaistre says.

Finally, here are a couple of Dr. LeMaistre's top tips for dealing with people who are chronically ill.

Listen to them. "Don't try to jolly them out of feeling bad," Dr. LeMaistre says. When they express pain and frustration, they aren't expecting you to fix it. They just want to know that you understand and care. Encourage them to talk about how they feel and what they are going through and trying to accomplish. Don't offer a lot of advice, but do ask questions that show that you understand what they are saying.

Encourage and recognize triumphs. It can be tasks formerly as routine as dressing or feeding themselves, if those are what they've been working on.

Banishing Loneliness

Make Connections for Life

It's one of those revered male traditions that dies hard. The loner. One man against the elements. Gary Cooper in *High Noon.* John Wayne in *Red River.* Sylvester Stallone in the Rambo movies. Clint Eastwood in the Dirty Harry flicks. But it was Madison Avenue that came up with an image of the single guy that has proven to be timeless: the Marlboro Man. Always on the roundup. Always in some enviably remote locale. Always in sweet solitude.

Of course, for all its appeal, the strong, silent type—who needs no one and nothing but his steed and his smokes—can be a stressful role to play. That's a weighty suit of armor to wear all day, and covering up all the chinks of vulnerability can be time-consuming. Even without the cigarette dangling Belmondo-style from your mouth, playing the loner who has no friends literally could be hazardous to your health. A number of studies have shown that the fewer the social relationships, the shorter the life expectancy.

"There's a whole body of behavioral medicine research that hammers home the notion that lack of good solid relationships is harmful to your immune system," says Stanford University's Dr. Robert Sapolsky.

And study after study has shown that people who lack supportive social ties are more likely to die early from heart disease, cancer and other major diseases, says Dr. Redford B. Williams of Duke University Medical Center.

The Buddy System

You don't really have any friends now, do you?

Psychologist Joel Block, Ph.D., of Long Island, New York, conducted a landmark study in the late 1970s and discovered that four men out of five don't have a close, personal male friend. Dr. Block and other psychologists we interviewed say that nothing has changed in this regard since the 1970s. We men may unload on our spouses and/or girlfriends some, but we don't spill our guts to other guys.

We have male playmates, says psychologist Dr. Paul J. Donoghue. Guys we bowl with or golf with. But it's a rare man who has a buddy with whom he discusses his deep, inner milieu and private, personal conflicts and doubts.

"There's a general devaluing of male friendship not just in society but in men's heads," laments Dr. Samuel Osherson of Harvard University Health Services. "We have a tendency to look on other men as competitors, not confidants. One of the last things you think about is making time for men friends."

The reason why men need other men as friends, Dr. Osherson says, is because they serve as "mirrors, great fact-checking systems. You can ask another guy, 'Am I seeing reality as it really is?' "

The obstacles that keep men from developing close friendships with other men are not insurmountable. If you've found yourself wishing that you could have a buddy like you did in high school or college—a pal with whom you could talk about anything and everything—here are some helpful tips.

Don't come on too strong. Remember that it's a big turnoff if you're too pushy. Men get suspicious that you want something, like a loan, or that you're really needy.

No matter how desperate you are for companionship, you must suppress that desperation, that neediness, says Arthur Wassmer, Ph.D., a psychologist in Seattle and author of *Making Contact.*

"Neediness isn't attractive," he says.

On the other hand, "everybody needs human contact." Recognize that and capitalize on it to overcome shyness. "Realize that you are a supplier of a needed commodity," Dr. Wassmer advises.

"Before going out to meet a group of people, practice self-talk. Remind yourself, 'They need me. I have something to give. I have kindness, love, gentleness, support and concern to share with people. I have admiration to share with people.'"

Stand on common ground. "Men are shy when it comes to emotions and feelings," Dr. Osherson says. "They're easily concerned about being embarrassed and exposed." If there's something serious that you want or need to discuss, don't start there. Ease into the difficult stuff after you've established some commonality.

Be a sport. "Some people think that men who do sports together are just barbarians," Dr. Osherson says. "That's not fair. Sports has emotional resonance to men. It might have been a major connection they had with their fathers or remind them of strong bonds from their past, a sense of camaraderie." It's a male proving ground, and that's part of why you're hanging out: to reinforce your manhood. So play now, talk later.

Keep an open mind. Fear of homosexuality can keep heterosexual men from forming friendships with other men, according to Dr. Osherson. It shouldn't be that way, but, unfortunately, it's part of our culture. While it harms gay men's self-esteem, it also "hinders all men's ability to allow themselves to develop close relationships with other men," Dr. Osherson says. "Don't confuse a gesture of closeness from another man with necessarily being a sexual come-on."

One Is the Loneliest Number

Men carry with them a high lonesomeness, a grief. Poet and philosopher Robert Bly has speculated that it may be part of our genetic makeup. Some of us, he has noted, carry more grief than others. And we seem to idealize this.

Our heroes and favorite movie characters may be resilient loners. But if we want to be healthy—physically and emotionally—we need substantial human contact, says Dr. Wassmer.

And anyone, other than the utterly "damaged," as psychologist and author Barbara Powell, Ph.D., of Block Island, Rhode Island, and New Canaan, Connecticut, puts it, can make friends.

Having lots of acquaintances and people around "can help ease the pain of loneliness," says Dr. Powell. "But I think the majority of the people are lonely if they don't have a personal relationship with somebody—even if they have a lot of friends."

We feel devastating loneliness when we lose a friend or confidante—whether to death, divorce, a job transfer or other cause.

A gnawing sense of loss and loneliness is likely to arise during any major life crisis and dredge up memories of fear and panic and aloneness that we experienced during other crises. And it is at such times that we welcome the soulful consolation and interaction that close friends can offer. If we do not have such a friend to turn to, we are less likely to resolve the loss quickly and move on productively, say grief counselors John James, co-founder of the Grief Recovery Institute in Los Angeles with about 1,700 chapters around the country and co-author of *The Grief Recovery Handbook,* and Helen Fitzgerald, founding director of the first grief and loss program in a public mental health clinic in the United States, based in a Virginia suburb of Washington, D.C., certified death educator and author of *The Mourning Handbook.*

Even in personal crises we can find new, trusted friends, notes Dr. JoAnn LeMaistre of

Stanford University School of Medicine. Relationships forged then may be especially meaningful because we tend during such times to seek friends who can accept us as the "damaged goods" that we are, Dr. LeMaistre says. Friends who do not expect us to always be "Good-Time Charlie playmates."

But where do you turn for contact if you're reeling from loneliness and confusion following a profound loss? Consider a support group for people experiencing the kind of loss that you're going through, suggest Fitzgerald and James.

And, as Dr. Wassmer says, offer the needed commodities—respect, admiration, support, concern, kindness and so on—to the precious souls like you who are clinging to the group as a lifeline.

Making Fast Friends

The secret to developing meaningful friendships is simple, says Dr. Wassmer. Be a friend.

"Human beings need admiration," he says. "They need respect. They need attention. They need affection. They need a sense of importance. We could probably develop the list more. But my point is this: Hold the awareness that all human beings need those things high in your consciousness, and then behave as a supplier of those things, and you'll rapidly become a rather important person to other people. Just as a dope dealer is a very important person to an addict."

In addition to seeming desperate or needy, men need to avoid "leading with your plumage"—in other words, strutting or trying to impress—if they want to make fast friends, according to Dr. Wassmer.

You say that you've never been very good

Stress and the Single Guy

About the time a single guy creeps into his mid-thirties, odds are that he'll look in the mirror one day and wonder, "What's the matter with me?"

Absolutely nothing, says Jed Diamond of the University of California at Berkeley.

In fact, many men choose to be single not because they can't find Ms. Right—or even Ms. Right Now—but because they truly prefer not having to be accountable and responsible to another person and not having to make sure that the toilet seat is down after every usage.

"We live in a time where we don't have to be in a relationship to live complete lives," Diamond says. "That's a choice, a positive option."

By the mid-1990s, there were 24.7 million single men in the United States. That's 27 percent of the male population, according to the U.S. Census Bureau. By the age of 29, more than half of us will have jumped the single male ship and gotten hitched. Beyond age 75, only about 4 percent of us are single.

"Being single is clearly a double-edged sword," Diamond says. There's an awful lot of freedom, but at some point, you're likely to feel some pressure—either from within or from family and friends—to settle down and get married.

The causes of stress for a single man change with age. "At 21, to be frank, your main concern is getting laid," says Diamond. "In your late twenties and early thirties, you suddenly get serious about work. Later, men worry about whether they'll ever find a good relationship. They start wondering, 'What's the matter with me.' "

at meeting people? Well, that does make it tougher to make friends. So here are some ideas.

Find that old-time religion. Or new-fangled spirituality. "Go to church," Dr. Powell

Whether there is a monogamous relationship in your future or not, Diamond advises, enjoy your single life. Remember: One of the keys to living a stress-free life is to live in the moment. Spend quality time on yourself— someone with whom you *will* have a lifelong relationship. Here are some ways to make that relationship more fulfilling and less stressful.

Create rituals. Do things that have special meaning to you and you alone. Then do them again. Take a trip to your old neighborhood on your birthday. Celebrate spring with a solo hike in the woods. Look through your photo album on New Year's Eve. "Rituals are a way of making things even more important, more meaningful," says Diamond. "They tell you that you're important to yourself."

Eat with others. "One of the most stressful things in life is eating alone," says Arthur Fischer, a former partner in an advertising agency and a single man. "You end up watching the news, which is stressful. You tend to eat the wrong things because nobody is watching. You eat standing up." All of which led him to start the Single Gourmet, a membership club in New York City. If you can't find a similar group where you live, start one of your own. Try out new restaurants. Arrange potlucks. It beats talking to yourself over a meal. Or, worse, talking back to the tube.

Be a mentor. Get involved with young people. Organizations like Big Brothers will make you feel as though you're making a contribution to the future. "Single guys can get too narcissistic," says Diamond. "We all need to give something back."

that interest you: lectures, poetry readings, book discussion groups, painting classes, language classes, whatever there is that is in your field of interest. There's adult education in every town; even the YMCA offers classes. You meet people, and everybody but the most reclusive will make friends."

Get professional. Join and get active in groups and organizations related to your profession, business or occupation. Or get involved in community groups, says Dr. Powell.

Specialize. Find a group that shares your personal special interest, whether it's poker, bicycling, weight lifting or coin collecting. "I suggest starting with a mixed group," says Dr. Osherson. "Men's groups are great, but there's a little danger in that men have a tendency to segregate, and an all-male setting may not give them a chance to deal with larger issues that affect our relationship to the opposite sex."

Use your time productively. Treat yourself with respect, says Dr. Powell. Use time alone to get to know yourself, find out what you really like to do, work on your self-esteem, improve abilities, develop talents, "practice creativity in all its forms," meditate, exercise and more. Avoid the temptation to "do nothing," to sleep around-the-clock, watch too much TV, mope and throw pity parties and overindulge in drugs, alcohol and eating.

Learn how to listen. "It's very simple," says Dr. Williams. "All you have to do is keep your mouth shut until the other guy seems to be finished." Then reflect back and say, "What I hear you saying is. . . ." People you do this with are more likely to listen to you and be a source of support when you need it.

advises. There's a brand for every taste. Shop around.

Try a little class. "Sign up for a class of some kind," says Dr. Powell. "Go to events

Coming to Terms with Grief

Let the Healing Begin

We grieve much in adulthood. Top the list with the death of a spouse. Mix in the death of a close family member or the death of a friend. Add in losses. Include loss of a job, loss of a marriage, loss of identity and loss of self-esteem. Consider the grief involved in financial collapse or in moving to a distant job, away from familiar faces, places and memories.

The starkness, agony and confusion of grief are real, painful and necessary. We can do grief well, or we can do it poorly. We American men tend to do it poorly, say the experts, simply because society does not encourage open and complete grieving.

Here we'll focus on how to do it well so that it does not haunt and color the years, even decades following a loss.

But consider this irony: "You break an arm, you get six weeks off work with full disability and everyone comes up to you and asks how it happened and how you feel," notes John James of the Grief Recovery Institute. "But if your mother dies, you get three days off work; and on the fourth day, you better be back in the office and never talk about it. Nobody comes up and asks you what happened or how you feel. And that's just ridiculous."

Deep, Murky Waters

Men are poorly equipped for resolving losses. We don't share feelings openly, nor do we have the strong support networks that women build, notes James. Instead we sort of push our grief down, subdue it, bury it and attempt to ignore it until it melts into and adheres to the generalized burden of sadness and fears that we secretly carry with us through life.

Poet and philosopher Robert Bly says that grief is an innate part of the human male. "Men don't always know what they are grieving about," Bly told Bill Moyers in the 1990 film documentary *A Gathering of Men.* "It's as if the grief is impersonal with men. It's always present. . . . It may be a grief that is in nature itself."

Soon, each new loss covertly dredges up all the pain and agony and a cavalcade of emotions from each previous, unresolved loss. And the burden becomes greater. And, as we said at the outset, these losses can wear many faces, besides the mask of death.

"It can be loss of identity, loss of health, loss of job, loss of financial stability, loss of friends, loss of freedom, loss of sexual dignity—some of the men I work with in jail have been raped," says grief counselor Helen Fitzgerald. "We even get into loss of childhood and innocence. . . . Men come up with a whole list of losses that they have had. These are just a few."

Picking Up the Pieces

How do you deal with a loss when it is fresh and the world is pressuring you to forget it and get on with things? Here are some steps recommended by James and Fitzgerald to begin the healing process.

Confront your feelings. First, say James and Fitzgerald, recognize that what you are feeling is grief and that it's natural.

"Just applying the label 'grief' to how we respond to

those losses helps people experiencing them to understand what they are feeling," Fitzgerald says. "Understanding that you are grieving or mourning a loss gives you permission to feel those feelings."

Accept the process. Two reactions to a profound loss are universal, says James. First, an immediate sensation of numbness, of being stunned; and second, a tendency to punch the rewind button and review in minutia your relationship with the person or thing you have lost. During this review, says James, we tend to "draw larger-than-life pictures—both positively and negatively—and say, 'Oh, my wife was a Mother Teresa,' or 'Oh, my father was the Devil incarnate'; and neither, of course, is true."

Identify the issues. We feel the sharpest sadness, says James, "over things we wish that we had done differently, better or more of with the person who is now gone."

We need to pinpoint those things and isolate precisely what it is that we are grieving over, he says.

Suddenly, our life has holes in it. Perhaps many holes. Pieces of us are missing. And we agonize and perhaps leak tears each time we realize that a piece is gone. Our job, in the short run, is not to plug or hide the holes or replace the missing pieces but to discover them, recognize them and acknowledge them, James and Fitzgerald say.

In the long run, we'll need to find ways to fill in, bridge over or otherwise supplant essential missing pieces that we realize contributed to our mental balance and general well-being. While we can never replace the person or precise personal experiences we shared with him or her, we can and should, over time, find new constructive ways

Pillars of Pain

We are wracked with pain, regrets, guilt and a whole spectrum of earthshaking emotions in the aftermath of a loss as magnified memories replay over and over in seemingly precise detail, notes John James of the Grief Recovery Institute.

If—and James recommends that we do—we explore closely the matters causing us the most torment, he says that we will find that they fall into one of the following categories. The process of healing, he says, begins once we are able to identify and express specifically what it is that we are hurting about. Then, he says, we can begin to find ways to move beyond the loss.

The pillars of pain, James says, are built on these six foundations.

- **Should haves. Things that I am sorry that I did or did not do.**
- **Unexpressed amnesty. Things that someone else did or didn't do that I wish I had forgiven.**
- **Significant emotional statements. Things that I was going to say and didn't, like "I was proud of you."**
- **Hopes shared with or involving the other person.**
- **Dreams shared with or involving the other person.**
- **Expectations shared with or involving the other person.**

to fill some of the same needs, say James and Fitzgerald.

Before we even consider filling or patching holes, we need to know what the holes are. The pain helps with that. When pain and hysteria hit, we need to look and listen and ask ourselves specifically, "Exactly what is it that we are missing?" advises James.

Express it. Once we've identified the sources of our pain, we need to express them. At that point, it helps to write them down— maybe in a letter to the person we are grieving—"or share some of that information with a trusted friend," says James. "If you do, there is a definite, almost-instantaneous benefit, a sense of overwhelming relief."

Above all, say James and Fitzgerald, a griever needs a sympathetic listener. This person needs to be someone "who takes an interest in how the griever feels and in what he remembers and who just listens—without giving advice and without trying to change the subject," James says.

People need to talk about what happened and what they are feeling, without being judged, James adds.

"Men aren't always equipped to express feelings orally because of how they have been raised," notes Fitzgerald. "They're raised to be tough. Talking about feelings and expressing feelings are considered a sign of weakness. Men still struggle with that."

When someone you know is grieving, you can practice being an interested, nonjudgmental listener. When you are grieving, find that listener, the experts advise.

Where are some places to find a sympathetic ear? Fitzgerald suggests calling a clergy person, a friend, a therapist or a support group.

James's organization operates, at no charge, a toll-free telephone service with trained volunteer grief counselors available to listen and to refer you to local support groups. Grief Recovery Institute counselors are available from 9 to 5 Pacific Time, Monday through Friday at 1-800-445-4808.

Taming the Angry Beast

Grief and anger are closely related, says Fitzgerald. We tend to feel angry when grieving, and the anger is a multiheaded beast, she says. We may vacillate from being angry at the world or universe or God for supposedly causing the grief.

We may feel angry at ourselves for things we did or didn't say or do. We may feel angry at the person who is gone, blaming him or her for the pain and confusion that we are feeling. And then we may feel angry and guilty for feeling that or any of the above.

Men best express and dissipate anger by taking physical action, says John Gray, Ph.D., author of *Men Are from Mars, Women Are from Venus* and other books. Work out anger physically, but in a productive manner, he advises. Jog, lift weights, build a house or chop wood.

"I know one fellow who went out and chopped wood and got all his winter's wood chopped in July because that's what he needed to do following the death of his son. He needed to physically work and chop and chop and chop until he was physically exhausted," says Fitzgerald.

Digging Up Old Bones

You can identify, confront and resolve long-buried, incomplete grief experiences, says James. It's not a finger-snap process. It takes time and a willingness to survey your life and locate, stir up and probe delicate, sometimes-painful memories and their effect on later actions.

In addition, you must have a desire to recover from those feelings of loss and emptiness. James and Frank Cherry offer a step-by-step process that has been followed by thousands of people. You can find their instructions in *The Grief Recovery Handbook*. If you can't find the book at a library or bookstore, write or call the Grief Recovery Institute, 8306 Wilshire Blvd. #21-A, Los Angeles, CA 90211, (213) 650-1234.

Part Four

Beating
Work-Related Stress

Managing Your Boss

How to Succeed in Business

A boss is life's greatest occupational hazard, and, until you hit the lottery, you'll probably always have one. Normally, this isn't too bad. Bosses are a necessary but tolerable evil.

What happens when the boss becomes an ogre? Or when the boss has office myopia when what's really needed is a global view? Suddenly, having a boss isn't just one of life's nuisances. It's an incredible source of stress.

"Job stress is far and away the leading cause of stress for American adults, and it's getting worse all the time," says Paul J. Rosch, M.D., president of the American Institute of Stress in Yonkers, New York, and clinical professor of medicine and psychiatry at New York Medical College in Valhalla. "One of the components of this rampant work stress is dealing with a troublesome boss."

Fortunately, Dr. Rosch adds, "there are as many ways to deal with this stress as there are different types of stressful bosses."

Who's the Boss?

Our experts have identified three common types of problem managers and have come up with suggestions for how to deal with them. See if one of these sounds familiar.

The Tyrant

Comic Sid Caesar once told a story about an office boy who was fired because he prayed for a raise. "I won't have anybody go over my head," the boss roared. That's the tyrant boss.

"The most stressful part is that these bulldozer types always think that they're right," says Elizabeth C. Johnson, co-owner of the Johnson Group, a management consulting firm in Yorktown, Virginia. Here's how to cope.

Remember your role. Commonsense egalitarianism says that we all have an equal right to an opinion, but for tyrants, the only opinion that counts is their own. That doesn't mean that your opinion won't necessarily be valued—it just has to be presented in the right way, Johnson says.

"As a tyrant boss, it's no fun to lead a parade if everyone goes in their own direction," she says. "You have to make sure that you come across as a team player, even if you disagree. The tyrant wants to make sure that everyone's working together."

Always be direct. While less aggressive bosses might respect diplomacy and tact, tyrant bosses value directness. So make everything crystal clear. If you want an audience with His Majesty, make an appointment—don't drop in. Schedule an exact time and specify your agenda by saying something like, "I'd like to talk to you about the third-quarter reports. Is 3:00 P.M. good?" Don't beat around the bush.

Don't despair. "If you have a jerk for a boss, there's little that you can do to keep your adrenal gland from going off regularly, but the real issue is how to cope," says Jim Laird, Ph.D., professor of psychology at Clark University in Worcester, Massachusetts, who studies emotions and stress.

"If you're constantly exposed to this type of stress, you might think that there's nothing you can do," Dr. Laird says. "But there's always a choice. Ultimately, you can leave your job. Or you can do a rational assessment of your life and maybe realize that your boss is worth putting up with for the money."

The Nitpicker

Nitpickers are never happy. But you can learn to appease without losing face.

Be fair. Play devil's advocate. Are your boss's criticisms on target? Ask a close friend or confidant to review your work to give you a reliable second opinion. Your boss could be going overboard with criticism, or you could be a little hypersensitive. Find out which it is.

Play dumb. Instead of getting all riled up over the next critique, pretend that you don't understand and say, "Now let me understand this. You think option B is better?" This makes you look open-minded. Plus, it leaves no room for nitpickers to weasel out of taking blame should their plan fail, because you've made it clear that you're both on the same page.

Pick your battles. You can lose a battle and still win the war. Arguing every point will brand you a troublemaker. Pick your real arguments wisely and make sure that you have plenty of ammo to back you up when you do choose to pipe up.

The Milquetoast

Milquetoast bosses are office invertebrates. Reporting to one can be exasperating for people who aren't wishy-washy. Here's how to make your styles blend.

Get specific. "Always pin down an indecisive boss," Johnson says. "You can still be assertive and savvy at the same time."

Don't be afraid to take the lead. But always do so with aplomb and diplomacy. Having to rely on Mr. Indecisive could make you look bad if it busts your deadline or makes you look like you're working slower than you should. If you have the leeway, push forward on a project with your boss's blessings. Just make sure that you remember the golden rule and be a team player. Otherwise, your initiative might be misinterpreted as mutiny.

The Danger of Anger

Unresolved anger at work, thanks to a boss who pushes your buttons, can be a runaway elevator that takes you straight down the corporate tower and into the mail room.

"Mismanagement of anger is the number one reason why fast-trackers get derailed," says psychologist Hendrie Weisinger, Ph.D., business professor at the University of California, Los Angeles, and New York University in New York City and author of *Anger at Work*.

Dr. Weisinger offers these tips on dealing with anger.

Don't read minds. When you're angry, all sorts of things pop into your head. That's because anger makes you irrational. So before you publicly accuse the boss of trying to sabotage your career by tabling your agenda item, view the facts objectively. What do you really know about the situation, and what are you assuming? Knowing the difference helps you respond appropriately.

Be a problem solver. View what's making you angry as a problem in need of a solution, not a personal affront in need of retribution. "Successful problem solvers manage themselves so that they do not respond automatically and inappropriately to problems," Dr. Weisinger says.

React—don't overreact. You spent six months working night and day to put the proposal together, and your boss didn't even look at it when you handed it to him. Now you're ready to blow a gasket. Before you pop your internal tubing, slowly take a few deep—very deep—breaths and collect yourself. Consciously slow yourself down when you feel your ears getting hot and your breathing rise.

Being More Assertive

Stand Up for Yourself

Sometimes, when stress gets really bad, you may find yourself wishing you were free as a bird, able to just fly away from it all. But if you indulge in such a fantasy, make sure that you don't imagine yourself a magpie in Andalusia, Spain. Otherwise, you'll have two more things to worry about: low self-esteem and organized crime.

Ecologists have discovered that great-spotted cuckoos are strong-arming magpies in Andalusia in what's been described as a Mafia-style protection racket. It seems that the cuckoos there aren't so cuckoo after all. They lay their eggs in a magpie nest, and, if anything should happen to their young, they come back and peck the magpie chicks to death.

It sounds like the plot of a Heckle and Jeckle cartoon directed by Martin Scorsese. But it's real life. If only those magpies would learn how to stand up for themselves and be assertive, they wouldn't have to worry about being bulldozed by some birdbrained bully. While we're packing our bags to teach those cuckoos a thing or two, we'll share with you some advice on assertiveness so that you don't go cuckoo over the stress in your life.

Power Plays

Experts say that the link between assertiveness and stress is rooted in the hierarchy of power that exists in nearly everything we do. This balance of power, for example, was clearly defined when we were children. We accepted virtually without question that adults were in charge and we were not. (At least until puberty.) But as adults, things aren't so clear. At home, you may be the boss, but at work you might be the lowest man on the totem pole. A doctor might be king in his office, but he's unnerved explaining his car's symptoms to a mechanic. At work, your manager might be ineffectual, but he's still the guy doing your annual review.

In the daily meanderings through these power structures, stress grows as we feel like we've lost control. Or worse, when we feel like we've never had control.

"A lot of people who have not developed assertiveness skills feel victimized by just about everything," says Elizabeth C. Johnson of the Johnson Group. "People feel like they're not authorized to stand up for themselves. That they're powerless to change anything."

Assertiveness initially was described as a personality trait that you either had or didn't have. The concept was coined by researcher Andrew Salter in the late 1940s. Today, experts believe that assertiveness is a skill that lets you claim your own rights without denying the rights of others. And it shouldn't be confused with aggression. "Aggression is standing up for yourself without caring about someone else," Johnson says.

In the workplace, assertiveness is a crucial skill to master. People who assert themselves without bulldozing others are more likely to build healthier relationships at work and at home, says Clark University's Dr. Jim Laird. Here's how to flex your assertive muscles without muscling others out of the picture.

Speak out. Know that it's okay to assert yourself, your values, your thoughts, your opinions and your beliefs. It doesn't matter if you're dealing with a weaselly mechanic or an ineffectual boss. If you assert yourself fairly—that is, without suppressing the other guy's right to assert himself—it doesn't mean

The Bill of Rights

Here's a guide to help you figure out your rights as an assertive guy. This list comes from *The Relaxation and Stress Reduction Workbook*, by Martha Davis, Ph.D., psychology professor in the Department of Psychiatry at Kaiser Permanente Medical Center in Santa Clara, California, and other experts.

Nonassertive Traditional View	Your Assertive Right
It's selfish to put your needs before others' needs.	You have a right to put yourself first sometimes.
If you can't convince others that your feelings are reasonable, then you must be wrong or maybe you're going crazy.	You have a right to be the final judge of your feelings and accept them as legitimate.
Respect the views of others, especially those in authority. Keep your differences to yourself. Listen and learn.	You have a right to have your own opinions and convictions.
You should always try to be logical and consistent.	You have a right to change your mind or decide on a different course of action.
You shouldn't take up others' valuable time with your complaints.	You have a right to ask for help or emotional support.
People don't want to hear you complaining, so keep it to yourself.	You have a right to express your feelings and pains.

that you're manipulative or domineering. "In fact, the payoff is that you feel better about yourself," Johnson says. "You feel like you're living up to your potential and that you're not a victim to someone else."

Make it a work in progress.
Becoming assertive doesn't happen overnight, and it's not a good idea to rush when you're learning a new interpersonal skill, says Dr. Laird, who's an expert in emotions and how they affect us. Go slow and work on being assertive one day at a time. Start by identifying good opportunities to be assertive. Then put the skills below to action.

Learn to say "no." This is hard to do, especially when you're competitive and hard-driving by nature. But saying "no" might be the best way to improve your productivity. "Trying to be perfect is a recipe for disaster," says business consultant Paulette Ensign, president of the National Association of Professional Organizers in Austin, Texas, and owner of Organizing Solutions, a consulting firm in Bedford Hills, New

York. Think about that the next time you're asked to organize the company Pencil Sharpening Olympics. Then assert yourself and politely decline.

Be an "I" guy. Say Ralph in research and development is wheedling you again to take on the Pencil Sharpening games. Express yourself in "I" terms. Don't couch your replies neutrally with, "It's not for me, Ralph." Start with "I," as in, "I don't have time right now."

Be fluent in assertive body language. More than half of all human communication is nonverbal. That means that your lips might be saying one thing but your eyes could be saying another—and so could your back, shoulders, feet, hands and head. When talking to someone, concentrate on the basics of assertive body language. Maintain good eye contact and an erect posture, deliver smooth hand gestures to complement your message and avoid extraneous movements, like foot tapping, hand jiggling, blinking or swaying.

Taking the "Dead" Out of Deadlines

Trade Stress for Success

Paulette Ensign of the National Association of Professional Organizers and of Organizing Solutions has a mission: "I am on a personal campaign to change the word *deadline* to *due date*," she says.

While noble, Ensign's work won't be easy. She faces staunch resistance from a phlegmatic corporate America that believes deadlines are the foundation of time management. And while the word *deadline* is quite young etymologically (see "Who Put the 'Dead' in Deadline?"), the concept is as old as time.

"Deadlines—getting something done by a certain time—have been around forever," says Ensign. "Unfortunately, deadline means death. Finished. *Finito*. Kaput. The end. Over. In reality, a deadline is usually a beginning. It's when a project ends one phase and enters another. It's a birth of sorts."

Beat the Clock

Coping with deadlines often gives birth to its own creation: the demon child we call stress.

"I see this in reporters a lot. They're constantly working under deadlines," says Dr. Paul J. Rosch of the American Institute of Stress and New York Medical College. Unchecked, this stress can be a huge source of internal angst, Dr. Rosch says, because "if your deadline is unrea-

sonable or if you're not on top of it, you feel like you have very little control over the finished product."

Compounding deadline stress is the notion of time itself. Without getting all New Agey and metaphysical, suffice it to say that time is a man-made concept that we interpret differently. Larry Dossey, M.D., an internist in Santa Fe, New Mexico, and author of *Meaning and Medicine*, has diagnosed "hurry sickness" in stressed-out executives by asking them to sit quietly and guess when one minute has passed. The Bundle of Nerves award goes to one executive who stopped the clock at just nine seconds.

Time for a Change

Erasing deadline stress can be easy with the right attitude and some sound time-management techniques. Here's how.

Take the one-minute test. Take Dr. Dossey's one-minute test, but remember that it isn't golf—the lowest score doesn't win. The point is to gauge how accurate your notion of time is and how high your stress levels are. Don't cheat by counting seconds in your brain—just relax and guess when you think a minute is up. If you're overstressed, you'll feel that time is passing too quickly. You might even beat that nine-second record. Take this test once in a while to gauge your perception of time and to assess the stress that you're under.

Use the three-strikes rule. Let's say that you're working on a five-year strategic plan for your boss. And you're more than a little stressed because your deadline is approaching and you still haven't made it through June of the first year. If you've put the project on your to-do list three times but never seem to get to it, hit the brakes.

"If I've transferred something to my to-do list three times and haven't done it, I stop and ask myself what the real problem is," Ensign says. "Sometimes you're afraid of the project, aren't prepared or aren't enjoying it. By recognizing what's going on in your head, you'll find the real reason why you're not getting work done, and you'll be able to get back on track."

Take a deadline vacation. Humorist Gene Perret has won three Emmy Awards as a comedy writer for *The Carol Burnett Show* and also has written material for Bob Hope, *The Bill Cosby Show* and *Welcome Back, Kotter*. When Perret got creatively constipated writing gags on deadline, he'd simply stop trying.

"Our answer always was, 'Let's go to lunch,'" Perret says. "We'd go for a walk, have a drink or two or just get goofy. You have to break the chain of stress, or else you can't produce. That's what writer's block is."

Make more deadlines. It sounds oxymoronic, but by breaking a deadline into manageable sub-deadlines, you'll make life easier, says Elizabeth C. Johnson of the Johnson Group. "It's like setting goals. You wouldn't realistically think that you'd become a millionaire without saving 1,000 bucks first, would you?" Johnson asks. "You have to work at deadlines a little at a time instead of getting overwhelmed by the big picture."

Do not disturb. Guard against interruptions by scheduling blocks of time dedicated solely to the matter at hand. Hold your calls. Don't accept visitors. Turn off the TV or radio. Instead, schedule these things as you would an appointment. For example, do phone work all in one block or take visitors only at a certain hour. If you do get interrupted—say, a phone call sneaks through—deal with it in a controlled rush and cut it short. Simply say, "Gee, sorry. I'm incredibly busy now. Let me call you back at 3:00."

Who Put the "Dead" in Deadline?

Some questions beg to be asked. Like who put the "dead" in deadline? And why is the word *deadline* so . . . morbid? For starters, if *deadline* weren't so ominous-sounding, we'd probably never get anything done on time. Imagine your boss screaming at you that your please-try-to-get-this-done-if-it's-not-too-much-trouble line was Friday. Not quite the same. It turns out that there's a logical explanation for management's favorite word. It dates back to the bloody Civil War.

According to Graham Donaldson and Sue Setterfield, who cataloged the etymology of *deadline* and other idioms in their book *Why Do We Say That?*, the word *deadline* comes from a prisoner-of-war camp in Andersonville, Georgia, in the 1860s. The camp had become so crowded that a line was drawn in the dirt around a wire fence holding prisoners. Any captive who crossed the line was shot dead. No questions asked. No "Freeze." No "Halt, or I'll shoot."

And you thought your deadline was tough.

Work smart. Looking to squeeze in some extra hours during that crunch time? Try waking an hour earlier in the morning. Or get work done at home with a laptop computer. Finish paperwork on your morning and afternoon commute—provided you're on a bus or train, not behind the wheel—or during business travel. Ask about flextime at work to make the most of your productive hours. Instead of working 9:00 A.M. to 5:00 P.M., try 7:00 A.M. to 3:00 P.M. if that's your most productive peak. Cut out TV and other time wasters. This nickel-and-diming strategy isn't good in the long term because it's robbing you of well-deserved downtime. But it's handy in meeting short-term goals so that you can breathe easier later.

Working Well with Others

How to Avoid Office Conflicts

Maybe it's Seymour, the ambitious back-stabber in marketing who took credit for that brilliant campaign you devised last year and was promoted for it. Or Rita the receptionist, who's so perky that you suspect that she mainlines amphetamines with her cereal. Or Sam, the slug who devotes all his energy each day to figuring out ways to get others to do his work for him.

Work is a colorful conglomeration of human beings. Although there are some people that we truly befriend, admire and respect, it's a safe bet that there's at least one person you see every day at work who really gets on your nerves. Dealing with these folks is enough to drive you into stress overload. So learning how to resolve conflicts with co-workers—whether it's over a specific incident or just a personality clash—is essential to lessening your workplace stress.

"When you don't know how to handle people, it puts you under tremendous stress, and when you walk around with hostility because of this, it's not good for your health," says Elizabeth C. Johnson of the Johnson Group.

But you don't have to be a walking time bomb at work. "There are some universal people skills that you can use in almost any social setting that are invaluable in dealing with others," Johnson adds. Including Seymour, Rita and Sam.

Getting Along

You don't need to be a psychologist, journalist or professional speaker to learn good people skills. Anyone can do it, and the payoff is worthwhile. Good communication makes you more effective personally and professionally, and it relieves stress by reducing the chance that you'll be misunderstood. "It also builds your credibility and power base at work," Johnson says.

It may even keep you out of court. A group of attorneys surveyed in 1994 responded that more than 80 percent of the lawsuits filed by patients against doctors resulted from miscommunication. Patients felt that their physicians were condescending or insensitive or that they both simply failed to understand each other.

"I gave a lecture in South Africa once called Negotiating with the Soviet Union and with Your Spouse—Is There a Difference?" recalls Roger Fisher, L.H.D., emeritus law professor at Harvard Law School, director of the Harvard Negotiation Project and author of numerous books on international law, negotiations and conflict resolution. "The answer is, not as much as you think. They both boil down to good communication."

Here's how to hone your people skills to stop stress from sapping your relationships at work.

Deal with it. So the new work assignments are handed down, and, much to your dismay, you're now teamed with that back-stabber Seymour on an important project for the next six months. Lost cause? Not necessarily.

"Because human behavior tends to be predictable and consistent for most people, the

sad truth is that if you had trouble with this person before, chances are that you'll have trouble again," Johnson says. "But that doesn't mean that your project is doomed.

"What you want to do is limit extraneous contact with that person. Limit your interaction strictly to the task at hand," she says. "A strategic way to do this diplomatically is to ask the other guy what parts of the project he wants to handle or how he would like to go about it.

"This way," Johnson says, "you're affirming his rights and making him feel good. It's a nice way of putting you both on equal footing and showing that you're willing to overlook your differences and support him for the cause."

Loosen up already. Try a little levity. "Humor doesn't take away from your strength. It's the biggest management tool that you're never taught," says humorist Gene Perret, Bob Hope's lead joke writer who started his comedy career giving retirement roasts at General Electric. "Humor makes for a good working atmosphere, which is nice, since most people on the clock won't let a smile cross their face."

Put yourself in the other guy's shoes. You can assume that people are jerks and that's why they act like they do, or you can take a moment to see what's really going on. This approach works exceedingly well for Lieutenant Hugh McGowan, chief hostage negotiator for the New York City Police Department. "We used to call the people I deal with psychos, but we try not to do that anymore because labeling is derogatory," Lt. McGowan says. "Understanding someone's feelings and why they're doing what they're doing is much more effective than labeling someone."

While that might not make up for the ethical shortcomings of Seymour stealing your idea, knowing that he was on the verge of bankruptcy and was being considered for termination might not make his taking your idea look so horrible when you know his motivation.

Uphold dignity. Another effective communication strategy of Lt. McGowan's is the importance of preserving the other guy's dignity. This works well on the street and in the office.

"It's really common sense. To establish good rapport with someone, you need to respect their self-esteem, their self-worth," he says. "For me, for example, I need to convince a suspect that we're not going to drag him out and treat him like an animal. I need to convince him that he should come out and discuss his problem with dignity. The only way that I can do this is to acknowledge and respect his sense of self."

Do your homework. You need credibility to work well with others. The most important thing that you can do to build your credibility is to do your homework and know what you're talking about. If you don't know something, admit it. Don't fake it. Knowing the facts allows you to justify your opinions emotionally, logically and intelligently. Doing this consistently lets people know that you're a man of integrity.

Don't act on impulse. Smedley, that snide self-aggrandizer in accounting, was promoted to a position that you rightfully earned. When the announcement is made, you storm into his office and blow your top, calling him every name in the book. You momentarily feel better—until you realize that you now report directly to Smedley and that he holds your career in his sweaty palms. Next time, try thinking first—not later.

"It's easy to give in to emotional impulses, especially when you're angry. But once you recognize your emotions, use self-control," says Clark University's Dr. Jim Laird. "When animals get mad, they fight. We can think about our reactions without acting on them."

Before you do or say something volatile, give yourself an hour to cool off. Do breathing exercises to lower your stress and relax. Don't speak out of anger, fear or jealousy. It just undermines your credibility and kills effective communication.

Keep secrets carefully. Office secrets are as common as paper clips, but superfluous ones extract a huge mental and emotional toll. "Habitual secrecy is an unrecognized cause of havoc in the business setting," writes Gerald Goodman, Ph.D., in *The Talk Book*. "Remembering what not to say costs energy and increases stress." If it's not truly important, don't lock your lips.

Getting What You Want

Win by Word of Mouth

What do booking a hotel room, buying a microwave oven and ordering a bottle of Chardonnay have in common? They're all excellent opportunities to negotiate.

"But, unfortunately, in America, we're afraid to negotiate. We think it's inappropriate, except for big-ticket items, like a house, a car or a new job," says international negotiating expert Roger Dawson, of La Habra Heights, California, professional lecturer, business consultant and author of *Roger Dawson's Secrets of Power Negotiating*.

Because we're so unaccustomed to negotiating in general, we seldom do it well when it really matters. As a result, when high stakes are riding on the outcome, stress levels soar. In reality, we negotiate every day in thousands of innocuous ways, from deciding what movie to watch with our spouses to presenting our ideas at work. Things just seem worse when a car, house or promotion is on the line.

"Negotiating, by definition, is the management of conflict," Dawson says. "If you aren't prepared to deal with it properly, it can be immensely stressful."

The Art of the Deal

If you're not managing your conflicts well, don't despair. Here are some tips to help you negotiate life more smoothly.

Fear no encounter.
Like we said, successful negotiating means realizing that there's nothing to be afraid of. This has to do with assertiveness. "People think that

assertiveness is bad, that it's being pushy or showing off," says Bonnie Jacobson, Ph.D., director of the Institute for Psychological Change in New York City. "It's not. It's sticking up for yourself. Expressing your needs."

Practice. Because negotiating doesn't come naturally, force yourself to practice when it doesn't matter so that you're confident when the stakes are high, Dawson says. Booking a hotel room? Ask for a discount—a reduced rate is better than a vacant room, isn't it? You get the idea.

Be clear. Clear, concise communication is critical in all negotiations. While there are verbal gymnastics that you can use, none is effective if your message is muddled. "In each and every case, you want to understand and be understood," says Dr. Roger Fisher of Harvard Law School and of the Harvard Negotiation Project. "Taking the stress out of conflicts like negotiations boils down, at some point, to just talking about your problems."

Know the psychological landscape.
"Everyone has a different personality style, and knowing about these styles can spell the difference between a deal and a deadlock," Dr. Jacobson says.

Be prepared. You might have skimmed through college without ever lifting a pencil, but you'll never get an A in negotiating without doing your homework. Before you step into the conference room, know everything that you possibly can about your opponent, his position, his options, your request, your options, what issues you're willing to concede and where you're going to draw the line. "People can tell when you've done your homework by your demeanor. If you've prepared, you'll feel and appear more confident," Dawson says.

Take time. Time is the enemy of successful negotiations, and the side with time to spare has enormous leverage. "The pressure of time in a negotiation causes stress. Postpone making a commitment whenever you can so that you can 'give it careful consideration,' " Dr. Fisher advises. The reason is twofold: It prevents you from answering rashly, and the other side will hear time ticking away.

Avoid committing first. Don't pin yourself down by committing to a bargaining position first. It narrows your options. Get the other side to state their position first. If you must commit first, hedge your bets by using the "appeal-to-higher-authority" defense. Tell the other side that your proposal is tentative and subject to the approval of your spouse, lawyer or accountant.

Ask for the moon—and the stars. This strategy is so old that you probably think that no one falls for it anymore. Not true. Asking for more than what you want gives you options to toy with, Dr. Fisher says. Every time you concede an option, make a stink and ask for a counter-concession. Asking for more up front gives you more wiggle room.

Stand your ground. Don't negotiate over the phone. Talk in your office, if you can. Being face-to-face, while more intimidating, allows you to watch facial expressions and body language carefully. Being in your office or home gives you the home-field advantage by placing the other side in a subordinate position.

Don't take it personally. Always be ready to walk away. Negotiations are professional, not personal. "Protect yourself from becoming too emotional," Dr. Fisher says. His advice is if the other side is angry, don't return fire. Rather, tell them that they appear upset and that you strongly believe that becoming emotional might impede your progress. If you become angry, ask to take a ten-minute break. Then do some deep breathing and calm down, Dr. Fisher says. Visu-alize your anger dissipating with each breath. Remember that once you become emotionally involved, your judgment is impaired. Keeping calm is the key to success. (For more tips on anger, see Overcoming Anger on page 24.)

Negotiating a Pay Raise

Asking for a raise is the toughest negotiation that the average guy ever tackles. It's you and the boss, *mano a mano*, and the issue is cold, hard cash. Instead of turning yellow or seeing red, get green—in your wallet.

Do one thing well. Before you ever foresee the need to ask for a raise, distinguish yourself on the job in at least one thing. Do your job better than anyone else, be the morale booster, be the problem solver or be the idea guy. "It doesn't have to be something major—just something the boss recognizes so that he realizes how hard you are to replace," says international negotiating expert Roger Dawson.

Role-play. Rehearse asking for a raise with a friend. Present your case clearly, concisely and quickly, and have your friend pretend to be the boss, Dawson says. Together, you can brainstorm most of your boss's typical reactions and prepare in advance.

Bide your time. Don't ask for an answer pronto, advises Dr. Roger Fisher of Harvard Law School and of the Harvard Negotiation Project. Tell the boss that you're simply sharing with him your feelings and that you're not expecting an answer right away. When you do this, he knows that the clock is ticking on your employment. He also knows that you could have résumés in circulation and another job on the line. By not demanding an answer right away, you're putting the onus of time on him. Plus, you're giving him time to sweat—and to loosen the purse strings. Follow up your talk in a week.

Steering Clear of Sexual Harassment

What You Need to Know

It's Friday morning, and you're in a great mood. Another eight hours and the weekend is finally here. As you stride to your office, you pass that attractive brunette who works in marketing.

You flash her your most engaging smile and say, "Good morning, Sue. You look nice today. That's a very attractive sweater you're wearing."

Sue flushes and glares at you, then stalks away, thinking, "What a pig. It's obvious what he has on his mind."

Meanwhile, you're left wondering, "What's with her?" After all, you were just trying to be friendly. Maybe with just a touch of innocent flirtation. But since when did that become a crime?

Welcome to the 1990s, where negotiating the sexual politics of the office can be as treacherous as a walk through a minefield and just as stressful. While it's contemptuous to think that a woman—maybe your wife or girlfriend—should endure some oaf's overtures at work, it's equally appalling that genteel men like yourself should live in fear of being friendly.

"In my experience as a labor lawyer, I have not come across anything as harmful as a sexual harassment allegation," says Frank Harty, a sexual harassment lawyer in Des Moines, Iowa. "It can be career-ending for both the accuser and the accused."

Law and Order

Sexual harassment charges filed with the federal government's Equal Employment Opportunity Commission (EEOC) skyrocketed from 6,127 complaints in 1990 to 15,545 in 1995. And the amount of monetary benefits that employers have had to shell out annually to victims during that period rose from $7.7 million to $24.3 million. The tide of complaints isn't likely to ebb, especially since women are making up larger chunks of the workforce. One study found that the number of women executives in the marketing industry alone rose from 19 percent in 1990 to 30 percent in 1994.

"In some ways you'd think that there'd be less complaints today, since we're supposed to be more politically correct," says Elaine Herskowitz, a senior attorney at the EEOC in Washington, D.C. "But, unfortunately, the problem is getting worse. We can't say for sure why, but it could be that people are becoming better informed as to what their rights are.

"While sexual harassment complaints put respectful men in an awkward position, hopefully men, in general, don't exaggerate the perils that they face, because the truth of the matter is that they shouldn't have problems as long they treat women the way they themselves would want to be treated," Herskowitz says.

Sexual harassment laws as we know them are rooted in Title VII of the Civil Rights Act of 1964. The act bans discrimination in hiring and employment on the basis of race, creed, sex, religion or ethnic origin. The sex part has been defined by the EEOC and subsequent law as anything that creates "a hostile environment" and any sexual advance occurring on a quid pro quo, or "something-for-something," basis.

Simply put, linking a person's career in any way with sexual favors is illegal. "Basically, this is where a supervisor says or implies,

'Sleep with me, or you're fired,' " Herskowitz says.

The concept of hostile environment is more nebulous. It's defined as when sexual advances, requests for sexual favors or similar actions unreasonably interfere with a person's work performance or create an intimidating or offensive working environment. It's the more common type of harassment charge filed these days. The case of the boss who fired a female employee for not playing strip poker, for example, would fit both definitions. (She, by the way, collected $1 million. His insurance company refused to cover intentional harassment.)

Sexual harassment isn't always so overt, especially when it involves a hostile environment. According to the American Medical Women's Association, numerous studies show that female physicians, medical students and residents repeatedly bump up against "a lack of gender fairness." A 1994 study found that sexual harassment affects 42 percent of women and 15 percent of men in occupational settings and 73 percent of women and 22 percent of men in medical settings. Just 1 percent to 7 percent file complaints, though more than 90 percent suffer mental and physical symptoms from the abuse.

Avoiding Trouble

While harassment charges could seem like a nightmare to any gainfully employed man, there's nothing to get stressed out about. If you keep your nose clean and treat people the way that you want to be treated, you shouldn't run into trouble. But just to be safe, here are some things that you should know.

Be informed. Understanding the law goes a long way toward keeping you out of trouble. Reread the section of this chapter that discusses the legal definitions of sexual harassment and hostile working environments and commit them to memory. For more information, contact the local EEOC office near you. They should be in the phone book under the "U.S. Government" listing.

Watch the wisecracks. Asking her to sit on the photocopier might be a joke to you, but she won't think that it was funny. Neither will a judge. So avoid sexual humor at work. There are plenty of other things to make fun of—at least until they ban bosses.

Confine compliments. Telling a female co-worker that she has drop-dead gorgeous legs might be a compliment, but it's inappropriate at work. If you wouldn't compliment a man that way, don't say it to a woman.

Don't be hostile. To avoid a hostile work environment, don't hang pictures of scantily clad women on office walls or engage in "boy talk" in the hallway. If you're the boss, make sure that everyone else does the same.

Hands off. Juries take touching very seriously. If it's more than a handshake, don't do it. Restrict backslapping to the verbal kind.

Watch customers. Hostile environment includes nonemployees. That means customers and clients, too. "A hostile environment can come from anyone. The difficult thing is figuring out when the employer is responsible for a nonemployee's conduct," Herskowitz says. Nevertheless, if your female employees are complaining about harassment from a customer or client, take their complaints seriously and do something about it.

Put it in writing. What if you're on the receiving end of sexual harassment? "Although women make up 90 percent of the official complaints, men do get harassed, and we take those complaints just as seriously," says Herskowitz.

Sometimes it's helpful to confront your harasser openly, candidly and nonthreateningly, says Herskowitz. Her advice is to write the person a memo and send it return receipt on e-mail, or return receipt via the U.S. Postal Service. This tells your harasser to back off. More important, it establishes a paper trail to substantiate your case. Which is handy, should you need to prove the harassment was ongoing and unwanted—two crucial ingredients to a successful prosecution.

Making Your Workspace Work

Be an Office Environmentalist

Your first peek into that alien place called the working world was actually the classroom. You didn't know it at the time, but when you backed your Toughskins-clad rear end into that tiny orange chair in kindergarten, you were really sitting in the teacher's office. Sure, it wasn't much as offices go. Her desk was messy, the carpet was cheap and she was surrounded by the Alphabet people and five-year-olds. Not exactly your typical corporate power center.

Now that you're grown up, you've probably seen and worked in many different places—some better, some worse than a kindergarten classroom. Working environments vary. Not everyone lands the corner office with the mahogany desk, wet bar and leather couch. But one thing that all workplaces share is that they can make you pretty miserable if you don't feel at home in the one place where you probably spend more time than home.

Schoolteachers may not be able to do much about the Alphabet people or five-year-olds, but they do brighten things up by placing apples or houseplants on their desks. You, too, can take liberties with your personal space, whether it's an office suite or a closet with a lightbulb and desk calendar. More important, sprucing up your workplace chips away chronic stress that you may never have known existed.

"The workplace can be insidiously stressing. Our office, for example, has a lot of paperwork to push and deadlines to meet; it's probably no better

than a newspaper office," says Roger C. Anderson, Ed.D., business consultant, lecturer and—in his spare time—president of Adirondack Community College in Queensbury, New York.

"When you're busy, your working environment matters that much more," adds Dr. Anderson, author of *Some Days You're the Pigeon, Some Days You're the Statue.*

Making Yourself at Home

Here's how to make your work environment less stressful.

Picture this. If you haven't already, decorate your work area with pictures, and among the snapshots of family, friends and vacations, include some postcard-style nature scenes. "There's a long chain of evidence that shows direct relaxation reactions to nature pictures—looking at them lowers your stress response," says psychiatrist Aaron Katcher, M.D., a pioneer of studies linking pets to good health and stress reduction, emeritus professor of psychiatry at the University of Pennsylvania in Philadelphia and consultant to the Devereux Foundation for animal therapy.

Buy a friend for work. Speaking of pets, think goldfish. Or, if you're really exotic, think anole, also called an American chameleon, for your desk. Office pets are great stress relievers, just like Rover is at home. Not only do they give you someone to vent to after your next budget meeting but they're also entertaining enough to keep your stress on ice, even when you should be boiling.

"I've found that having a few fish at work is very useful when taking annoying phone calls. It's very relaxing to watch fish when some colleague is yammering away," Dr. Katcher says.

Pop off. No, we're not recommending that you tell your boss off. Rather, head to your company mail room for some bubble wrap, the kind that merchandise is shipped in. (Or buy it at a United Parcel Service or wrap-and-pack store for about $5 a sheet.) Keep a sheet or two in your bottom draw and pop stress away when it's getting the best of you. A study at Western New England College in Springfield, Massachusetts, found that bursting these little bubbles banishes stress that's bubbling up inside. "Bubble popping relaxes your muscles," says Kathy M. Dillon, Ph.D., professor of psychology at the college and author of the study.

Turn on, tune in. If you can't bring a radio to the office and play it softly, buy an inexpensive personal stereo and headphones. "Relaxing by listening to music is one thing that anybody can do to make his workplace a little less stressful," says Al Bumanis, director of communications for the National Association for Music Therapy in Silver Springs, Maryland. "Putting some thought into the music you're listening to goes a long way in creating a mindset that's conducive to wellness."

Color-coordinate your mood. The color of your working environment subtly influences your mood, experts say. Red, orange and yellow, for example, have been shown to rev up our bodies. Blue, green and bubblegum pink mellow us out. Just look at the walls of your doctor's waiting room next time. If they're not a neutral white, they'll probably be soft pastel blue.

Put in a plug. Excessive noise on the job can also cause stress. And although a woman's hearing is more acute than yours, you're still susceptible to the barrage of noise that assaults your ears every day at work. In pioneering studies done on monkeys in the 1980s, doctors found that monkeys exposed to noise for extended periods—at a rate similar to what you'd expect at a construction site—had significantly higher blood pressure than monkeys who lived in low-noise conditions. Heed this monkey business by eliminating excessive noise when you're on the clock. If you work in a factory or at a construction site, wear foam earplugs—the kind you'd wear on a pistol range.

Stop On-the-Job Straining

Back injuries account for 16 percent of all workers' compensation claims. Here's how to avoid the perils of back injuries, courtesy of Malcolm H. Pope, D.M.Sc., Ph.D., of the Spinal Research Center at the University of Iowa in Iowa City, and Jeffrey Young, M.D., assistant professor of physical medicine and rehabilitation at Northwestern University Medical School in Chicago.

Call for backup. Go for contoured secretary-style chairs, which provide maximal lumbar (lower-back) support. If your chair doesn't measure up, roll a small towel up and put it in the small of your back for additional support.

Drop your drawers. Put stuff that you hardly use in the bottom filing cabinet drawers. This keeps the things that you use most up high, minimizing the risk that you'll hurt your back by continually bending over to get what you need.

Seat yourself. Adjust the height of your chair seat so that your knees are extended two to three inches over the edge and your knees form 90-degree angles when your feet are firmly on the floor. Properly positioned, you shouldn't feel your feet on the floor because the pressure should be evenly distributed over your feet, legs and butt.

Compute on the level. Place your computer monitor at eye level so that you can look directly at it without craning your neck or bunching your shoulders. With good posture and a good ergonomic setup, your head remains over your shoulders while you're working, not tilted forward or looking down.

Resolving Ethical Conflicts

Make Your Stand against Stress

The first time that the boss said something about kickback, you thought that he was telling you to slow down, sit back and put your feet up. Then you discovered that he wasn't telling you to take it easy. He was telling you to take it sleazy, and suddenly your dream of being a vice-president was flying out the window of the corner office that you coveted.

Okay, that's an extreme example, and one that you're never likely to encounter. But there are countless smaller ethical conflicts that workers face every day. And some slip by unrecognized. What if one of your co-workers asks you to punch him in on the time clock when he's going to be late for work? Does the reason make a difference? Is it okay if your buddy has to take his sick kid to the doctor but not if he's just suffering from a hangover?

What about the guy in the next office who justifies taking home office supplies on a weekly basis because the company's not really paying him enough? Or what if the boss asks you to pretend that you share a common interest with a highly prized job recruit—even though you couldn't care less about the topic? Clearly, a little angst in your ethics can be a tremendous source of stress on the job.

"The problem comes when your goals and values are not consistent or compatible with those of your employer, and it's happening more and more these days," says Dr. Paul J. Rosch of the American Institute of Stress and of New York Medical College. "Ethical considerations are a big problem in today's world."

The Theory of Relativity

Part of what makes this such a murky area is that different people have different ethical standards. Something that creates tremendous stress for one individual wouldn't even register with another.

In a study they conducted on American ethics, researchers Michael C. Kearl, Ph.D., professor of sociology at Trinity University in San Antonio, Texas, and Daniel Rigney, Ph.D., associate professor of sociology and director of the honors program at St. Mary's University, also in San Antonio, drew two significant conclusions: First, they found that 85 percent of Americans feel that ethics and morals are ambiguous. Second, they found that 67 percent of Americans feel that morals are personal and that society should not "force everyone to follow one standard."

As the saying goes, it's all relative. What's considered ethical conduct in one situation may not be viewed as ethical in another. While this sounds like a recipe for ethical anarchy, the researchers, writing in the *Journal of Social Philosophy*, encouragingly think otherwise.

"The widespread sense of moral ambiguity that prevails in the United States does not necessarily mean that Americans have abandoned all sense of right and wrong," they say. "Rather, it suggests that Americans generally recognize that moral judgments are often complex and difficult. . . . To acknowledge moral ambiguities may well be a mark of moral maturity rather than moral confusion."

Sentiments like these are critical when it comes to the stressfulness of ethical problems at work, because it acknowledges that there are no easy answers. Not everyone's going to feel the same way about the same thing. This is especially trying when one of those someones is a lowly drone like you and the other is the queen bee in charge of that comb of the corporate hive.

"It's always difficult when your values clash with your boss's or your workplace. Who's to say that you're right and they're wrong?" says consultant Elizabeth C. Johnson of the Johnson Group. Acknowledging this harsh reality is vital in dealing with your stress productively, however. The alternative—fighting your feelings—can leave you feeling stressed out and morally bankrupt.

A Working Set of Ethics

Here are some suggestions to help you stay on the high road.

Get personal. The best way to handle ethical concerns is to personalize them, Johnson says. Stating the problem in hypothetical terms—for example, "Should a person deposit company money in a personal account?"—can lead to an ambiguous answer. But if you say, "I don't feel comfortable putting company money into your account," there is little room for ambiguity, Johnson says.

Stall for time. If you're asked to do something that makes you uncomfortable, say that you need time to think about it. This does two things: It gives the appearance that you're seriously mulling the situation over, and it gives you time to reflect. If you're still not comfortable, then politely decline the next day, Johnson says. "Just say, 'You ought to leave me out of this one,'" she says. If they ask why, simply respond, "I don't feel comfortable with this."

"Sometimes just by doing that, you'll get the other person to reconsider what he's proposing. Or you might get more information that can change your mind," Johnson says.

Be assertive. Sticking to your guns is the most important thing that you can do when

---

The Value of Values

Ethical problems that conflict with your core values can cause lasting damage. "It's okay if you want to drop your values on your own—that's your decision—but don't let anyone compromise your values for you," says Elizabeth C. Johnson of the Johnson Group.

The first step in avoiding that is to focus on your values so that you know what they are. Start by listing 20 things that are important to you—fundamentally important and at the core of your being. For example, your list might include "honesty, to be loved, family support and financial success." Now choose a half-dozen of these that seem most important, and concisely describe them in one paragraph. For example, your definition of financial success might be to make enough money to pay the bills so that you can spend quality time with your friends and family. Or it might be to be a millionaire by age 40 so that you can retire early.

Such self-introspection is critical for personal growth. Once you've identified the most important values in your life, you'll know where you stand when your ethical framework is being rocked at work.

---

you feel an ethical migraine coming on. If you're weak in this area, brush up on assertiveness skills (for more information, see Being More Assertive on page 108).

Be realistic. Recognize that some ethical problems these days are the result of companies making unreasonable demands on employees. "Employers are more interested in quantity work than quality work," Dr. Rosch says. "Companies count your keystrokes but don't care how many mistakes you make. They monitor the number of customer service calls you handle but don't care if you got the problem taken care of."

Keeping Up with Technology

Merge onto the Information Superhighway

For years, you managed to do your job just fine with only a typewriter, telephone and adding machine on your desk. Now, the work tools that you used most of your life are viewed as relics fit only for the Smithsonian Institution. And you're beginning to feel like your fate is to be stuffed as part of the exhibit titled "Primitive American Worker, Circa 1970s." Just pray that they don't dress you in a leisure suit.

Or perhaps you've merged successfully into the fast lane of the Information Superhighway. The only problem is that you're finding it nearly impossible to keep up with the traffic around you. Just when you think that you know everything you need to about the latest technology, it's no longer the latest technology.

We live in an age of previously unfathomable technological change. And stress is all about how we cope with change. If you're having trouble coping with the dizzying pace of the technological revolution, you're likely feeling a lot of stress.

"Technostress at work can be devastating," says Dr. Martha Davis of the Kaiser Permanente Medical Center. "For the middle-age man, it can be especially difficult, because younger people are seen as better because they're more technologically savvy," she says. "If you're older, unless you're reasonably intelligent and can stay on top, it's used against you."

Adapting to the Computer Age

A birthday card that plays a tinny, annoying version of "Happy Birthday" holds more computer power than any corporation had before 1950. That's how far and how fast technology has evolved in the last half of the twentieth century.

And keeping up hasn't been easy. Just look at the growth of the Internet, the world's largest computer network. Similar technological explosions throughout the telecommunications industry have radically changed the way that many companies do business. "Job stress is getting worse all the time, especially because of the way that workplace technology is advancing," says Dr. Paul J. Rosch of the American Institute of Stress and of New York Medical College.

But dealing with the stress of technology can be easier than many other forms of stress, because the antidotes in most cases—positive mental attitude and education—are within your grasp. Here's how to cure what ails you if things just aren't computing.

Read widely. Take an active interest in technology instead of shunning it, suggests Elizabeth C. Johnson of the Johnson Group. Start by reading. Head to a local newsstand and pick up a few computer magazines. Or buy some industry magazines and pay close attention to the technology departments and features. Another option is to go to a local library some Saturday morning, especially a large municipal or university library, and simply browse. Make a list of what's available and what interests you. The next Saturday, spend more time studying the topics in detail and check out some books to read in your spare time at home.

Make allies. You'll only magnify your stress if you're hostile to the younger guys in the office, who seem to have been born with a joystick in their hands. It's not their fault that they grew up with computers. You're better-off aligning yourself with them in a symbiotic relationship. They can show you the ins and outs of the technology that you need to know, and you can be a mentor for them in their career development.

Take the pressure off. Don't feel like you have to know it all. In fact, it's impossible to know it all. "Once you accept this, it takes a lot of pressure off your shoulders," says Ann McGee-Cooper, Ed.D., international creativity consultant, lecturer and author of several books, including *You Don't Have to Go Home from Work Exhausted!* and *Building Brain Power.*

"No doubt, technology can cause stress," Dr. Davis says. "But you always need to remember that technology is your friend, not a prison warden.

Go back to school. Sure, experience means a lot, but you won't get ahead if you're still using that old Royal typewriter while everyone else is zipping along on the latest version of Word. Being computer-savvy is a basic job requirement at most places, and the best way to bring you up to speed is to take a few classes at your local college or career-development center. Dr. Rosch suggests starting by making a list of five technology-related job skills that you need at work. Then scour the Yellow Pages and make some calls to see how you can update or advance your knowledge.

Be assertive with your job training. "Often, you'll see someone who's expected to learn new technology at work but who's not given the time, educational training or finances to get on board," Dr. Davis says. If this is your story, brush up on your assertiveness skills first.

On the Net

It's the fastest-growing community in the United States and the world. It's cyberspace, specifically that online computer community of the Internet. The Internet was created decades ago as a way for scientists to keep in touch throughout the world. It has since attracted the eyes (and keyboards) of the public and grown accordingly. One estimate showed that 4.9 million computers were connected to the Internet in January 1995—more than double from the previous year.

But who uses the Internet and why? According to *Interactive Age* magazine, here's a demographic snapshot from the third World Wide Web survey conducted in April and May 1995 by the Graphic, Visualization and Usability Center at the Georgia Institute of Technology in Atlanta. (The World Wide Web is the most popular and most accessible portion of the Internet's global computer network.) More than 13,000 people responded to the online survey.

- Average age of Internet user: 35
- Gender: 82 percent male worldwide; 80 percent male in the United States
- Average income: $69,000
- 31 percent have been on the Internet for less than six months; 29 percent for one to three years; 23 percent for four or more years
- 50 percent explore two to six hours a week; 45 percent explore more often

Then see just how much your boss and company will help. Maybe they'll give you flex-time for classes, or perhaps you'll get reimbursed for tuition.

"The important thing is to recognize whether you're being encouraged and empowered to get ahead," Dr. Davis says. "If you're not, that'll only add to your stress."

Mastering Public Speaking

Talk the Talk with Style

Do you think that public speaking is stressful? Well, think what it must have been like to have to follow Mark Twain, one of America's sharpest wits and finest speakers. A man named Chauncey Depew did just that at a banquet once. Twain had just delivered a rousing 20-minute speech that was received with great enthusiasm. Depew, the next scheduled speaker, slowly rose as the applause for Twain died down.

"Mr. Toastmaster, ladies and gentlemen," Depew said. "Before this dinner, Mr. Twain and I made an agreement to trade speeches. He has just delivered mine and I'm grateful for the reception you have accorded it. I regret that I lost his speech and cannot recall a thing he had to say." With that, Depew sat down to thunderous applause, having survived the stress of the best speech never given.

Scared Speechless

Public speaking can be the most uncomfortable thing that you do in your life. According to one study of 3,000 Americans, it ranked first among our greatest fears—ahead of such trivial matters as getting married and death. Yet, public speaking needn't be a mortal enemy. Rather, it's a chance to shine, to show the world what you're made of and to share your thoughts, feelings, perspectives and sense of humor. And, as Depew showed, even the most daunting speaking conditions can be overcome.

"Public speaking is a type of performance, and, as with any performance, there's an energy between you and your audience. You can feed off this energy," says Mark Brown, a systems analyst at *Reader's Digest* who, in 1995, spoke his way to a world title in oration through Toastmasters International, an international speaking organization.

Now that reports of Twain's demise are no longer in the least bit exaggerated, you don't have to worry about finding yourself in Depew's shoes. But that still doesn't make public speaking easy. The prospect of speaking to a large group can be overwhelming and cause serious apprehension, stressing our system mentally and physically.

The mental stress may result from memories of previous speeches. "Most people, at one time or another, have had the unfortunate experience of being laughed at when they were speaking," says Joel Goodman, Ed.D., director of The HUMOR Project in Saratoga Springs, New York, and a humor specialist who writes and lectures widely. "Even if it was in elementary school, people learn to shut up because of these experiences."

The physical stress, on the other hand, is a purely natural reaction. It's our inborn fight-or-flight response kicking in, says Steve Allen, Jr., M.D., a humor specialist and physician in Ithaca, New York, who lectures widely on the benefits of humor and creativity.

But this physical reaction can be turned in our favor, says Earl Mindell, Ph.D., registered pharmacist, nutrition professor at Pacific Western University in Los Angeles and worldwide lecturer on health and nutrition. "People mentally talk themselves scared when it comes to speaking, instead of concentrating on the positive aspects of their message."

To do that takes practice. Here's how to get started.

Go through the looking glass. Professional magicians practice their tricks in front of a mirror so that they can see themselves from the audience's point of view. This strategy works well for speaking, too. By watching yourself in the looking glass, you'll know when you're slouching, looking down, stuffing your hands in your pockets or shuffling from foot to foot. Pay attention to your eye contact. Reach everyone in the audience. And move your hands naturally to complement your message. Don't gesture so zealously that it looks like you're sending semaphore. If you do these things enough, they'll become natural, even in front of 1,000 people.

Go to the videotape. Another way to watch your own speech is to videotape it, suggests Redford B. Williams, M.D., professor of psychiatry and director of the Behavioral Medicine Research Center at Duke University Medical Center in Durham, North Carolina. By doing this, you can see exactly how natural you look and sound.

Don't read your speech. It takes real skill to read a speech well. More often than not, a read speech comes off as boring and monotonous as the narration to high-school biology filmstrips. Instead, try to speak extemporaneously, that is, with a rough outline of the topics that you want to talk about and in what order—but not exactly what you plan to say. Memorize the beginning and ending, but leave yourself the latitude to ad-lib the heart of the speech. In other words, deliver most of your message personally, as if you were talking to each member of the audience one-on-one.

Take it personally. Speak on a topic that means something to you on a personal level. If you can't, try to find a personal angle to the topic that you're addressing. Not doing so is like taking black-and-white pictures of a rainbow: You might have a beautiful

---

Leave 'em Laughing

Sprucing up speeches with good-natured humor makes your speeches memorable and makes you look like a polished pro.

"Humor gets and keeps an audience's attention, and that's half the battle," says Dr. Joel Goodman of The HUMOR Project. "Somebody who's able to use humor in public speaking has the audience in the palm of his hand. If that's not power, I don't know what is."

Here's how to leaven your oration with levity.

Warm 'em up with a custom intro. If you're going to be introduced, say, at a formal function, write your own introduction and cram it with a gaggle of gags. That way, whoever introduces you will warm up the audience before you ever step on stage.

Be the punch line. Laughing at yourself gives others permission to laugh. At you, themselves and everything.

Have a saving grace. Remember when Johnny Carson was king of late night? He could summon up raucous laughter even after a bad joke. Why? He had a bag of tricks for just such occasions: raised eyebrows, deadpan stares, cracks about the joke writers, banter about the audience's poor humor standards. By doing the same, you can salvage a failed joke and look funnier in the process. Be warned, though. Doing this well takes practice and a strong delivery. And it could backfire.

---

opportunity, but the end result is devoid of the color of passion.

Leave time for questions. Often, it's easier to address the masses in an informal question-and-answer session—if you know your subject material. If you feel more comfortable doing this, leave the last half of your allotted time for some personal dialogue.

Commuting with Nature

Don't Let It Drive You Crazy

It's 7:30 A.M. in Pleasantville, and Mr. Jones is leaving for work. He strides down the front walk, admires his well-manicured lawn and hops into his conservative-yet-sporty sedan (that's also very roomy, gets great gas mileage and is cheap to insure). Birds are singing, the sun is shining and somewhere, someone is whistling the *Leave It to Beaver* theme song.

Shortly after he pulls onto the two-lane road that connects his immaculate home to his gleaming office building, Mr. Jones's morning reverie is rudely interrupted when he has to slam on his brakes to avoid rear-ending a car that's crawling along at 25 miles per hour (mph) in a 55 mph zone. For the next ten miles, Mr. Jones feels like he's in a funeral procession. Whenever he comes to a passing zone, there's a steady stream of oncoming traffic. The only time that the other lane is clear is when the road is divided by a solid double yellow line.

As his blood reaches the boiling point, our hero sees a momentary opening and whizzes by—but not without spewing invective out his rolled-down window and flashing a one-finger salute. After a half-dozen similar encounters, the *Leave It to Beaver* soundtrack has been replaced with the sinister theme from *Dark Shadows*, the sky has clouded over (as has his mood) and Mr. Jones wishes that he was driving a Humvee with a 105 mm. howitzer on the hood instead of a consumer digest winner.

As he pulls in to work, Mr. Jones contemplates firing

someone just to make him feel better. Just another day in commuter paradise.

On the Road—Again

Whether you drive to work, carpool or take public transportation, commuting can be one of the most stressful parts of your day. Consider these disconcerting statistics.

• The average work-related commute is 11 miles one-way; average work-related business travel is 28 miles.

• Work travel accounts for 32 percent of all miles driven in a car or truck.

• 38 percent of all U.S. households owned two cars in 1990. All told, there are an estimated 147 million cars on U.S. roads and 48 million trucks and buses, for a total 195 million vehicles.

"No doubt about it, commuting can be a real stressor if you let it," says Dr. Paul J. Rosch of the American Institute of Stress and of New York Medical College and a former colleague of stress research pioneer Hans Selye, M.D., author of *Stress without Distress*.

Of course, it doesn't take a medical degree to figure that out. Just ask Mike Morrissey. He's public-relations manager for the American Automobile Association national headquarters. He's also a brave road warrior of the ultra-congested I-4 interstate in Orlando, Florida.

"I would say that commuting is the most regular source of stress in our lives," Morrissey says. "Unfortunately, it's also one of life's necessary evils. You just have to accept it and plan for it."

Surviving Life in the Fast Lane

Here's how to make it through your commute without getting run down, run over or run through by stress.

Take respiration vacations.
Concentrate on breathing fully and
deeply, especially when you're stuck
in traffic or when your train's late.
"Breathing keeps stress under control,"
Dr. Rosch says. It eases tension and
oxygenizes your system, which makes
you feel refreshed and relaxed.
Breathe in for a count of three
seconds, pause a second, then breathe
out for a three count. Odds are that
after several minutes of this, you'll lose
the urge to disembowel someone.

Do some body work. While
you're breathing deeply and slowly,
scan your body from head to toe for
tense spots, advises Phil Nuernberger,
Ph.D., president of Mind Resource
Technologies, an executive consulting
firm in Honesdale, Pennsylvania, and
author of the tape-cassette package
*Taming the Beast: Driving without
Stress.* When you find a tense spot, say,
in your jaw muscles or furrowed brow,
breathe deeply and relax it. (Periodic
full-body scans are also useful during
the day.)

Go with the flow. Let's say that
you have 30 miles to cover on a
freeway in which traffic is going 60
mph. You can go with the flow and
mindlessly warble along with the
radio, or you can tense your whole
body and start weaving in and out,
surging to 70 mph for a few moments
before slamming the brakes and then
looking for the next opportunity to cut
someone off. What will it gain you?
Even if you manage to go 70 mph half
the time, you'll be lucky to have
shaved two minutes from your drive. Is
all that stress worth two minutes?

Accept it. Fighting against adversaries
whom you have no control over is not only
useless but also bad for your health. The same
is true on the road. You can't control the car in

Operator, Get Me a Tow Truck

As you close in on the clown ahead of you doing 35
miles per hour (mph) in a 55 mph zone, you notice his
BMW swerving back and forth over the center line.
When you get close enough to see the driver, you notice
that he has a cellular phone in his left hand while he's
gesticulating wildly with his right hand. This guy, you
think, is an accident waiting to happen.

You're right. Researchers at the Rochester Institute
of Technology in New York and the State University of
New York at Buffalo say that drivers who use cellular
phones get into 33 percent more accidents than other drivers. In a 1996 study, cellular phone users who made 50
minutes' worth of calls a month while driving were 5½
times more likely to get into an accident than other
drivers. Not surprising, the odds of an accident mounted
when you coupled talking on the phone with drinking,
lighting a smoke or taking your hands off the wheel.

The study was based on accident data from the New
York Department of Motor Vehicles. Although the group of
phone users was small—just 14 people—the findings suggest that phone use while driving can be dangerous.

So use your common sense when you use your cellular phone, says Mike Morrissey of the American Automobile Association. Keep conversations short and
unemotional for safety's sake. Your attention needs to
be on the road, not on the other end of a phone call.

---

front of you, the traffic lights or the crowded
freeway. Why get angry at them? Change what
you can—the time of day in which you
commute, your route, where you live or where
you work—and leave the freeway conditions to
someone else to get angry over.

Taking the Hassles Out of Business Travel

How to Be a Zen Road Warrior

If you're one of those corporate road warriors who's convinced that "business travel" is a kind euphemism for "physically beaten, mentally battered and emotionally bruised," you're standing, once again, in the long line.

There was a time when business travel sounded like a perquisite of reaching middle or upper management. Excellent cuisine, four-star accommodations—the picture seemed sublime. You even got to be out of the office. That was before corporate downsizing forced everyone to hit the road at speeds that Superman would resent. From Duluth to Tacoma to Dallas to Boston—and it isn't even Wednesday yet.

Of course, you're not alone. Joining you on the road are your constant traveling companions: headaches and stiff backs, indigestion and insomnia, jet lag, dry throat, dry lips, red eyes and the sniffles plus, at no extra charge, general anxiety and depression. If you were a kid, you'd call it homesickness. But because you're a grown-up, you call it life—and then you call a cab.

Life in the Fast Lane

Today's business traveler is a fast-lane version of American playwright Arthur Miller's Willy Loman, the lonely traveler in *Death of a Salesman*. Except that the new business traveler racks up a lot more frequent-flyer miles. By the mid-1990s, more than a quarter of

Americans were traveling for business. And that number is only expected to rise. Nowadays, it takes a lot of savvy to cover your territory. Roll Davy Crockett, Indiana Jones and Luke Skywalker into Willy Loman and you may be able to make it back to the home office just in time for a staff meeting.

"If you think of travel stress as your response to situations outside of your control, you'll have a better chance of breaking the downward spiral that it triggers," suggests Jon Kabat-Zinn, Ph.D., director of the Stress Reduction Clinic at the University of Massachusetts Medical Center in Worcester who is also an associate professor of medicine, lecturer and author of *Wherever You Go, There You Are* and *Full Catastrophe Living: Using the Wisdom of Your Body and Mind to Face Stress, Pain and Illness*. Dr. Kabat-Zinn travels extensively, lecturing and visiting other stress-reduction clinics throughout the country. And he admits that it's not always an easy endeavor, even for someone who has developed successful stress-reduction techniques.

While you may not be able to prevent flight delays or hotel reservation foul-ups or be guaranteed that your long journey will pay off with a signed contract, you can change the way that you respond to both the physical and mental travails of travel. Here's how.

Keep perspective. As you approach the front of a long line after your flight has been canceled or after some similar mishap, repeat this: "It's not their fault. It's not their fault."

"It does no good to get overwhelmed by anxiety when things don't go as planned or to blow up in anger at some hapless employee who didn't cause the problem and can't do anything about it," advises psychologist Daniel Goleman, Ph.D., behavior writer for the *New York Times* and author of *Emotional Intelligence*. "If you're swept up in anger, you're going to say some things that you'll regret, you'll hurt your chance of getting what you do want and you'll waste time that you should be spending thinking of smart alternatives." He recommends slow breathing as an effective antidote to stress. Inhale and exhale deeply for just a few rounds and notice the difference: a clear mind and a slower pulse. And breathing can be done anywhere, anytime—a big plus, since stress generally knows no boundaries or time zones.

Plan ahead. Debi Tracy Hirsch has the right idea. "I never try to hail a taxi, especially when I know that I'm going to be on a tight schedule," says the New York City–based professional meeting planner who logs more than 75,000 miles a year for her company, Blessed Events. "I call a shuttle or private car service the night before."

Another example is to learn to live for days out of one carry-on bag. That's what the real pros do. That may minimize your ability to make a fashion statement, but you'll never land on one coast while your bags land on the other. Also, if delayed, instead of fretting over missed appointments, run to a phone and let whoever's waiting for you know that you'll be late. You'll relieve stress on both ends.

Say "yes" to yoga. "The habit of becoming aware of your body's tension creates the habit of preventive care," says Judith Lasater, Ph.D., author of *Relax and Renew: Restful Yoga for Stressful Times.* "Yoga helps stop stress before it starts." Her "restorative yoga" positions are surprisingly easy and especially adaptive to a hotel room or even while standing in line.

To ease neck stress, slowly raise your shoulders to your ears. Slowly lower them again. In hotels, Dr. Lasater recommends the "legs-up-the-wall" pose. You'll need only a floor, a wall and, oh yes, a pair of legs. Sit upright on the floor, one shoulder against the wall, legs straight out in front of you parallel to the wall. As you lie back, turn your body and swing your legs up the wall. Be sure that your lower back maintains contact with the floor. Keep your legs straight but not locked, arms out to the sides. Close your eyes and breathe for ten minutes. Fluids accumulated by long-term sitting drain away.

Blood flow is directed back to your vital organs.

For a guided yoga class in your hotel room, bring a yoga video that you can throw into the VCR (call ahead to request one).

Put time on your side. When your body time clock goes off its natural beat, all hormonal hell breaks lose. Commonly called jet lag, the malady occurs when you cross time zones. This can prove particularly disastrous for the business traveler who must be "on" for the duration of his trip. One successful approach is to quickly adapt to the time zone that you're in. Wake up when they wake, go to bed when they do (pretend to sleep if you can't sleep).

The so-called jet-lag diet tries to accomplish this with carbohydrates, which help you sleep, and protein, which helps keep you up. If the conventioneers are ready for bed and you're just hitting your stride the first night, have a bowl of pasta. If you're struggling to stay in an upright position during your client's presentation, grab a protein bar, a slice of cheese or a fish meal (hold the starch).

Phone home, E.T. Part of the stress of business travel is feeling alone, lonely and missing your home base—the things and people that comfort you. Bring a favorite mug or call home. Check in with your wife or girlfriend—if desperate you can even buzz your parents. If you're a parent of a youngster, the separation hurts from both sides. Hearing your kid's laughter can brighten almost any miserable day of travel. Sometimes even hearing them cry reminds you that you're connected to someone, someplace where the scenery is not always moving.

Beware the food trap. Frequent business travelers tend to fall into the trap of overeating, says Evelyn Tribole, R.N., a nutritionist in Beverly Hills, California, and author of *Eating on the Run* and *Healthy Homestyle Cooking.* "Many people pig out from boredom, due to their inability to handle downtime between appointments," she says. Her advice is to amuse yourself with things other than food. Call someone at home, make use of a hotel gym or get a massage.

Changing Careers

Shift Occupational Gears

For all the griping, groaning and moaning that we do about work, there's a tiny indisputable fact behind all this protest. Deep down inside, many of us love bringing home the bacon. The very act of working is empowering.

And that's what makes the prospect of changing our line of work incredibly stressful. "A career change can be devastating for a man. It can be a real source of agonizing stress, especially if it's an involuntary change," says international creativity consultant Dr. Ann McGee-Cooper.

Men tend to define themselves by their work. Put a couple of guys together in a room and, guaranteed, one of the first questions will be, "So, what do you do for a living?" The question itself makes the connection between work and living.

And that's a double-edged sword: When work is good, life is great; when work is bad, life is almost unbearable. Even more dangerous is the notion that if you lose your job, you lose your self-worth.

Contemplating a career change, then, can cause considerable stress. For all the good that work does in our lives, it does just as much harm when our career identity is called into question. It's then that we feel that the double-edged sword has run us through. And if we're not careful, we picture a host of entities as the sneering swordsmen—bosses, society, spouses and ourselves.

"If you're not sure why you want to change careers—say, you're wrestling with the realization that you're bored—it's easy to let that turn into steam that you blow off in any direction," cautions Dr. Martha Davis of Kaiser Permanente Medical Center.

Taking the Plunge

Handling career changes adroitly starts with realizing why you're considering jumping ship in the first place. You also need to recognize what you're longing for. Here's how to do both.

Learn and grow. Maybe you're the top dog at work. Maybe you're an entry-level pup. It doesn't matter. If you're unhappy, you're unhappy—and nothing more. "It's easy to interpret as failure the fact that you don't enjoy your work or feel particularly successful in life," says Kendall Dudley of Lifeworks, a life-planning consulting business in Cambridge, Massachusetts. See your unpleasantness as a time of personal growth, not as time served.

Don't play the blame game. Even if your workplace is perfect, don't blame yourself if you are unsatisfied. Most of us choose career paths when we're young and relatively inexperienced in life. "Decisions made early in life were often made to please peers or parents instead of ourselves," Dudley says. Lamenting the past just keeps you from building your future.

Ask yourself the tough questions. "I believe that we keep ourselves chained, while clutching the keys in our hands," Dr. McGee-Cooper says. The key to unlocking the chains lies in self-exploration by asking yourself some tough questions: What makes you truly happy? What outrages you? What are the most important things in your life? What attributes do you most prize? If your life—mistakes and all—could talk, what lessons would it impart? These answers aren't easy, but finding them helps you find

---

yourself. They'll also point you in the right direction career-wise.

Write the wrong. Write about things you've done that have brought you true satisfaction. Maybe it was addressing the local school board on a controversial issue or writing a letter to the editor that got published. After you've written about these events, examine them to find out exactly what it was that you enjoyed: Public speaking? Getting published? Resolving conflict? Writing focuses your feelings and allows you to take a more objective look at your life.

Brainstorm options. Just because you're dissatisfied with engineering, for example, doesn't mean that you need to leave the field entirely. Ask some trusted friends or colleagues to help you brainstorm possibilities. Maybe you don't need to change fields—just jobs. Perhaps you can teach your trade or go into consulting, suggests international negotiating expert Roger Dawson.

Volunteer first. Volunteering is a good way to explore optional careers safely, without losing your day job. Put a few hours into an avocation that you really enjoy to see if it's what you'd like to do full-time.

Make change. Maybe you do need to change jobs. Or, as Dawson calls it, to have an occupational face-lift. Dawson remembers confronting the head of a retail chain that he once worked at as a young man with ambitions of becoming store manager. "He could tell that I didn't have any other options by the way I was talking," Dawson says. "I was so insulted by his attitude that I left two weeks later. It was the best move that I ever made in my life."

Changing careers is scary. But "the vast majority of people who leave something that's depressing them wind up happier and most

often financially better-off in the end," Dr. McGee-Cooper says. "Don't be fooled by what seems like a difficult job market. There will always be a market for talented people with imagination and a sense of purpose."

Odd Jobs

Tired of buttoned-down, wing-tipped corporate America? Maybe you need an odd job. Might we suggest one of the following?

• **Chicken shooter:** At Virginia's Langley Air Force Base, air safety technicians man 20-foot cannons to shoot four-pound, dead chickens at aircrafts whizzing by at 700 miles per hour. Why? So that pilots can practice evading live birds that often fly in front of planes and cause accidents.

• **Ant catcher:** Digs up live ants for ant farms.

• **Egg breaker:** Separates the yolks and whites of eggs for use in food products.

• **Flush tester:** Tests toilet bowls' flushing power by flushing rags down the channels.

• **Grips, gaffers and best boys:** They're always mentioned at the end of a movie, but just what do they do? Grips lay down camera rails, lug equipment around, assemble sets and arrange props. Gaffers are lighting experts. Their job includes a fair amount of acrobatics, since they must hang lighting in unique places. Best boy is the gaffer's right-hand man. That means that he does most of the grunt work and climbing.

• **Lump inspector:** Inspects lumps of tobacco for defects in the wrapper leaf; repairs tears and holes with glue and pieces of another leaf.

• **Weed farmer:** Grows weeds to sell for herbicide research.

• **Tufter:** Puts the tufts of padding into bed mattresses.

• **Glass bender:** Manipulates four-foot-long glass tubes into letters and words for neon signs.

• **Croupier:** Runs the gambling tables at casinos, standing behind a gaming table for up to ten hours a day with a short break every hour.

Surviving Downsizing

How to Rebound after Restructuring

Not that long ago, there was no such thing as downsizing. Companies laid people off or fired them. But if you're the one getting tossed out on the street, it doesn't much matter whether you've just been downsized or laid off.

"I heard a newscast the other day that said that it used to be that when a company reduced its workforce, it was something to be sad over," says Dr. Martha Davis of Kaiser Permanente Medical Center. "Now, it's something to be proud of. Wall Street cheers. Unfortunately, it seems to be a sign of the times."

The Silver Lining

The word *downsizing* originally was coined to define the scaling down of car sizes by automobile manufacturers. The term took on its "layoff" definition in the 1980s when businesses began making major workforce reductions in response to a recessionary economy.

Does downsizing really improve a company's overall business? In the short term, probably not. Morale suffers, productivity suffers, confusion reigns. Most economists say that it takes years before a company truly realizes the benefits of its downsizing, according to a report by *U.S. News & World Report.* Rather, the greatest gains in productivity occur in companies that are growing, because it's there that employees are most confident and more likely to be productive.

As for the individual, experts agree that downsizing can be a tremendous source of stress. But, says international creativity consultant Dr. Ann McGee-Cooper, there's usually a silver lining to the cloud.

"Downsizing can be the most important gift that you'll ever get in your working life," says Dr. McGee-Cooper.

"Downsizing might finally break you loose from something that you've never really enjoyed but would never walk away from on your own," she says. "It's an opportunity to look elsewhere—to look within and to make any necessary changes to your working life."

Turning Your Life Around

Here's what the experts recommend for dealing with the shock and stress of downsizing and turning it around in your favor.

Feel the pain. It's okay to be devastated if you're suddenly thrown out of work—for a while. Our identities are integrally tied up with our careers. In many ways, jobs are how we define ourselves and how we're defined by society. "But a bad attitude never helped anyone," says Elizabeth C. Johnson of the Johnson Group. You'll eventually have to get over your shock, swing into action and make a recovery.

Get a mood ring. In times of flux, scientists have discovered, our thoughts and feelings tend to mirror our current mood. It's called mood-congruent emotion, says Clark University's Dr. Jim Laird. "What it means is that you're most likely to recall sad moments when you're feeling sad, and happy moments when you're feeling happy," Dr. Laird says. Give this a downsizing spin, and it means that you can really sabotage your self-esteem if you let your stress and depression get out of hand.

Embrace your nonworking life. Don't become so absorbed in your layoff that you're neglecting the other facets of life: health, family, fun time and exercise. "It's critical that people who are looking for jobs spend a certain amount of time doing stress management, exercising and spending quality time with family and friends," Dr. Davis says.

Assess things clearly. One of the most unsettling things about downsizing is that you feel so out of control. To survive these devastating feelings, realize what's beyond your control—the company's decision to downsize—and what's in your control—your ability to turn these lemons into lemonade.

"Focus on what you can change, not on what you can't. This takes the fear out of downsizing," Dr. McGee-Cooper says. "It's like facing a terminal illness. The important thing in coping is realizing what's in your control, what's not and where your priorities are."

Work on your next job. Despite being jobless, you're not without a job: Your biggest job now is finding another one. Treat this responsibility just like you would any other assignment, were you still on the clock. "Some days you won't feel like doing it, but you must," suggests Kate Wendleton in her book *Through the Brick Wall: How to Job-Hunt in a Tight Market.* "Make a phone call. Write a proposal. Research a company. Do your best every day, no matter how you feel."

Brush up on your job-search skills. It may have been a while since you've had to jump through the hoops of finding a job. Make sure that you're prepared: Update your résumé, practice interviewing techniques and make sure that your wardrobe hasn't atrophied. If you need to, buy a couple of job-search books or find a seminar in your area catering to professionals who are back in the job market.

The Terminator

It's always tough firing someone, but firing a friend—especially when it's because of downsizing and not because of poor work performance—is downright traumatizing for both of you. Take this advice and make it easier on yourselves.

Practice. **Rehearse, just like you would for an important job interview. Delivery is key in keeping your dignity and his intact.**

Go to lunch. **Or some other neutral place to break the news. Don't do it in your office or on campus if you can help it.**

Look him in the eye. **Never fire someone, especially a friend, over the phone. Do it in person and maintain eye contact. Looking anywhere else makes you look like a weenie.**

Admit how tough it is. **It's okay to keep eye contact and speak firmly, but don't come off as snide or distant. Rather, confide in your friend that what you're doing is killing you. There's no harm in admitting that you're human.**

Keep it short and sweet. **Don't prolong the news. Break it to him in the first five to ten minutes. Skip the small talk.**

Listen and empathize. **After you've done your managerial duty, be a friend. Listen to him; let him vent.**

Help out. **After you've done the dirty deed, uphold your end of the friendship by giving him a hand. Offer to be a superlative reference, network for him and tell him about job openings you've heard of.**

Avoiding Burnout

Keep Hope Alive

You just can't do it anymore. It used to be fun. You knew what you were supposed to do and did it. But since the latest downsizing, you're supposed to do your job and—now that they're gone but their responsibilities remain—Tom and Dick's, too.

You can't say "no." You have a family and a mortgage. But you keep getting colds and headaches, and your marriage is in trouble because you're constantly snarling at your wife. Your kids are wondering what they did to turn their fun, piggyback ride–giving dad into an absent brooder.

In today's world of downsizing and job insecurity, burnout is scary. Luckily, experts agree that you can bust out of burnout and get back to business by taking control of your situation.

Getting Overwork under Control

You're working so hard that you can barely remember your own name. And we're telling you to slow down and take charge? Yep. Slowing down will help you reorder priorities in your life and on the job so that you can better beat burnout.

How do you know if you've crossed the line from stress to burnout? Experts say that it occurs when hope and energy fade, when you believe that your job is meaningless and that nothing can happen to change that.

How do you keep from crossing that line? Read on.

Clarify your role. "Write down your top ten major responsibilities in order from most to least critical," says Stan Silverman, professor of social sciences at the University of Akron in Ohio and co-author with Kenneth Wexley of *Working Scared: Achieving Success in Trying Times.*

Then take the list to your manager and arrange a time to discuss your priorities. Together, you should be able to agree on what tasks must be done and what you shouldn't be sweating.

Just say "no." It's tough. The company just got rid of half its employees, and you have to tell your supervisor that you can't do it all. But unless you're certain that saying "no" will cost you your job, you may lose your job if you don't tell, warns Kenneth Wetcher, M.D., psychiatrist and medical director of the Wetcher Clinic in Houston.

"If you try to do too much, it will impair your job performance," Dr. Wetcher says. "If you don't set limits, your supervisor will assume that you're handling all your assignments well, and then you will get blamed if you don't follow through."

Lighten your own load. "You may not need to apply to your manager if you can figure out how to trim your workload on your own by streamlining priorities," Dr. Wetcher says. At the very least, you may be able to make the work less burdensome by making your work area more pleasant with music or art.

Manage yourself. You're not the only one with more responsibilities since the cutbacks. Chances are that your manager also has more than he can handle.

So, if you're not getting the attention and direction that you crave, become your own manager, advises Beverly

Potter, Ph.D., a psychologist in Berkeley, California, and author of *Beating Job Burnout.* "Set goals and give yourself feedback," Dr. Potter suggests. "Acknowledge what you're doing well. Don't dwell on the negative."

Nurture your manager. "Everybody works best when they feel needed, noticed and nurtured," says Hamilton Parker, an organizational consultant in San Diego.

That includes your manager. You'll win points and have a better time on the job if you let your manager know when he does something right, instead of carping about what's wrong, Parker says. Honey goes a lot further than hostility.

Get real. "Realistically appraise your abilities," says John Howard, Ph.D., management psychologist and professor of business administration at the University of Western Ontario in London, Ontario. "People often overestimate and expect too much of themselves. Strive for your highest attainable aim, but don't put up resistance in vain."

Let a Smile Be Your Umbrella

We know that it sounds trite. But it really is true. If you look at the bright side, chances are that life will start looking up, experts say. It takes practice, but you can do it. Here's how.

Accentuate the positive. Is the glass entirely empty or at least half-full? When work is going badly, we make it even worse by stressing everything that's rotten and forgetting anything that's good, Silverman says.

And that creates a vicious cycle

Warning Signs

Here are the common signals that burnout is becoming a problem.

Negative emotions. It's normal to feel frustrated, angry, depressed, dissatisfied or anxious occasionally. But if you're caught in the burnout cycle, you'll feel these emotions more often, until they become chronic and you experience emotional fatigue.

Interpersonal problems. When you feel emotionally drained, it's harder to deal with others. When conflicts arise, you may overreact with an emotional outburst or intense hostility. This makes communicating with co-workers, friends and family increasingly difficult.

Health problems. As your emotional reserves become depleted and the quality of your relationships deteriorates, your physical resilience declines. You may experience frequent colds, headaches, insomnia, backaches and other minor ailments. In general, you feel tired and run-down.

Below-par performance. You may become bored with your job or lose enthusiasm for your projects. Or you may find it difficult to concentrate. You become less productives and the quality of your work declines.

Substance abuse. To cope with the stress of burnout, you may start to drink or use drugs, eat a lot more or less, drink more coffee or smoke cigarettes. Substance abuse further compounds your problems.

Feelings of meaninglessness. Increasingly, you find yourself asking, "So what?" and "Why bother?" This is particularly common among burnout victims who were once very enthusiastic and dedicated. Your former idealism and enthusiasm is replaced by cynicism, and work seems pointless.

of stress and negativity. Despite the changes, chances are that there's some part of your job that you really enjoy and maybe even a new challenge ahead. Focus on the bright side, and you may roll out of bed a little less depressed.

Don't jump to conclusions. Before the merger, you used to supervise ten workers. Now, you still have your job, but you report to a manager. "Don't leap to the conclusion that you're no longer a supervisor because you're incompetent," Silverman says. "When companies merge and downsize, such decisions are frequently arbitrary, so don't waste energy blaming yourself." Instead, focus on the new challenges of your job.

Nix nostalgia. Negativity feeds on itself. So, you start out thinking, "I liked it better before," and voilà, you've blown up the changes into catastrophe. You think, "Our company used to be so wonderful. It was a family. I'll be miserable the rest of my work life."

You're so unhappy that you can't focus on your job, but just walking through it because you're burned out isn't a good survival tactic. Instead of giving in to nostalgia, "refocus on how to make work work for you in the new order of things," says Silverman.

Get a Life

Work is important. You may spend more time there than at home. But work isn't everything. You have a life. If not, perhaps you ought to get one, says Ronald Drabman, Ph.D., professor and director of the clinical psychology department at the University of Mississippi Medical Center in Jackson. When you have other joys in your life, your problems at work will become less significant.

Am I Burning Out?

Read each of the following statements and rate how often it is true for you on a scale of 1 (rarely true) through 5 (usually true). Then add up your score.

1. *I feel tired even when I've had adequate sleep.*

2. *I am dissatisfied with my work.*

3. *I feel sad for no apparent reason.*

4. *I am forgetful.*

5. *I am irritable and snap at people.*

6. *I avoid people at work and in my private life.*

7. *I have trouble sleeping because I worry about work.*

8. *I get sick more than I used to.*

9. *My attitude about work is "why bother?"*

10. *I often get into conflicts.*

11. *My job performance is not up to par.*

12. *I use alcohol or drugs to feel better.*

13. *Communicating with others is a strain.*

14. *I cannot concentrate on my work as well as I used to.*

Embrace meaninglessness. No, we're not going existential on you here. Maybe your problem isn't overwork but boredom. You've gone as far as you're going to go in your career. You could do it all standing on your head with your eyes closed. Work seems meaningless, but you can't afford to quit. Embrace it, says Dr. Wetcher.

"Acknowledge that it's a dead-end situation, and find stuff outside of work that's challenging and enjoyable, such as mentoring," Dr. Wetcher says. "Contribute by helping a young person in your field, or go to the Chamber of Commerce and ask about people in start-up businesses. Lots could use advice from an experienced hand." Or use other nonbusiness skills:

15. *I am easily bored with my work.*

16. *I work hard but accomplish little.*

17. *I feel frustrated with my work.*

18. *I don't like going to work.*

19. *Social activities are draining.*

20. *Sex is not worth the effort.*

21. *I watch television most of the time when I'm not working.*

22. *I don't have much to look forward to in my work.*

23. *I worry about work during my off-hours.*

24. *Feelings about work interfere with my personal life.*

25. *My work seems pointless.*

Scoring

25–50: You're doing well.

51–75: You're okay if you take preventive action.

76–100: You're a candidate for burnout.

101–125: You're burning out.

Help out a troubled kid by becoming a Big Brother, teach literacy or even tutor in some subject that you were good at in school.

Energize your outside life. Is work the only thing that matters to you? How about family, children, hobbies or volunteer work? "Once you figure out what's important to you, put more energy into the areas that you've neglected," Dr. Drabman says.

Doing that will make you feel better about yourself and much less stressed out over work, says Dr. Drabman. Don't give in to the temptation to take out your problems on your family and friends. Rather, make them a source of support.

Turn off the TV. Do you feel too drained to do anything after a grueling 12-hour day except veg out in front of the boob tube with a six-pack?

That's the surest way to increase the stress and lack of energy that feed burnout, warns Dr. Wetcher. "Research has shown that hobbies and other activities energize you and make you feel rejuvenated, while sitting in front of the television makes you tired and depressed," Dr. Wetcher says.

Activities can be anything that makes you happy, from stamp collecting to karate to playing with your kids.

Do something wild. "You've always wanted to go bungee jumping or hike the back paths of the Grand Canyon, but one thing or another kept you from carrying through. Do it now," says Dr. Drabman. You'll forget about hating your job while you're focused on a new and exciting activity.

And don't let overwork stand in your way. "Change requires you to force yourself to do something, even if you don't want to," says Dr. Drabman.

Work it out. Good exercise can significantly lessen or even eliminate stress, says Dr. Wetcher. "It's especially vital if you work a desk job with long hours. When you work a desk job and don't get exercise, you're increasing the toxins in your body." If you exercise, you're also likely to alleviate the health problems that often accompany burnout.

Start small if you have to, exercising 20 minutes a day, three times a week. "Everybody can find 20 minutes," Dr. Wetcher says.

Eat right. Good nutrition relieves stress, strengthens your immune system so that you're less likely to get sick and gives you more energy, says Dr. Wetcher. You never cook? You eat out of foam containers and food wrapped in paper? No excuse. "Even fast-food restaurants have salad," Dr. Wetcher says.

Enjoying Retirement

How to Make It Work for You

Most people know that legendary University of Alabama football coach Bear Bryant dropped dead within a year of retirement. The myth is this: See? Workaholic. Couldn't work anymore. Kaput.

The truth is that he retired because he was sick. Within a year, Bryant was dead of congestive heart failure.

"Subsequent studies have shown no link between retirement, illness and early death," says Robert Atchley, Ph.D., director of Scripps Gerontology Center at Miami University in Oxford, Ohio.

So forget any notion that you might have that if you quit working, you'll drop dead. Sure, it could happen. But it won't be because you retired. If you take care of your physical and financial health today, you can have a lot of bright tomorrows, experts say.

But with the future of Social Security pensions in doubt, will you be able to afford your retirement years? And, after a lifetime of going to school and then to work all day, will you be able to fill your leisure hours without going crazy from boredom?

It's making you nervous and stressed just to think about it, right?

But thinking about it is exactly what you need to do. The goal is simple. You've probably heard Mr. Spock say it dozens of times on *Star Trek* reruns: "Live long and prosper." So calm down and take second things first. Let's start with the part about prospering.

Putting the "Gold" in Your Golden Years

"People think of retirement as the first day of retirement, but you're really planning the last day of your life, and you don't want to outlive your resources," says Mary Sue Wechsler, a certified financial planner who is regional director of Watson Wyattt Worldwide financial services in Washington, D.C.

The rule of thumb is that to retire with 100 percent of your income, you have to save between 10 percent and 20 percent of your gross income for about 25 years, says Richard Kraner, partner and personal financial counselor at Ernst and Young in St. Louis.

You have rent to pay, your children's tuition to save for and myriad other expenses. So how do you sock away 15 percent of your income? With discipline and planning, it may not be as hard as you fear.

Turn dreams to goals. If retirement planning crosses your mind at all, you probably think, "I want to retire someday."

Guess what? Thinking won't make it so, Wechsler says.

Instead, you need to set a specific goal: "I want to retire in 15 years at 100 percent of my current salary adjusted for inflation."

The earlier you set a goal, the less stressful it'll be to reach it, Wechsler says. "Having 20 to 25 years to achieve your goals is easier than five."

Start now. Once you have a goal, start meeting it, Wechsler says. If you work for a company that offers 401(k) or other pension plans, take the maximum benefit, she says. And put money into a tax-deductible individual retirement account as well.

Trim your spending. For most people, company pension plans won't give you enough to retire on, Wechsler says, so you have to figure out where you'll make up the short-

fall. Ask yourself where you can find more resources.

"Don't look so much at cutting the $500 items each month, as at the little things—the $2 cappuccino you buy every morning or the three meals you eat out each week."

Make allowances. Oh, cash machines. What a wonderful invention. Money just flows from them any time.

And out of your savings.

"Instead of just drawing out money whenever you feel the need, budget," says Wechsler. One fast way to save money is to give yourself a weekly allowance, like your parents did when you were kids. "Live enough below your means not to outlive your means tomorrow," Wechsler says.

Take control of your spending. "Literally go through a two-month sampling of your checkbook," Kraner advises. It'll show you what you spend money on and give you ideas of what to cut.

Then, draw up a realistic budget covering all your expenses and stick to it. Or, try a computer program such as Prosper (available from Ernst and Young for about $60), which can calculate your retirement needs based on current assets.

Stock up. When you are 40, if you put $100,000 into a guaranteed interest account like a certificate of deposit at a rate of 6 percent, you'll have $429,000 at age 65. "If you put it in a diversified equity fund like a mutual fund, you'll have more than $1 million," says Peter Marmaras, a certified and chartered financial planner and co-owner of Marmaras and Woolf Associates in Allentown, Pennsylvania.

Don't think you have the money? Anyone can start a mutual fund program for $25 to $75 monthly, Marmaras says.

Look into Your Future

Most of us see retirement as a short-lived but non-stop stream of dry martinis, loud Bermuda shorts and chip shots off the ninth hole. Ken Dychtwald, Ph.D., president of Age Wave, a communications, marketing and consulting firm in Emeryville, California, and author of numerous books, including *Age Wave* and *Bodymind*, sees something different.

"'Never trust anyone under 50' will be the battle cry in 2020," says Dr. Dychtwald. "Legions of experienced and active older men and women will have taken over more and more of America until they're lodged in nearly every position of control," he predicts.

Obviously, this will change the scope of retirement, says Dr. Dychtwald, winner of the prestigious 1996 American Society on Aging Award. "The traditional 'linear life' paradigm of education-work-retirement will be replaced by a more cyclical approach," he says. "It'll be normal for 50-year-olds to go back to school and for 70-year-olds to start new careers."

Dr. Dychtwald predicts that the average guy's "first" retirement will rise from the current age of 62 to age 70 in 2020. Moreover, "rehirement"—not retirement—will be the norm, as thousands of healthy, seasoned workers decide that their longer life spans are better spent working than playing Bingo.

"A thousand years ago, the average life expectancy was only 25," Dr. Dychtwald says. "Today, thanks to advances in civilization, particularly medicine, the average man will live to be 83 in the twenty-first century."

Pay yourself first. Treat yourself like your mortgage company. No matter what, put your savings aside first. "Whatever's left can be considered disposable income," Marmaras says.

Put extras away. Every time you get a salary increase, put half of it in a savings plan, Marmaras says.

Or, let's say that you have a three-year car loan but only buy a new car every six years. After you've paid off your vehicle, invest the money that you had been budgeting each month for car payments, says Wechsler.

To Your Health

Okay, your money's intact, but that's only half the equation. Now, you want to live long enough to enjoy it. Here are some ideas to help you turn back the clock.

Get pumped. Keeping physically fit will help you remain healthy, active and better able to enjoy your retirement, says Erdman Palmore, Ph.D., professor emeritus of medical sociology at Duke University Medical Center in Durham, North Carolina.

"I have taken up weight lifting since retirement," Dr. Palmore says. "Most people think of retirement as a euphemism for deterioration. I'm trying to prove that you can improve with age. I'm getting stronger, putting on muscle mass and outgrowing jackets. I feel great about it every morning when I look in the mirror."

Don't forget aerobics. Some of the benefits of aerobic exercise are improved flexibility, balance, strength, endurance, weight control, sleep and heart functioning and an overall sense of well-being, experts say.

Aerobic—or heart-pumping activity—can include swimming, walking, jogging and other sports. Exercise at least three times a week for 30 minutes for maximum benefits.

Cut the fat. By lowering the fat intake in your diet to less than 30 percent of your daily calories, you'll reduce the risk of heart disease and cancer and improve your weight control, experts say.

Cut out the fat by cooking with olive and canola oils. Eat a lot of fruit and vegetables and complex carbohydrates such as whole-wheat bread and brown rice. Cut down on red meat and replace it with poultry and beans.

Making Retirement Count

So, you're healthy and wealthy, but how do you get wise as to how to spend all your leisure time? You're used to going to work all day and don't know what you'll do with yourself when you suddenly have nothing but time on your hands. How are you going to deal with it?

Keep working. If you like what you do, you don't need to give up your career entirely, Dr. Palmore says. "Large numbers continue to work part-time or as consultants," says Dr. Palmore.

Get involved. If money isn't an issue, retirement might be the time to use some of your skills to help the less fortunate, Dr. Palmore says. Volunteer through your religious or civic groups, help out with your grandkids or try something independent, such as Meals on Wheels (for the elderly or people with AIDS).

"Volunteering can be even more rewarding than a career," says Dr. Palmore.

If you'd like to do something, but are not sure exactly what it might be, write to the American Association of Retired Persons, 601 E St. NW, Washington, DC 20049, and ask to be part of their volunteer talent bank—a nationwide pool that matches your skills to available jobs in your area, suggests Louise Piazza, senior program specialist at the American Association of Retired Persons in Washington, D.C.

Lobby for special interests. "Even if you work part-time or consult, you'll still have more time on your hands than you do now," Dr. Palmore notes. No clue what to do when you're not working? Spend the time between now and retirement developing hobbies, skills and interests that you can bring into retirement, or browse through the many different sections in a bookstore (such as home repair, photography, computers) to look for ideas.

Choose a mentor. "Seek out a retired friend whose life you admire, and ask him what he's done to create an enjoyable, high-octane retirement. Then model your retirement on him," Piazza says.

Part Five

Real-Life Scenarios

Quest for the Best

They have risen to the pinnacle of their public professions. Through the years, performing under pressure has become a way of life for these men. Here are their secrets to turning stress into success.

You Can Do It!

These guys work hard, often under enormous pressure. Just like you. They have learned to deal with stress in a positive way and to take control of their lives. So can you.

Male Makeovers

Everywhere you turn these days, stress is lurking. And it's not always easy figuring out what you need to do to live a happier and healthier life. So we asked the experts for advice on how to deal with some of the most typical problems that men face. Here's what they said.

Quest for the Best They have risen to the pinnacle of their public professions. Through the years, performing under pressure has become a way of life for these men. Here are their secrets to turning stress into success.

Phil Jackson, Chicago Bulls Coach

Meditations on the Fast Break

To be a coach in the NBA would be enough stress for most men. For Phil Jackson, there is the added pressure of leading the Chicago Bulls, a team blessed with a bunch of physical magicians and monumental egos that is expected to win every time it takes the floor.

Newsweek magazine said that his "masterful handling of the team's disparate egos and temperaments should earn him an NBA lifetime achievement award." In conversation, Jackson laughs off the compliment with characteristic humility.

"I don't know about all that," he says, speaking from the team practice facility in Deerfield, Illinois. "The major stress in a coach's life is getting the best performance out of a team."

How do you do that? Not, as you might suspect, by practice, practice, practice, says Jackson. But by process, process, process. "It's a combination of developing a compatibility among the players and a workability with the coach," he says. "Beyond that, everything else—losses and wins—can be worked out. That all comes together if the team plays hard and likes to work together.

"It's come down to some very basic male stuff—guys enjoying hanging out with guys. It's a delicate juggling act, keeping the guys productive and cohesive as a group, to remind them that it's more than just making money and being on an ego trip and to remind them of the rewards of group process."

Zen and the Art of Coaching

Convincing a squad of players whose egos match or exceed their considerable talents to work together as a group may seem a daunting task. But Jackson, who has coached the Bulls to four NBA titles and was himself a former championship player with the New York Knicks from 1967 to 1978, manages to pull it off with considerable aplomb. He achieves a level of equilibrium by breathing deeply at critical moments, by practicing Zen meditation each morning and by keeping basketball in metaphorical perspective.

"Basketball is a game, a journey, a dance—not a fight to the death," says the 6-foot-8 native of Montana. "It's life just as it is."

Jackson, author of *Sacred Hoops: Spiritual Lessons of a Hardwood Warrior*, takes his own inspirational lessons from an eclectic assortment of thinkers—from Japanese Zen master Suzuki Roshi to Sioux Indian Black Elk to British novelist Rudyard Kipling to Don Juan devotee

Carlos Castaneda to Jon Kabat-Zinn, Ph.D., director of the Stress Reduction Clinic at the University of Massachusetts Medical Center in Worcester who is also an associate professor of medicine, lecturer and author of *Full Catastrophe Living: Using the Wisdom of Your Body and Mind to Face Stress, Pain and Illness* and *Wherever You Go, There You Are*.

The son of Pentecostal

preachers, Jackson has been meditating regularly for more than 20 years.

"Meditation is a discipline first and foremost," he explains. "I enjoy doing it first thing in the morning instead of jumping fast forward into life. With 101 things to do in the day, it's easy to immediately stress or become activated about them. Meditation allows you to sit and let the mind realize who's in control. Thoughts come and go, but you don't let them possess you. It gives you a chance to enter the day with peacefulness and also with compassion. That's one reason. The other one is to wake up—to be conscious and alert. One of the things that I teach in basketball is that alertness is the key, so I apply it to that."

It's difficult to imagine how Jackson maintains his cool in the midst of a fast-paced game, pacing up and down the sidelines with refs making bad calls and plays unraveling before his eyes.

"In those tense moments, when anger or frustration comes up, I usually feel tension in my shoulders and neck," he says. "That's a signal that I'm holding my breath. The key for me in getting through those situations without blowing my top is breathing. I take a deep breath, let it go and keep going on. That's one of the things that you teach yourself through meditation—watching your breath."

The hard part, admits Jackson, is finding the time to meditate in a busy schedule on the road. "Nowadays I carry a foldable wooden meditation stool and I sit first thing in the morning. That's how I make sure that it's a necessary part of my life."

Because of injuries incurred during his playing career—first a torn shoulder from his high-school pitching days and later a debilitating double-herniated disk with the Knicks that sidelined him for two seasons—his ability to work out stress through exercise is severely limited. Now in his early fifties, Jackson's regimen consists largely of walking—when the pain is not too great.

"I lost a nerve in my leg after that injury in 1968," he says, "so when I can't walk, I meditate. Basically because of the limits of time and my own body, I can only do one."

A Balancing Act

There's another stressor that basketball professionals face. Being on the road 100 days a year takes a toll on family life. "The biggest stress is balancing family and work," Jackson says. "It's not just being away that causes stress. It's the little work stresses that keep me from being attentive to my kids. Trading deadlines, watching game tapes at home, all those niggling things that come along and create a little more job pressure, which force you to put in a few extra hours. Then suddenly, you don't know your kids' teachers, you're unfamiliar with their classes and you don't know their friends' names. You realize that you're not participating in their lives. For me that was a big part of what stressed me."

His first marriage fell apart—a casualty of life on the road. Now he and his wife of 20 years pay careful attention to maintaining a strong marriage. The secret? "The secret is no secret," Jackson says. "The secret of making it work is working at making it work."

Early in his second marriage, he woke up one morning and realized that they had four children—all under the age of five. "Talk about stress," he says. "Plus, it was the end of my career, so I was dealing with the loss of a role—the loss of an identity—as well as the loss of a livelihood." He dealt with it by not dealing with it, by retreating in a certain respect.

"I basically retired, got away from basketball for a couple of years and became a housekeeper and a hands-on father," he explains. "I became immersed in the family aspect, and that brought me right back to the base level. It was very healing for me."

Ultimately, whether in family or basketball, for Phil Jackson, dealing with stress comes down to awareness and selfless compassion. As he puts it in *Sacred Hoops,* "The power of We is stronger than the power of Me."

Jon Kabat-Zinn, Ph.D., Stress Reduction Clinic Director

Mainstreaming Meditation

If misery loves very good company, then the following news flash should come as some relief to those tightly wound coils among us trying to pass for mellowed-out men: Dr. Jon Kabat-Zinn gets stressed out, too. This would not be a big deal if he wasn't founder and director of the highly regarded Stress Reduction Clinic at the University of Massachusetts Medical Center in Worcester; a pioneer who introduced the Eastern practices of meditation and yoga techniques into a traditional Western medical setting with resounding results and acceptance; an associate professor of medicine at the University of Massachusetts Medical Center; the author of two successful books, *Full Catastrophe Living: Using the Wisdom of Your Body and Mind to Face Stress, Pain and Illness* and *Wherever You Go, There You Are* and the subject of a popular Bill Moyers PBS TV special, "Healing and the Mind."

The success of the clinic and the media attention have made him a highly sought-after speaker and consultant. Dr. Kabat-Zinn travels constantly, giving talks and lectures, advising up to 60 other hospital stress clinics whose programs are based on the model that he developed. He appreciates the opportunity to increase awareness of the benefits of what he calls mindfulness meditation, but it admittedly takes a toll on his personal life.

"Sure, I feel stress," says Dr. Kabat-Zinn, whose Ph.D. is in molecular biology from the Massachusetts Institute of Tech-

nology (MIT) in Cambridge. Now in his early fifties, he has a youthful face and equally youthful torso. He speaks sincerely with precision and a no-nonsense New York accent. You get the sense that he sees himself as one of the guys. There's no big ego here. "I feel anxiety, ambivalence, frustration and all sorts of things." The difference between him and many others who face equal amounts of pressure is his willingness to name it and work with it.

Meditation and yoga are not just techniques that he teaches or clinical approaches that he has shown to be effective in helping people deal with chronic pain and everyday stress. They are integral parts of his life; he makes time every day to fit them in—wherever he finds himself.

A Breath of Fresh Air

"The practice of meditation is not about learning to relax or be still but about realizing that they're both here all the time and about learning to do what we do from a deep, still place," he says. "It's not something that you can magically do; that's why we call it practice. And that's not to say that if you meditate, you won't ever feel stress."

When he feels stress, the bridge that he uses to bring himself back to his own balance point of "stillness" is his breathing. "I bring a heightened level of awareness to my breathing, and within two or three breaths, tension either dissolves or is held by me differently," he says. "If I find myself very tense, I'll lie down on the floor and go into total stillness in the 'corpse' pose. I let my body totally relax into the floor, as if I'm melting, becoming as transparent as possible. This feeling reminds me that whatever I'm going through is just a tiny little nothing in the whole scale of things.

"I remember and perceive that things are always in flux, always changing, and that not everything has to get solved in that moment. We men have a particularly hard time with this, because very often we want very tight control over situations. In meditation you learn that a loose control is sometimes a lot better. Very often when you take that attitude, new and unexpected options open up."

It was in what could easily have been dubbed the Stressful Sixties that Dr. Kabat-Zinn was introduced to Eastern practices. At MIT, straddling the worlds of humanist and scientist; reading British novelist/molecular physicist C. P. Snow, on one hand, and anything about Zen that he could find, on the other and studying karate and yoga, he became active in the anti–Vietnam War movement, eventually helping to start the Union of Concerned Scientists (an organization still in existence).

"At that time in my life I was rebellious and defiant," he recalls. "There were lots of things going on politically that I was very unhappy with—inconsistencies and contradictions, horrors that were being perpetrated in Vietnam and also around the Civil Rights movement." He feels strongly that the new-old, mind-body disciplines he was learning played an important part in his political activism.

"Before organizing meetings, we'd get down on the floor and do yoga and be silent," he says. "That definitely helped us focus. Our political strategy came out of the deep space of stillness that we had experienced as a group practicing together."

A Life in the Balance

The 1990s, as countercultural clown and Woodstock emcee Wavy Gravy has said, are the 1960s standing on its head. And in the 1990s Dr. Kabat-Zinn faces other causes of stress. "The main stressor in my life nowadays is having more things coming at me than I can possibly do," he says. "That's a challenge."

On the work front, Dr. Kabat-Zinn says, "it's very stressful to run a stress-reduction clinic, especially in a major hospital. It's stressful just to work in health care these days. The problem for us is getting our service paid for now by HMOs. The irony is that, in many cases, if people were to go to a stress-reduction clinic up front, they would cost their insurance companies a lot less down the road.

"Lacking time to do it all and having to prioritize and say 'no' to important things are big stressors," he says. "And, of course, the effort to balance work with family life and quiet time for contemplation can also be a big challenge."

Family Time

One thing that Dr. Kabat-Zinn and his wife, Myla, do to keep stress from tearing their family apart is to have dinner together every night with their three children. "I've seen statistics that show that it's very rare these days for father, mother and children to all sit down together to dinner," he says. "It's a great ritual. We often light candles at the table. The subdued lighting helps create a relaxed atmosphere.

That doesn't mean that it's always relaxed. Kids are kids, so there's the usual teasing and fighting and chaos. But at least we make an attempt to bring a certain amount of regularity to family time. And over the years, that has paid off for us."

The "heart of parenting is very simple," he says, "but, of course, it's very, very complicated. We're not saying that there's one way to parent. We're saying that there are thousands of ways. Find the conscious and mindful way that works for you. Especially when you're under stress, it's easy to not be conscious, to not see your kids for who they really are. That can make family life very difficult."

Nick Meglin and John Ficarra, *Mad* Magazine Editors

Behind the Funhouse Mirror

To anyone born after about 1940—especially would-be class clowns with tendencies toward irreverence—he is as much a part of the American ethos as apple pie and the Fourth of July. Though the pie would probably end up in *his* face and the fireworks would probably blow up in *his* pocket.

He is the class klutz, the nitwit, the guy least likely to succeed, the kid picked last for the team, the misfit who was so unfit that he didn't even know that he didn't fit, the trickster who questioned every question, the joker who took nothing seriously—not even himself.

But ultimately he is the guy who deals with stress better than anyone we know. Zen monks and therapists alike aspire to emulate his response to every stressful situation: "What, me worry?"

He, of course, is Alfred E. Neuman, the mascot and alter ego of *Mad* magazine.

"*Mad* is a fun-house mirror," says Nick Meglin, co-editor, who joined the magazine in 1956. "We don't create fads or trends. We just reflect back society with our own unique perspective. To poke holes in balloons of pretentiousness—that's what we love to do."

And Neuman, as the embodiment of the *Mad* philosophy, is the idiot savant of stress. "Neuman is the eternal optimist," says John Ficarra, the other co-editor of *Mad*. "No matter what situation he's in, he has that 'What, me worry?' smile. In that expression, he's saying that we can complain and find fault but that we can't do much about it."

A World Gone Mad

Asking *Mad*'s editorial staff to sit around their Manhattan offices to discuss stress is like inviting the proverbial bull into a china shop and asking it not to break anything. Their responses vary between surprisingly serious and silly, a mix of profundities and verbal pratfalls. Listening to their banter is like watching a game of verbal table tennis played by the masters of one-liners.

"Actually, stress is good for you," says Meglin. "We've found that writers and artists who move from the highly stressful environment of New York to mellow California lose that edge that makes our material so good."

But maintaining that edge isn't easy. Meglin goes to a therapist to deal with some of his stress. "I was lucky because my therapist also played tennis and suggested it as a physical release and as a wonderful microcosm of the issues that you deal with in life. But the trick is not to play it competitively. I play for fun."

Ficarra kibitzes: "Some people would say that that's an elaborate rationalization for you being a lousy tennis player."

"Gee," Meglin retorts, "I lost in straight sets to Stevie Wonder in a celebrity tournament, and they won't let me forget it."

All kidding aside, Ficarra admits that he doesn't deal with stress as well as Meglin. "I don't do sports, and I don't exercise," confesses Ficarra. "As a result, over the years I've been racked with various stress-related problems—migraine headaches, colitis, prostate problems, a bad back and borderline high blood pressure."

He now has discovered two remedies for stress. One is working on handicraft projects in his basement. The other is "being close to nature," he says. "Visiting the Alps once was like peeling layers of stress off me."

"That was a case of mind over Matterhorn," quips Meglin.

"And God Alps those who Alps themselves," Ficarra counters.

Once again Meglin tries to get serious. "That kind of interplay among us is a great stress reliever," he says. "We are merciless on ourselves. We're the same way with each other—but with a great deal of affection. We really have fun, and we think that that gets on the pages of *Mad*. John usually finishes my sentences for me unless I'm in quicksand. Then he watches me go down."

Ficarra corrects Meglin: "When I see you in quicksand, I throw you an anvil."

One of the real stressors for the *Mad* staff is working under a corporate structure. In the beginning, under founder Bill Gaines, the whole operation was one big whirlwind of creative chaos. Now working under the same roof as its owner, Time Warner, things have changed. The boys at *Mad* have had to grow up. "In the past we were able to control our environment," comments Meglin. "Now we don't. That's inherently stressful."

"In 15 years of working for Bill Gaines I never saw a memo," adds Ficarra. "In the corporate world, everybody is looking to cover their butts. So they want a paper trail. Now there are memos. Memos take time. The bean counters are watching."

Mad, however, remains as irreverent as it ever was. ("We still take potshots at corporate in *Mad*," boasts Meglin.) And the magazine continues to hold up that fun-house mirror to society.

"The biggest stress is the falling apart of the American dream," Ficarra says on a serious note. "Kids today don't believe that if they finish school or work hard, they'll be better-off than

What, Him Worry?

One of the stressors in the life of Alfred E. Neuman, the mascot of *Mad* magazine, is that he gets to actually say so little. The only place where he's quoted is in pithy one-liners found in every issue of *Mad* on the contents page. Here is some of the pithier thtuff that has tumbled out of his toothy mouth.

"A plastic surgeon's office is the only place where no one gets offended when you pick your nose."

"Teenagers are people who act like babies if they're not treated like adults!"

"It takes one to know one—and vice versa!"

"How come stealing from one book is plagiarism, but stealing from many is research?"

"Who says nothing is impossible? Some people do it every day!"

"These days a balanced diet is when every McNugget weighs the same!"

their parents." That attitude is reflected in a cover that showed Neuman in a cap and gown, with the message: "Congratulations Class of '96: By the Way, You're Doomed!"

Because Alfred E. Neuman (we're told that the E. stands for either enigma or enema) cannot speak for himself, we asked his creators to speak on his behalf on some important topics. Here, through his interpreters, are his responses.

• On the stress of doing satire: "Imagine picking up the *Congressional Record* and seeing a much more humorous magazine than anything he appears in."

• On his biggest stress: "Being mistaken all the time for David Letterman and Ted Koppel."

• On his truly biggest stress: "Having people like us as his spokesmen."

Steve Allen, Comedian, Author and Songwriter

Doing What He Loves

Bring up stress with Steve Allen and he's likely to say in his velvety, resonating radio voice that stress is something he doesn't know much about and that he's naturally resistant to it. He describes himself as the "Perry Como of comedy," because a mellow, easy-going attitude shields him, like titanium armor, against the slings and arrows of mundane misfortune. But Allen squarely concedes that, while resistant, he's hardly immune to stress. The stress that he feels, however, is a unique strain usually reserved for philosophers, poets and pundits.

"Although I'm not an easily stressed person, I admit that I am conscious of being bugged by injustice," Allen says matter-of-factly. "For example, when I read about children born into poverty, I'm conscious of feeling angry. It seems like such a damnable way of running a world. More people are in trouble than are doing well.

"Sometimes life is a vale of tears. The essence of the human predicament is tragic, and I find that greatly annoying."

Comedy's Renaissance Man

Allen is truly a man who needs no introduction. He's one of comedy's elder statesmen, from an era where being funny didn't mean using abusive or foul language. His professional and artistic accomplishments exhibit amazing depth and breadth. Among the highlights are:

• Creating and hosting the original *Tonight Show* in 1954

• Writing nearly 50 books, from murder mysteries to academic analyses

• Writing more than 6,000 songs—including the smash hit, "This Could Be the Start of Something Big"—earning him a spot in *The Guinness Book of World Records* as the world's most prolific composer and songwriter

• Creating, writing and hosting the critically acclaimed, award-winning PBS series *Meeting of the Minds*

• Starring in motion pictures (notably *The Benny Goodman Story*) and on stage (Broadway's *The Pink Elephant*)

Allen has moved effortlessly between the many artistic roles that he has played, finding little to be stressed about on a personal level. Doing live TV shows, performing on stage, writing humor on deadline and speaking in public don't seem to faze him at all.

"Of course, there are many annoying things in show business that can be stressful if you let them," he says. "But, for me, they're mostly human-relations issues. Egos and personalities. In the industry confines, they're the same people problems that you deal with whether you're selling cars or hawking toothpaste.

"I do get stressed if I run out of gas or spill coffee on my shirt, but these are normal circumstances that all human beings share," he says.

When Allen does feel stress, it's on that cosmic scale. His global concerns have manifested themselves in a variety of ways. He's written books on America's declining intellectualism; analyses on the Bible, religion and morality and articles and essays on what he sees as society's ills, including a massive campaign against TV violence and an 11-page critical essay on pop singer Madonna, which he published in the *Journal of Pop Culture*.

"Most of these works were of little profit to me. In fact, with some of them, I might have been better-off public relations–wise not writing them at all," he says. "But to hell with that. I see injustice, I have ideas and opinions and I have access to media.

"The real irony here is if I want to get something published, it generally gets published, whereas the average guy might have the same reaction I do, or even superior ideas, and he won't get the ear of a publisher. He won't get on radio or television.

"Being able to vent my frustrations is, in a sense, a major stress reliever for me," Allen says. "Reducing stress wasn't an objective for me from the start, yet, in retrospect, it's turned out that way."

Living the Good Life

Born in New York City in 1921, the son of vaudeville performers, Allen grew up on the road. By the time he graduated from high school, he had attended 16 different schools. Allen began radio broadcasting in 1941 in Phoenix before moving to Los Angeles in 1945. It was in Los Angeles that he hitched his star to the budding medium of television and soon won a national following.

Although Allen, now in his mid-seventies, is comfortably set for life, he still keeps busy every day writing, composing, recording, crafting jokes and doing performances.

"I think one of the big reasons why I'm generally not very stressed is because I love my job and always have," he says. "I work seven days a week—and love it. My brain, my soul and my heart have a marvelous time writing songs, writing jokes, getting laughs, doing TV and Broadway and all that stuff.

"I'm fortunate, because I think that most people don't like what they do for a living," he says. "They need time off. I prefer to work constantly."

Allen's personal life has had its share of stressors. He had cancer over a decade ago, has been divorced and, most recently, suffered the passing of Audrey Meadows, sister of Jayne Meadows, his beloved wife of more than 40 years.

Although understandably shaken by the cancer, Allen has come to terms with it. "I'm just a man who had cancer, just as I'm a man with opinions," he says. "It's just that when you're a public figure, what you feel or do gets into the media.

"As for dying, I have no morbid fear of death. Death as such doesn't matter much to me, but the circumstances surrounding it certainly do," he says. "If God told me that I was going to die because an alligator will bite off my leg, I'd be scared.

"On the other hand, if God said, 'Don't make any plans for next Friday,' I'd take care of some business and personal things, but it wouldn't matter much at all," Allen says. "It's no news that death is going to come. It happens to everyone."

In the meantime, Allen divides his time between working and giving an occasional lecture with his son, Steve Allen, Jr., M.D., a humor specialist and physician in Ithaca, New York, who lectures widely on the benefits of humor and creativity.

On his downtime, Allen exercises—ideally, a little every day—by spending an hour or so in his pool. "I'm a terrible swimmer. I'm a natural sinker, so I just move around in the water," he says. "I do it consciously for health reasons, not to reduce stress, though it has that effect.

"Of course, like a lot of people, I find exercise boring, so I keep a dictation machine at the poolside to record thoughts and ideas or to work on a book, comedy routine or musical number that I'm composing," he says.

"Being busy and creative energizes me. Quite a few of my books—the ones that have nothing to do with humor—have been created by using the energy that I feel from my sense of the world's injustice," he says. "If I get an idea for a poem, for example, there's a pressure in me for something to be born from it. It's born out of my mind, and it has to be vented, even if you write it on a wall.

"Eventually, I'm able to put many of these products of my creativity to practical or commercial use," he says.

Gene Perret, Emmy Award–Winning Comedy Writer

Stress Can Be a Laughing Matter

If laughter is the best medicine, then Gene Perret is a pharmacist who's spent the last 30 years doling out prescriptions for levity. Audiences of all ages have come to trust him, letting Perret into their homes night after night. In return, he fills their lives with laughter—even though almost nobody has a clue who he is.

Perret is a professional comedy writer. You may not know him, but you almost surely know his work. He's written some of the funniest shows on TV, including *The Carol Burnett Show,* for which he won three Emmy Awards. He also was Bob Hope's chief gag writer and has authored 20 books on humor.

But life hasn't been a never-ending laugh track for Perret. He knows stress. Getting grins and guffaws is tough enough, let alone doing it week after week on deadline.

"In Hollywood, when you're working on a TV show, it's extremely stressful because of deadlines and people," Perret says. "Not only are you working with some big egos, but you have to get the work done on time.

"Sometimes you can't think funny, so instead of finding something to write about, you spend your time worrying," he says. "After a 10- or 12-hour day, you blame it on your partner, and it's always his fault. You get angry, and you can get pretty mean."

Fortunately, along with the stress comes a crash course in stress management.

"Instead of fighting about it, our answer was—and it always worked—let's go to lunch, let's go for a walk or let's have a drink," Perret says. "Just doing something took the pres-sure off. You need to know when you need a break."

Another solution—one that you'd expect from professional gag writers—was to get goofy.

"Getting goofy breaks the chain of stress that's keeping you from producing," Perret says. "Even though you have a deadline, it's more productive to take a break and get goofy than it is to sit there worrying about your work."

Retirement Roaster to Hollywood Star

Gene Perret, Emmy Award–winning comedy writer, started out as the funny guy in the engineering department at General Electric (GE) in his native Philadelphia.

"I was an electrical drafting apprentice at GE, and I worked my way up while going to Drexel University night school," he says.

If not for an exodus of retiring employees and support from his managers, Perret might still be an obscure office jokester.

"I was asked one time to emcee a retirement party, and I did a Bob Hope–style monologue. It went over well, and soon I was doing three or four a month," says Perret, who now lives in Westlake Village, California.

"Those monologues were good training. I couldn't use the same material because I had the same audience each time," he recalls. "Plus, I was performing for my co-workers, which can be difficult. It was a great apprenticeship."

Perret soon spun his workplace wit into  part-time gag writing by moonlighting for nightclub performers. His first clients were Phyllis Diller and Slappy White. When Hollywood heard of the young drafter's superlative sauciness, producers signed him on for the *The Jim Nabors Hour.* That led to a staff assignment for *Laugh-In,* head writing duties at *The Bill Cosby Show* and five years on *The Carol Burnett Show.* When Burnett retired, Perret produced *Welcome Back, Kotter, The Tim Conway Show* and *Three's Company*, one of the most successful shows of its time.

The Wit and Wisdom of Comedy

As a professional comedy writer, Perret has learned the value of taking chances and following his dreams.

"Professionals—comics and writers—have the courage to have someone look at their stuff and say, 'This is the worst thing I've ever seen,'" Perret says. "I ask aspiring writers all the time what jokes they've tried to get published, and they say, 'Oh, I'm not good enough to send my stuff out.'

"You have to believe in yourself if you want to succeed," he says. "When I was at GE, I was funny, and people loved me. GE was influential in getting me into this business, but I was working at it very hard, too. I was going out and meeting people. I risked getting kicked in the teeth."

Perret has also learned a lot about the serious side of humor and how helpful it is in real life, especially in dealing with stress.

"I believe that stress is vicious if you don't recognize it for what it is," he says. "Humor helps you do that. When you have a sense of humor, you see the facts for what they are, but you're not letting them bother you.

"A lot of stress comes from fighting the truth. Fighting the facts," Perret says. "When you loosen up and see the humor in a situation, no matter how horrible it looks, it puts things in perspective. The answer to most of our stress is seeing the truth, and I think that humor is one of the best ways to do that."

One thing that Perret is having a hard time finding humor in is the direction in which his industry is heading. He counts it among his biggest stressors these days.

"I feel that the industry is going in a

Thanks for the Memories

When Bob Hope hit the road to entertain the troops, Gene Perret went along for the ride. Whether it was the war zones of Beirut, Lebanon; the Persian Gulf or Saudi Arabia, Perret was there. He also was there in times of peace, like when Hope took his show on the road to Moscow and Berlin to celebrate the dismantling of the Berlin Wall.

"My job for Bob when we traveled was to talk to people and find out what was going on," Perret says. "When we'd do the USO (United Service Organizations) tours, I'd ask the enlisted men and women what they laughed about. Then I'd write material on it, and Bob would deliver it. Half the time he didn't really know what he was talking about because he didn't do the research—but he trusted me."

wrong direction," Perret says. "The goal nowadays seems to be to shock and offend. That's being confused with humor."

What about the launch of his career, a life that started with retirement roasts?

"When I did those roasts, they were basically insulting, but the guest of honor always came over to ask for a copy of the script," Perret says. "It was Will Rogers–style humor. Will Rogers changed politics by poking fun, but he did it without hurting anyone's feelings. He was truly funny. His goal wasn't to shock or offend."

Of today's comics, Perret singles out Jerry Seinfeld and Paul Reiser as keepers of the old flame. Both of them, Perret says, "see the humor in everyday life."

"That's funny—when you can take anything and find humor in it," Perret says. "When you hear that type of humor, it's like looking at a Van Gogh painting. You recognize the mind and the creativity behind it. The other stuff is cheap and sophomoric."

Jeff Braun, Chief Executive Officer, Maxis

Taking Care of Business

There was never any doubt in Jeff Braun's mind about what he wanted to be when he grew up.

Rich. Filthy rich.

"In college I used to tell people that my major was pre-millionaire," he recalls. So it was with equal parts wonder and horror that Braun found himself, in his mid-thirties, rich beyond his wildest dreams—and absolutely miserable.

Maxis, the computer software company that Braun co-founded in 1987, was worth millions of dollars and was growing almost exponentially. But the stress of running a spectacularly successful company took its toll. He started experiencing health problems. He became a belligerent boss. And his girlfriend dumped him.

Broken-hearted, depressed and lethargic, Braun went to a doctor in the early 1990s with a slew of symptoms. "It's stress-related," the doctor told him. "Have you tried diet and exercise?" Braun still laughs at himself; the suggestion was so obvious that he hadn't even thought of it.

Since then, Braun has made changes in his life that have made him healthier and happier.

"Essentially, stress is when things get out of control. I was out of control," he candidly admits. "Antistress is when things are in control. I decided to focus on the things that I could control. I couldn't control my business. I couldn't control my girlfriend. But if I took care of myself, I trusted that the rest would come around again."

Clearly, he was right.

The Price of Success

Braun's odyssey from a scrawny under-achieving geek with a fascination for video games and a bunch of California dreams to multimillionaire is peculiarly American.

The Los Angeles native wandered through several colleges over eight years without ever getting a degree. Gigs working for a video games distributor and installing bar-code readers went nowhere. Then he met game designer Will Wright, and the pair formed Maxis in 1987.

Working for several years out of Braun's apartment, they brought out a computer simulation game called SimCity in 1989. It was an instant success and spawned a series—which includes SimEarth, SimFarm, SimAnt and SimIsle—that demonstrated that computer games don't have to be violent to be popular.

Over the next seven years, the company went from $3 million in revenues and 9 employees to $55 million and more than 200 employees. When the company went public in 1995, Braun found himself the modern version of a forty-niner. He hadn't just struck it rich. He had become the bank. At age 40, he was suddenly worth $79 million—at least on paper.

As the company took off in the late 1980s, Braun wondered whether his wish had become a curse. "I had always longed for the big hit," Braun says. "Then the next thing I knew, I had 25 employees, and the responsibilities had increased exponentially. Everything came down to me, and there wasn't enough of me to go around."

And just as success was upon him, all that glittered turned to . . . gunk. A thin six-footer all his life, he started adding pounds like they were video game bonus points. In no time at all, he had ballooned from 160 to 205 pounds. He also grew increasingly short-tempered. "Typically, when you start a business, you trust other people to do important things," he explained. "When they were mishandled, I'd lose it. I'd freak. I'd yell and scream. I was a pretty tough boss."

When his girlfriend dumped him "because she said that everything I did was for the business," he recalls, he hit rock bottom.

Changing His Life

He was living the entrepreneur's dream life, but it had become a nightmare. Not that he didn't have the best of intentions. He had opened Maxis's offices in Moraga, California, near a bike path so that he could take exercise breaks. But those 18-hour days never seemed to allow time for that. As for his eating habits, call his the Silicon Valley Startup Diet: a well-balanced assortment of coffee and doughnuts, chips and salsa, late-night pizzas and the latest gourmet sodas, heavy on the sugar.

After discussing his health with his doctor, Braun attacked the situation like a true venture capitalist. He did a lot of research, tested his options and developed a phase-in plan with built-in intermittent reviews. First, he cut out sugar. Then dairy. "Then I thought I'd go off the deep end and give up red meat," he says. "I told myself that if I felt better after a month, I'd continue. . . . At the end of 30 days I felt great, so I went another 30. By the third month, with most of my stress symptoms gone, I was sold."

Eventually, he became a vegan, one step beyond vegetarian (no dairy or other animal products). Now he frequently eats only raw vegetables, and from time to time, he abstains altogether, fasting on just juices for several days at a time. He boosts those eatless stretches with nutritional, herbal and vitamin supplements.

It's a far cry from his meat-and-potatoes early life. "I try to keep a flexible mind while I enjoy my life," he adds. "The idea is to keep it all in balance."

Although he once had been an avid sports enthusiast—getting away into Northern California's mountain wilderness regions to ski, backpack or bike—all of that had fallen away in the rush to strike it rich. When his doctor urged him to exercise, Braun put his considerable mental skills to the task first.

"After doing a lot of reading, I decided that oxygen is the key benefit of exercise. Think about it: How long can you live without food? A couple of weeks. How long can you live without water? A couple of days. How long can you live without breathing? A couple of minutes. Oxygen is the most important thing that you need for your metabolism. It helps build your immune system. And then I read that one way to get that oxygen hit I'm talking about was through trampolining, which provides a real aerobic workout."

Trampolining, whether on those living room–size contraptions or the little circles that kids bounce on, is easy on the knees, ankles, hips and joints. You can do it in any weather. You can do it alone. And you don't have to be a multimillionaire. It requires no expensive designer gear or attire.

"For me, ten minutes on a trampoline is equal to running a mile in terms of getting my heart rate up," Braun says. "If I do those ten minutes, I have enough energy to work until 6:00. If I don't, I'm pooped out by 2:00 in the afternoon." His investment in a healthy diet and exercise regime has paid huge dividends. "I feel 17 years old. I have the same shape, size and stamina that I did then," Braun boasts. "I don't feel old or fatigued, and I've had no major sickness since I changed my ways."

There's something else new is his life: a woman. "When I found myself and felt comfortable with that person," he says, "then—logically—I attracted someone whom I feel totally in tune with." Sachi Enochty had been a software company general manager before she resigned to study acupuncture. She's a vegetarian as well. "I saw my old girlfriend a while back," he recalls, "and you know, it's funny, but she wasn't someone whom I'd be attracted to now."

You Can Do It! These guys work hard, often under enormous pressure. Just like you. They have learned to deal with stress in a positive way and to take control of their lives. So can you.

Speaking of Passion

Mark Brown,
Mount Vernon, New York

Date of birth: Aug. 17, 1961

Height and weight: 6-foot-1½, 203 pounds

Profession: Systems analyst, *Reader's Digest*

I've heard that public speaking is something that no one wants to do and that it ranks even higher than death on our list of greatest fears. I've never really understood this. I've tried to empathize with what other people go through, but public speaking has never been stressful for me. I'll talk to 5, 10, 1,000 or 2,000 people, and it's all the same. Sure, I get nerves, but I feed off that energy. That's what enabled me to win the Toastmasters International 1995 World Championship of Public Speaking.

When you're on stage or in front of a group it's just you against the crowd. The problem with most people is that the first thing to cross their minds is fear—fear of not being accepted. And the worst part is that we let this fear make us feel that what we have to say has no value or importance.

Everybody's important in their own way. Everyone has value, and so do their thoughts, feelings and opinions. We need to hear from each other. We need to speak.

The last few years have been a real wake-up call for me, mostly because I almost died from what's called multiple pulmonary emboli—blood clots—in my lungs. It was June 1993, and I was in a supermarket parking lot. Next thing I know, I'm lying facedown on the cement and then in a hospital. I spent ten days in the hospital (five in the critical-care unit) and needed two months to recover. It was a real

scare and a shock, because I didn't drink, I didn't smoke, I was in reasonably good shape and I was refereeing high school soccer.

The guy who read my lung x-rays said that they looked like a textbook case of a dead person. To this day, I still can't figure out why I had the blood clots, but I'm thankful that God saved my life. It was a brush with death, and it opened my eyes in so many ways. It gave me a new perspective on life. Now I have a passion to share my story and feelings with other people. That's why I love speaking.

This all happened about two years before the world finals and before I got serious about public speaking. When I started to prepare for the 1995 Toastmasters competition, I was a man on a mission. I was competing against the best speakers in the world and had already gone through the area, division, district and regional contests. Finally, there I was in San Diego on stage with eight other people in front of an audience of 2,100. I had memorized a script that I followed religiously in practice. My son timed my speeches, and my wife and daughter listened and critiqued. I did a lot of rehearsing, and boy did I put my VCR to the test.

After the competition, I realized that speaking is my passion and has always been my gift. Before, I was at work, doing my job, but I was restless. When I started to get into speaking, it made me feel alive. It became a fire in my gut, and I can't describe the depth of emotion that I feel for it. I daresay that something magical happens to me when I speak. Something that I can't explain. But when I stand before an audience of 10 or 10,000, I feel like I connect. Something inside says that I'm doing what I was meant to do, and aside from my family and God, it's the deepest sense of satisfaction and purpose I know.

Chopping Down Stress

Robert Luoto, Jr., McMinnville, Oregon

Date of birth: Oct. 1, 1951

Height and weight: 5-foot-10, 225 pounds

Profession: Owner of Luoto Logging and president of Associated Oregon Loggers

I've been working in the logging industry since I was a teenager. Logging is listed by occupational safety agencies as among the highest-risk jobs when you consider such factors as the odds of fatality. It's an intense physical job. I think that we work harder than any athlete. I'd drag what are called chokers that weigh 50 to 75 pounds through three feet of brush and hook them up to logs all day. The physical stress is unimaginable. You need upper-body and lower-leg strength and incredible endurance. We'd work in temperatures from 15° to 100°F. We'd do that nine hours a day, every day.

Every second you have to be aware of things falling on you, of things being dragged over you and of cables breaking. You have to look around you—really pay attention—all the time, know where you're standing and know what's happening every moment.

But those stresses are nothing compared to the pressures that I deal with now. I help manage our company. We employ 40 people. I hire crews, inspect several thousand acres a year and purchase equipment. It never stops.

I used to deal with the stress very poorly. I had been chewing Copenhagen, a very strong chewing tobacco, since I was 19. I also drank tons of coffee, always caffeinated, and I usually polished off a Thermosful by lunch. My diet—well, I was raised on beef and raise some cattle myself. As a result, I've eaten red meat almost every day of my life.

My body and my family paid the toll. For years I had serious migraine headaches, especially on weekends when I didn't drink coffee. I had severe neck pains. I went to a chiropractor who told me I had done some permanent damage to my neck and vertebrae from handling heavy weights at work. It's called a logger's neck. At home in the evening after a long day, my wife and two kids suffered the consequences of my stress. I had a short temper and would yell at them for the smallest reason.

When I realized that I was jeopardizing my family's emotional health as much as my own physical health, I decided to try to turn things around with the help of my wife. The first step was to renew my faith in God. We are strong Christians. We worship as a family, and that's really important. Basically, I turn the stress over to God, and I have faith that He'll take care of it. I've learned that I don't have to go through the fire alone. When you're weak, you can become stronger if you ask the Lord to help you. And He gives us the strength to get through.

We also have visited a family therapist, and I find that that helps me express my pent-up feelings in a safe and understanding context. Now I don't seem to blow up as easily. We're learning how to communicate better and support each other.

On the eating front, my motto is moderation. I noticed as I got older that coffee tensed me out. Now I'm down to two cups in the morning, and I don't drink caffeinated coffee after noon. Instead of fatty snacks, I'm eating apples and oranges like crazy. My weakness is taco chips, but I'm working on trying to like chips with 1 gram of fat rather than 9 grams. I'm also trying to eat more chicken and fish.

As for my body, I've started working out in a gym. For an aerobic workout, I walk for 20 to 30 minutes on a treadmill set on high incline, high speed. I do sit-ups, lift free weights and do bench presses and curls, concentrating on leg work and upper-body strength. At about 225 pounds, I'm a few pounds over my goal. I'm aiming for 205. More important, the headaches and neck pains are gone, and I have more energy.

All of it taken together adds up to a lot more relief for me. I feel more balance and more focus in my life.

Negotiating with Stress

Lieutenant Hugh McGowan, New York, New York

Date of birth: July 28, 1942

Height and weight: 5-foot-10, 200 pounds

Profession: Police lieutenant/hostage negotiator; adjunct college professor, Ph.D. doctoral candidate

As chief hostage negotiator for the New York City Police Department, people often ask me what's the worst situation I've ever faced. I usually tell them that it's the next situation. That's the one that we haven't gotten through yet. That's the one that's a big question mark, where you wonder if you have the right people available and if you'll do what it takes to resolve it peacefully. It's the unknowns in this job that cause the most stress. To survive, you need confidence in yourself and in your team. Luckily, confidence is contagious.

But fear can be contagious, too. It's transmitted over the phone. When you're in a hostage situation, it's important to lower anxiety, both on the police side and in the person that we're trying to take into custody. When you get to a hostage/barricade situation, there are two sets of disturbed people: the suspects and the cops. The officers, especially the junior officers, are all keyed up. They're almost as stressed out as the suspect, and this doesn't help. There have been plenty of times where I felt stress because superiors were asking questions that I couldn't immediately answer. They were asking, for example, how long a situation was going to take and how we were going to handle it. Just when you say that things seem to be going well and that it should end soon, you hear what sounds like a gunshot. Talk about stress!

One of the best ways that I diffuse the stress is humor. Humor at work or home is one of my greatest escape valves. It can really break the tension. And since for years I've been known to tell bad jokes, I'm a natural for this job. My children—kiddingly, I hope—can't believe that the police department put me in charge of talking to people who've barricaded themselves in a house. I've told them that I keep telling bad jokes until they give up. If that doesn't work, what would? But, seriously, if everybody's overwrought, how is that ever going to help anyone?

There's one other secret that I have about stress. I guess it's not really a secret, because my family can't keep secrets, but it's naps. I love to take naps. I'm a great believer in them. They're especially helpful if I'm called in to work in the middle of the night or on the weekends. At least if I've had a nap in the afternoon, I feel a little better about being awake all night. And when I found out that Winston Churchill was a great napper, I knew I was onto something good.

I became a cop because it was something that I always saw as a worthwhile job. I started out as a uniform officer, did plainclothes work, got promoted to sergeant and worked six years in the Bomb Squad. The Bomb Squad taught me a lot about staying calm under pressure.

Besides being a police officer, I'm an adjunct professor in criminal justice at John Jay College in New York City. I'm a doctoral candidate in criminal justice, and I'm also working toward completing my dissertation. I've been in graduate school for six years, and my mother and father, I hope, would be proud if they were alive. I won't be able to write a prescription, but I'll be a doctor some day.

I'm also a parent and a husband. I have four children—three beautiful daughters and a terrific son. Parenting is a different kind of stress. The younger kids see what has been and hasn't been allowed with the older ones, so they can be more difficult to deal with. The best answer is to be consistent and as fair as possible. I remember learning that from an older cop when I was a rookie. He said that the way you deal with people is important—you can't be good cop one day, bad cop the next and expect respect.

Running Free

Steve Nowling, New York, New York

Date of birth: Nov. 23, 1950

Height and weight: 5-foot-6, 140 pounds

Profession: Nurse practitioner on an AIDS unit

I've always wanted to be proactive in my life. But there's a toll that you pay for that, physically and emotionally. I work on the AIDS Unit at St. Vincent's Hospital in Greenwich Village, caring for people during acute phases of their illness. After a stressed-out day, I go out for a run. It breaks you from what was happening. When you're finished, you're refreshed again. It requires discipline, but I've turned it into something that I can use to completely wash away my worries and concerns.

I started running in January 1987. I remember this period of my life as rush, rush, rush. There was no time to do anything. One morning at 5:00 A.M., I suddenly awoke, totally stressed out, obsessing. Out of the blue, I remember thinking, "Well, I could run. It's free, and you can do it anywhere, anytime." I just got up, put on some sneakers and sweats and ran from my apartment to Washington Square, all of about ten blocks—a half-mile. I was exhausted. But it was a good exhaustion—physical exhaustion rather than emotional exhaustion.

Then each run got a little longer. One time I ducked into Central Park, and I discovered a whole new experience: rolling hills, vistas, no traffic. The park is wonderful, gorgeous. Now a typical run takes me on a six-mile loop around Central Park.

But even with all that, sometimes it's boring to run by yourself, so eventually I joined a running club for gay men, Front Runners. I had come "out of the closet" with my homosexuality in 1975, and that was a major stressor. The gay movement was pretty public, so it was kind of safe. But I was living in Louisville at the time, where there were about five gay bars but no gay community to speak of—and no one to speak to.

Joining Front Runners made running more fun. You can kibitz and run. The social thing was sustaining. Then I discovered the fun of competition. And I found that I enjoyed that part of it, the competitive part. In June of that first year, I ran in the Gay Pride Run.

I've never had one of those endorphin highs. But for me the thrill is zooming through New York City—the center of the world—on foot and passing people. I've now completed seven marathons.

I deal with some of the stress of work by talking with my colleagues at lunch. Just commiserating with someone who knows exactly what you're going through at work takes away some of the pressure and strain. I also deal with work stress by remembering something that I learned in nursing school that I think also applies to my own life. We're taught the difference between sympathy and empathy. They warned us against sympathy—that is, vicariously having the feelings, thoughts and experience of another. You get invested, and it keeps you from working effectively. When you empathize, you can recognize someone's pain, and you can do something constructive about it. Now, my lover, John, is dying of AIDS. And I find myself handling it pretty well. I separate sympathy from empathy. Knowing what to expect actually relieves some of the stress. That helps me keep perspective.

I think the secret to dealing with stress is to find something that interests you outside your regular interests, something that separates you from normal life, that's intrinsically satisfying to help refocus your energy.

I've found that stress pulls you into yourself. When that happens, what you need to do is focus outside yourself—whether it's books, music or, in my case, running races that I haven't run yet. That pulls you forward. It's something to look forward to, something that breaks your mind from the downward stress spiral. I'm still not sure exactly how it works, but I know that it works.

Male Makeovers

Everywhere you turn these days, stress is lurking. And it's not always easy figuring out what you need to do to live a happier and healthier life. So we asked the experts for advice on how to deal with some of the most typical problems that men face. Here's what they said.

The Young and the Hopeless

The Scenario

Jack's youth seems to be passing him by—at 26, he already feels tired and jaded. The job that he landed as a phone jockey in a customer service center is not at all what he dreamed of during four years of college.

Outside of work, Jack feels a real need to blow off steam. He prefers his music loud and furiously fast—Metallica is his favorite band. On Friday nights, his tightly wound temper and tendency to drink too much get him into more than his share of fistfights.

Naturally lean and wiry in college, his poor eating habits are starting to catch up with him. Living and eating alone gives Jack an excuse to eat takeout every night of the week.

He used to love playing basketball but hasn't touched a ball or engaged in any other exercise in a couple of years. Aside from fatigue, his main health complaint is frequent, troubling back pain from hours of sitting at his desk.

The Solution

Jack needs to seriously examine his drinking habit and consider the very real possibility that he may be addicted. For many people, alcohol addiction can be the beginning of a downward spiral of physical and mental health problems. In addition to alcohol's ability to increase depression and create disease, getting into barroom brawls on a regular basis is a potentially lethal hobby. Going sober right now would be a big step in the right direction.

Jack also needs to get back into physical activity, such as the basketball playing that he used to enjoy. It'll help him feel better about himself and give him a boost mentally and emotionally. If he's not up to playing ball, he should start with something simple like walking, which can help lift mild depression. He could try substituting a workout or a long walk for a night of heavy drinking. Jack might even want to consider using a punching bag to defuse some of his pent-up anger.

Being unhappy at work is like being unlucky in love—it can happen to anyone. Jack's dissatisfaction at work is probably being compounded by his real lack of any outside interests. He should review what's going on in his personal life, especially in the realm of relationships.

He needs to balance the seeming drudgery of his work with positive activities and people that could give his life a sense of fullness and connectedness. Support groups and stress-management classes would be good places for Jack to consider meeting others who are also interested in creative ways of handling stress.

—Keith Sedlacek, M.D., director of the Stress Regulation Institute in New York City

The Reluctant Retiree

The Scenario

At 63, Marty's golden years aren't looking so bright. As part of his company's downsizing plan, he has been asked to take early retirement and accept a reduced pension. He and his wife, Louise, now face living on a fixed income far below their expectations. He always promised Louise a Caribbean cruise after his retirement. Marty doesn't see how that will be possible under their current circumstances. He hates to let her down.

Almost as bad is the anxiety that he feels about not getting up and going to work every day. It's all that he's ever known. Sure, he fishes and enjoys model building, but he has always defined himself by the work that he does and the daily contribution that he makes.

A meat-and-potatoes kind of guy, Marty—for the first time in his life—is concerned about his health. Recently, a routine rectal exam indicated abnormalities in his prostate. His doctor wants to see him again to run more tests. There's talk of cancer. With this on his horizon and a bulging belly over his belt, Marty feels like the life that he worked so hard to build is falling apart around him.

The Solution

I have several suggestions to make to Marty, starting with his health. He should certainly proceed with the tests that his doctor wants to do to check out his prostate. These will undoubtedly include a prostate-specific antigen blood test, which may indicate inflammation of his prostate or, perhaps, even a tumor, both of which are treatable. Then he may be referred for a sonogram—a sound-generated picture of the prostate—and a biopsy, all of which can be done right in the doctor's office. Marty shouldn't worry too much just yet, because at this stage of the game, chances are that it isn't cancer. But even if it is, there are effective treatments for prostate cancer today, which his doctor will explain to him if necessary.

Then there's the matter of his weight. If Marty wants to enjoy a long and healthy life, it would be very smart of him to start a regular program of exercise and alter his eating habits to lose a few pounds. By exercising he will not only feel stronger, in general, but will also learn to enjoy a new healthy routine. The same is true for eating; Marty may be surprised to find out that he likes nutritious foods—even broccoli—more than he might expect.

Finally, this is a good time for Marty to take stock of himself as a person. His wife may well not feel anything more than ordinary disappointment at not being able to do some of the things they'd planned on, like a Caribbean vacation. It wouldn't hurt to review their finances with a financial counselor to see how they can make the most of the money that they have.

As for a sense of personal worth, Marty should consider some kind of volunteer work or a part-time job to restore his sense of making a contribution. But more important, he should come to understand that it is not the work that one does that defines who one is. A sense of our own values derives from being human, having led lives marked by honesty, courage, generosity, faith and love.

—Frederic Flach, M.D., adjunct associate professor of psychiatry at Cornell University Medical College and attending psychiatrist at New York Hospital–Cornell Medical Center, both in New York City, and author of *Putting the Pieces Together Again* and *The Secret Strength of Depression*

Time Isn't on His Side

The Scenario

As the general manager of a four-star hotel in the heart of the city, Jerry, 48, would seem to have it made. But his life is becoming frayed at the edges. After his wife of 15 years asked for a divorce, Jerry got a condo in the suburbs so that he could continue the after-work tutoring that helped his three children earn honor roll status in school. The hour-long daily commute, however, is wearing him down.

On weekends Jerry juggles "quality time" with the kids while answering pages from his beeper, a constant and demanding companion these days. Between handling hotel crises over the phone, keeping in touch with friends and trying to be the perfect part-time dad, he barely has time to relax before—sigh—Monday morning rolls around again.

A former runner, Jerry rarely exercises, except for an occasional game of tennis with a client, which the client usually wins. More and more he has come to realize that his fitness level isn't what it used to be, especially when he considers his slowly but surely expanding waistline. He's heard that time to relax and do nothing is good for your health, but he just can't seem to fit it into his life.

The Solution

This man needs to reorient his priorities and examine his personal desires. If his own basic needs for leisure and exercise aren't being met, burnout could become a real possibility.

The first thing that Jerry should do is stop the after-school tutoring. He's done a great job so far, but he needs to let go. By giving his kids a chance to follow through on their own, he'll open his schedule a bit and, at the same time, set an example of self-sufficiency. Second, he should consider moving closer to the city to eliminate a very stressful commute. Like many divorced dads, he can still spend weekend time with his kids, along with maybe one night during the week.

Instead of juggling quality time, Jerry needs to keep work separate from the rest of his life whenever possible. He should be able to be unavailable to his job at certain times. If he knows that he will have, say, three hours free on a Saturday morning, then that's it. He shouldn't feel the need to bring his beeper with him if he's made special plans with his kids.

As a former runner, Jerry should already know about the real "cost-effectiveness" of a regular exercise routine. Consistent workouts will pay him back with more overall energy, help get his weight under control again and decrease tension. By waking up a half-hour earlier each day, he could make the time for a brisk run. The sleep lost will be more than made up in the form of a real energy boost.

Basically, Jerry needs to learn to put himself first so that he can be in better shape to carry out his other responsibilities. Rather than seeing these changes as self-indulgent, he should use these tactics as part of a maintenance program. Over time, these preventive measures will help him to avoid burning out.

—Reed C. Moskowitz, M.D., clinical assistant professor of psychiatry and director of the Stress Disorders Medical Services Program at New York University in New York City and author of *Your Healing Mind*

The Weary Road Warrior

The Scenario

As a photographer for one the nation's top travel magazines, Clyde gets paid to fly to exotic places and photograph palm trees on windswept stretches of desolate beach. He has a beautiful wife, great kids and a house in the country. What's not to like?

Well, Clyde's life isn't exactly as glamorous as it may seem. About 80 percent of his on-the-job time is spent traveling. His wife, Marlene, complains that he's never around to help out with their two children. The closeness that they once shared has become a chasm that sometimes feels as vast as the thousands of miles that often separate them.

On the days that Clyde is home, he attends baseball games with his son, reads storybooks to his daughter and even cooks dinner so that his wife can rest. But just when he feels like he's bonding, it's time to go. His lifestyle precludes any kind of routine, and that includes exercise, sleep and meals. He's often irritable and almost always tired.

The Solution

Clyde would do well to set a time aside with his wife, possibly with a counselor, to clarify their goals and brainstorm some resolutions to this surprisingly stressful situation. Before the meeting, Clyde might spend some time meditating and delineating his artistic, financial, family, physical and spiritual priorities.

It's very likely that he's too busy pursuing his goals to ask whether they are, indeed, still his goals. He might do well to ask himself, "What would I do if this were the last six months of my life?" At the meeting he might want to ask his wife what it is that troubles her most about their life and listen in the same receptive way as he photographs.

The focus should then shift to solution talk rather than problem talk, with small changes leading to larger ones. For example, they might ask, "If a miracle happened and the problem was solved, what would we be doing differently tomorrow, next week, next month and next year?"

The small changes might involve arranging overnight babysitting for romantic candlelight dinners and local hotel sojourns when he returns home. Perhaps the couple could arrange more extended child care or visits to grandparents so that Marlene could accompany him on his job, possibly as a tax-deductible assistant. During the summer, the whole family might take advantage of Clyde's job-related travel.

Meditating or walking whenever and wherever Clyde is traveling is manageable and advisable. He might look into some exercise bands to carry in his suitcase for use in his hotel room. Clyde might also try sleeping on his home schedule regardless of where he finds himself and then try taking naps if early or late photography shoots require shifting his sleep pattern. Calling home spontaneously might help maintain the long-distance emotional bonding with his family. Finally, the largest changes might involve career-management counseling for Clyde and/or Marlene.

—Ronald G. Nathan, Ph.D., clinical psychologist and professor in the Department of Family Practice at Albany Medical College in New York and author or co-author of three books on stress, including *Coping with the Stressed-Out People in Your Life*

On the Firing Line

The Scenario

Matt is what you'd call a typical nice guy. A hard worker, at age 35 he had never really done anyone a bad turn. Never, that is, until his company merged with a larger firm and started laying people off. Suddenly, this mild-mannered man found himself saddled with the role of middle-management executioner.

Compounding the guilt that he feels over handing out pink slips is the fear that he may be the next to go. At work, he's paranoid—convinced that anything that he does wrong will be fuel for the fire. Combining his nervousness with five cups of coffee a day, Matt finds it hard to look at his situation realistically. At home, things aren't much better. His wife, initially very supportive and understanding, has started to tire of Matt's constant worrying. She feels that his anxiety is affecting their home life too much— from their sex life to raising their two small children.

To top it all off, Matt has returned to an old destructive habit: cigarette smoking. Having quit cold turkey years ago, he believes that he'll be able to stop again when he gets over this hurdle.

The Solution

It is clear that Matt is under stress—he's having a lot of trouble coping successfully with problems, both at work and at home. In my opinion, he probably doesn't need traditional psychotherapy. He could really benefit from a competent "stress coach," someone who can show him what is wrong with his current ways of coping and then point him in the direction of other strategies that could increase his well-being. Five to ten therapeutic sessions might be all that it takes for him to turn things around.

If Matt came to me for help, I would focus on some very specific issues. To start, he needs to recognize and deal with the guilt and the very normal feelings of worry surrounding his position at work. He needs to know that most people in his situation would feel the same—he's not unusual in this. He also needs to plan for the future in two ways. In the event that he doesn't get fired, Matt should identify and begin learning the new skills that he would need to survive the restructuring of his company. On the other hand, to help alleviate the anxiety of the unknown, he should also positively prepare—financially and emotionally—for the possibility of job loss and unemployment.

Regarding his home life, Matt should stop neglecting the needs of his wife and family. Turning the focus on them will pay off, in spite of the pressure that he's feeling. He needs to remember and experience the fact that a strong family support system can be a great help in times of stress.

Finally, Matt needs to stop smoking immediately. He's fooling himself if he thinks that a return to smoking, even for a brief period, will yield any benefits. He then needs to force himself to develop other, healthier ways of dealing with his anxieties.

If he's successful at achieving these goals, Matt not only will solve his immediate problems but also will have acquired new skills for handling stress in the future. This is how a negative or stressful situation can be transformed into a positive outcome that can enrich the rest of a person's life.

—**Morton Orman, M.D., author of *The 14-Day Stress Cure*. Informative reports on stress and how to handle it can be found at http://www.stresscure.com.**

Credits

Index

Note: <u>Underscored</u> page references indicate boxed text. **Boldface** page references indicate main discussion of topic.